AMERICA AT WAR

KOREA AND VIETNAM

Douglas Waitley

Glencoe Publishing Company
Mission Hills, California

Technical Consultant
Thomas Koberna

Send all inquiries to:
Glencoe Publishing Company
15319 Chatsworth Street, P.O. Box 9509
Mission Hills, California 91345-9509

Library of Congress Catalog Card Number: 74-84792

ISBN 0-02-648930-9

5 6 7 8 9   91 90 89 88 87

Acknowledgments

Grateful acknowledgment is made to the authors and publishers who kindly granted us permission to reprint excerpts from the following copyrighted material:

From *War in Korea*, copyright 1951 by Marguerite Higgins. Reprinted by permission of Doubleday & Company, Inc.

From *Reminiscences* by General of the Army Douglas MacArthur, McGraw-Hill Book Co., © 1964 Time Inc. Reprinted with permission.

From *Soldier* by Anthony B. Herbert with James T. Wooten. Copyright © 1973 by Anthony B. Herbert and James T. Wooten. Reprinted by permission of Holt, Rinehart and Winston, Publishers.

From *Plain Speaking: An Oral Biography of Harry S. Truman* by Merle Miller. Copyright © 1973, 1974 by Merle Miller. Reprinted by permission of Berkley Publishing Corporation.

From *The Last Parallel: A Marine's War Journal* by Martin Russ. Copyright © 1957 by Martin Russ. Reprinted by permission of Holt, Rinehart and Winston, Publishers.

From *Vietnam: History, Documents, and Opinions*, edited by Marvin E. Gettleman. Copyright © 1970 by Marvin E. Gettleman. Reprinted by permission of Joan Daves.

From *The Ugly American* by William J. Lederer and Eugene Burdick. By permission of W. W. Norton & Company, Inc. Copyright © 1958 by William J. Lederer and Eugene Burdick.

From *Ho Chi Minh on Revolution: Selected Writings, 1920–66*, edited and with an introduction by Bernard B. Fall. © 1967 by Frederick A. Praeger, Inc., New York.

From *The Pentagon Papers*, edited by Neil Sheehan, Hedrick Smith, E. W. Kenworthy, and Fox Butterfield. Reprinted by permission of Bantam Books, Inc.

From *The New Legions* by Donald Duncan. Copyright © 1967 by Donald Duncan. Reprinted by permission of Random House, Inc.

From *The Military Half: An Account of Destruction in Quang Ngai and Quang Tin* by Jonathan Schell. Copyright © 1968 by Jonathan Schell. Reprinted by permission of Alfred A. Knopf, Inc.

From *Lieutenant Calley: His Own Story* by William L. Calley, Jr., and John Sack. Copyright © 1971 by William L. Calley, Jr., and John Sack. Reprinted by permission of The Viking Press, Inc.

From newspaper stories appearing in the *Chicago Daily News* (April 21 and May 1, 5, and 6, 1975) by Bob Tamarkin. Reprinted by permission of the *Chicago Daily News*.

Picture Credits

Brown Brothers
34

Burton Holmes Collection/Stockmarket, Los Angeles
101

Cleveland Plain Dealer
133, 206

Defense Department/Marine Corps
52, 53, 61, 143, 148, 150, 155, 159, 181, 184, 204, 232, 258, 264

Jean-Claude LeJeune/Stockmarket, Los Angeles
214

Library of Congress
30

Louise Knaiger Shorr
236

United Nations
24, 32, 87, 89, 111

United Press International
20, 26, 64, 94, 96, 103, 105, 108, 116, 117, 120, 123, 124, 128, 135, 141, 170, 176, 183, 189, 192, 195, 198, 201, 210, 211, 216, 219, 226, 234, 241, 244, 252, 255, 261

U.S. Air Force
68, 114, 152, 168, 185, 186 (top and bottom), 203, 228

U.S. Army
18, 28, 38, 40, 42, 46, 54, 58, 59, 60, 63, 65, 70, 72, 74, 75, 76, 77, 78, 80, 81, 86, 88, 153

U.S. Navy
44, 47, 82, 139, 162, 164, 173, 178, 223, 230, 239, 246

Vietnam News Agency
229

Contents

Let the Bugles Sound!

When you first think of it, war seems simple. "Forward, the Light Brigade," shouted the officers in Lord Tennyson's stirring poem. Then "flashed all the sabres bare, flashed as they turned in air." The men of the Light Brigade thundered across the plain, drove their horses into the enemy ranks, fought savagely hand to hand—and conquered!

Modern wars, however, are not neat, precise operations in which victory is won by valor alone. They are great movements of large masses of men across often confused lines of march. Behind them stretch lengthy lines of supply vehicles: wagons, trucks, freight trains. And farther back are the factories in which all the complex instruments of war must originate. Wars are intricate enterprises that require detailed planning and mountains of paperwork. Individual battles may sometimes be won by the heroics of soldiers in the field. But wars are usually won by elderly men in quiet rooms planning the strategy or organizing the involved logistics that will have the right troops with the right weapons in the right place at the right time.

Warfare is conducted in four phases. First come the grand strategy sessions where the top leaders—the emperors, presidents, prime ministers, and their advisers—decide what are to be the overall objectives. Here, for example, the Kaiser determines that German troops will defeat France before Russia, or Hitler decides that he will conquer Russia before subduing England, or Ho Chi Minh decides that he will send guerrillas rather than uniformed regulars against South Vietnam.

Once the grand strategy is determined, matters move to specific strategy. Here the admirals and four-star generals plan the actual operations that will achieve the goals set by their leaders. These planners of the specific strategy have spent their lives in military service. They have gone to the top military schools, and they have sharpened their knowledge and intuition through active duty in earlier campaigns. Now they distribute symbols of their army divisions and naval flotillas on huge maps. They move them like chess pieces until they arrive at the desired positions, positions from which they can do the most damage to the enemy. Then they organize the logistic support, make alternate troop dispositions to delude the enemy, and provide for reserves in case a battle goes temporarily against them.

In the specific strategy sessions we see men like the German chief of staff, General Helmuth von Moltke, completely outwitting the French by overbalancing his right flank, then blasting through to beyond Paris. And we see the American general, Douglas MacArthur, ending the first phase of the Korean War in a single day after the success of his behind-the-lines landing at Inchon.

With the strategy settled, the war moves forward another notch to battle tactics. Here the field army generals decide exactly how and when they will fight their segments of the strategic battle. Battle tactics occupy the thoughts of the lower generals, men like George Patton, whom we recall for breaking out of the Normandy peninsula in 1944 on a dashing and dangerous encircling movement which cost the Germans an entire army.

Finally we come to the fourth phase of the war: the actual combat. This phase is the one most emphasized in accounts of the fighting. We see GIs leaping out of the trenches with artillery shells exploding overhead and machine guns spitting bullets from the ground. In the sky fighter-bombers scream on death dives. Gallantry, bravery, fear, cowardice—here is where we encounter them, often intermingling in a single solder in a single moment.

Grand strategy, specific strategy, battle tactics, and combat: these are the ingredients of war. How they are put together determines, in large measure, whether the war is lost or won.

THE ARMY

The organization of the United States Army, like that of most other armies, is complex. There are two groups of soldiers: enlisted men and officers. The enlisted men go to a basic training camp for several months, then are sent to their permanent stations. An enlisted man begins as a private, moves up to private, first class, then to corporal. After some time, should he display exceptional ability, he is promoted to sergeant. There are various grades of sergeant, the highest being master sergeant. This is as high as an enlisted man can go under normal circumstances.

Officers either come out of college or from special officers' training schools. They begin as second lieutenants, quickly become first lieutenants, and somewhat more slowly are promoted to captain. From there the going is more difficult. A few captains rise to become majors and fewer majors make lieutenant colonel, then colonel. A tiny minority of colonels jump to brigadier general. Then there are two more general grades to pass through before an officer can reach the rank of four-star general. The only officer above a four-star general is the General of the Army. Of the thousands of army officers, only one goes this high.

Army units are organized in a tight pyramid similar to that outlined in Chart 1. In actual combat situations, the number of men in each unit may be far lower than that indicated on the chart. Battle casualties, furloughs, desertions, and lost stragglers can reduce a company to fewer than sixty men and a division to fewer than ten thousand. It should be pointed out, too, that U.S. divisions are about twice as large as those of the British, German, and most other armies.

The division is the basic fighting unit. It is the smallest army grouping that has all the necessary elements for independent movement in battle situations. A typical division would be composed of about three infantry combat regiments, three or four battalions of light artillery, one battalion of heavy artillery, and a battalion of anti-aircraft artillery. There would also be a battalion or two of armor, which would include several hundred tanks, and a battalion of engineers for road maintenance, bridge construction, and so on. In addition, the division would contain smaller units performing such duties as enemy intelligence, reconnaissance, communications, transportation, supplies, ammunition, and medical services.

Divisions, being mobile, can be transferred to various sectors of the front or held in reserve to plug some hole that develops as the result of an enemy breakthrough. Usually divisions work within the framework of an army corps, which is a command post coordinating the activities of three or more divisions. If the number of divisions involved requires a larger command framework, four or five army corps are incorporated into a field army. There were, for example, five German field armies operating during the great offensive of 1914.

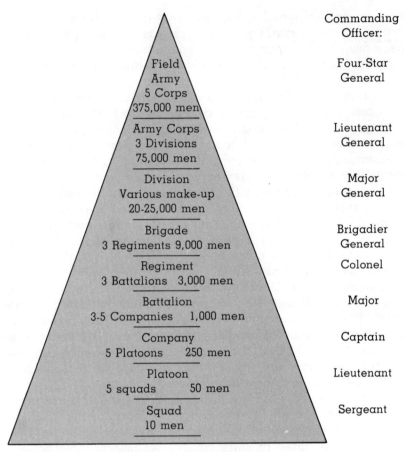

	Commanding Officer:
Field Army 5 Corps 375,000 men	Four-Star General
Army Corps 3 Divisions 75,000 men	Lieutenant General
Division Various make-up 20-25,000 men	Major General
Brigade 3 Regiments 9,000 men	Brigadier General
Regiment 3 Battalions 3,000 men	Colonel
Battalion 3-5 Companies 1,000 men	Major
Company 5 Platoons 250 men	Captain
Platoon 5 squads 50 men	Lieutenant
Squad 10 men	Sergeant

Chart 1. The structure of an American field army.

THE NAVY

Of course, wars are not fought on the ground alone. In each of America's four twentieth-century wars, the nation had to rely on the United States Navy and merchant marine (commercial vessels and their crews) to transport the millions of troops and countless tons of equipment and supplies to the battle areas. The transport ships had to be guarded by hundreds of destroyers, destroyer escorts, and planes operating from small convoy carriers. Navy warships and carrier planes were also essential in bombarding enemy shore installations and in providing support for invasion troops being ferried ashore in landing craft. The Marine Corps, which is part of the naval establishment, was often the land-combat spearhead for these invasions.

The traditional navy heavyweight has been the battleship. A battleship weighs around forty thousand tons and carries nine huge sixteen-inch guns in three rotating turrets. (For comparison, the standard seventy-five-millimeter artillery piece used by the army is only about three inches in diameter, and a heavy tank's cannon is about four inches.) Adding to the battleship's immense firepower are five turrets on its sides, each containing two five-inch guns. For defense against enemy bombers, the ship also has sixty or more emplacements of twenty- and forty-millimeter machine guns. A crew of nearly three thousand mans this impressive floating fortress.

The cruiser is second in strength to the battleship. A heavy cruiser weighs about fourteen thousand tons and carries nine eight-inch guns in three rotating turrets as well as twelve five-inch guns in side turrets. In addition, it mounts an array of twenty- and forty-millimeter machine guns. A light cruiser weighs ten thousand tons and carries six-inch guns as its main weapons. A cruiser's complement runs around thirteen hundred men.

Destroyers are much smaller than cruisers. These ships are only about two thousand tons and are armed with just four to six five-inch guns. But a destroyer will have a great number of anti-aircraft guns as well as a stock of depth charges for use against submarines. It will also carry ten to fifteen deadly torpedoes. A junior edition of the destroyer is the destroyer escort, weighing about thirteen hundred tons.

Even smaller than the destroyer is the patrol torpedo boat (PT-boat), which weighs barely forty-five tons. The PT-boat has a crew of fourteen men and races along at forty-eight miles an hour. It carries four torpedoes as well as some twenty-millimeter guns. The PT-boat's mobility is its great advantage, but it also has disadvantages. It is constructed of wood and is easily sunk by enemy fire. It is also incapable of weathering heavy seas and for this reason is restricted to duty close to shore.

Each class of warship is designed to perform certain functions. The battleship's function is to blow up enemy fleets. Its guns can hurl shells as far as twenty-five miles (although at such range accuracy is rare). No cruiser's or destroyer's hull can withstand the impact of a battleship's sixteen-inchers. Only other battleships can take a direct hit from a sixteen-inch gun and survive. Indeed, much of a battleship's weight results from the thick steel armor which encases it like a coat of mail.

In their heyday during World War II, most battleships could survive ten or even twenty torpedoes and a score or more of

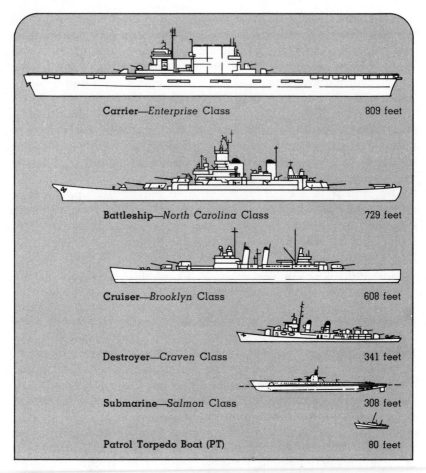

Carrier—*Enterprise* Class · 809 feet

Battleship—*North Carolina* Class · 729 feet

Cruiser—*Brooklyn* Class · 608 feet

Destroyer—*Craven* Class · 341 feet

Submarine—*Salmon* Class · 308 feet

Patrol Torpedo Boat (PT) · 80 feet

Chart 2. Representative warships used by the United States Navy in World War II. In 1945, the American fleet contained 37 carriers, 16 battleships, 69 cruisers, 353 destroyers and destroyer escorts, and 186 submarines.

bombs without sinking. Such was their strength that not a single U.S. battleship was sunk after the attack on Pearl Harbor, although many were pounded by enemy bombers and submarines.

The battleships' disadvantages are that they are slower than most other warships, they are very expensive to build, and their firepower is unnecessary in many situations. To hit shore installations and protect amphibious landings, cruisers are often preferred. Cruisers, being two-thirds lighter than battleships, can operate in much shallower water and can therefore get a closer, more accurate range on enemy targets. Another advantage of cruisers over battleships is monetary: one battleship costs as much to build as four cruisers. Cruisers are also more mobile, being able to travel at thirty-seven miles an hour compared to most battleships' thirty-two miles an hour. By investing in four cruisers rather than one battleship, the navy can cover a much wider area.

But cruisers have their drawbacks, too. The most serious is their lack of armor. To achieve economy, speed, and lightness, cruisers must sacrifice the thick steel plates that make battleships almost impregnable. Cruisers are particularly vulnerable to torpedoes. For this reason, they nearly always operate in conjunction with a squadron of destroyers.

Destroyers have two main functions. The most important is to hunt and destroy submarines. Destroyers can race at speeds of forty-two miles an hour, several times faster than the average sub. They are equipped with devices which enable them to locate submarines and with depth charges which can explode the subs. Because of their sub-sinking capability, destroyers are not only vital in protecting cruisers and carriers but also in convoying cargo and troop ships through war zones.

Destroyers are also useful in surface combat. Their five-inch guns are strong enough to do considerable damage to enemy shore positions. Although they are largely ineffective against battleships, their torpedoes make them formidable against cruisers and carriers when they are able to get within launching range. However, the destroyer has only minimal protective armor and is extremely vulnerable to the cruiser's long-range six-inch and eight-inch guns, to say nothing of the battleship's sixteen-inchers.

Destroyers are far cheaper to build than battleships or cruisers. This fact, together with their importance in convoy duty, makes them the most numerous type of warship in the navy's arsenal.

The navy's undersea arm has sometimes played a significant part in American military operations. This was particularly true in the war with the Japanese. Japan, being an island nation, depended on shipping for supplies. American subs were highly effective in sinking vessels bound for Japan.

However, the submarine has been mainly a German weapon. During World Wars I and II, German submarine attacks on Atlantic shipping nearly succeeded in reducing Great Britain to submission. But the German subs were very slow and therefore could be hunted down by destroyers. Once under attack, a sub's thin hull could not withstand depth-charge explosions. In both wars, after the Allies concentrated their resources on undersea defenses, the German submarines were gradually eliminated as major menaces.

One of the most radical changes in naval history came with the development of the aircraft carrier. During World War II, the function of battleships in fleet combat was largely taken over by aircraft launched from carriers. Because a big carrier could put a swarm of eighty or more planes into the air and send them toward targets several hundred miles away, it was generally more effective than a battleship with a much smaller range. The American fleet had no battleships at all in the crucial Battle of Midway—the Japanese fleet was disabled while still 175 miles distant by bombs and torpedoes dropped from U.S. carrier planes. During the wars in Korea and Vietnam, American carrier planes were responsible for a large percentage of the bombing attacks against enemy positions on land.

Despite its great value, the aircraft carrier has some serious liabilities: it has only a dozen or so five-inch guns and some machine guns with which to defend itself; its flat landing surface presents an ideal target for enemy bombers; and its thinly plated hull is easily penetrated by torpedoes. During the launching period, when the deck is filled with planes gassed and loaded with explosives, the ship is a virtual tinderbox, ready to be blasted apart should enemy planes swoop upon it. The carrier therefore requires a screen of destroyers to ward off submarines and to provide additional anti-aircraft firepower.

One part of the naval command which deserves special mention is the Marine Corps. Marines are the soldiers of the sea. When islands must be taken or beachheads established, it is usually the marines who do the job. Because their duties include the toughest assaults, they are one of America's elite fighting units. In the war against Japan, marines played a spectacular role—particularly in the vicious fighting at Guadalcanal, Iwo Jima, and Okinawa.

While the Marine Corps uses the same officer designations as the army, the navy has its own designations of rank:

Navy Ranking	Army Equivalent
Admiral	General
Captain	Colonel
Commander	Lieutenant Colonel
Lieutenant Commander	Major
Lieutenant	Captain
Lieutenant, Junior Grade	First Lieutenant
Ensign	Second Lieutenant

There are various grades of admiral. One of the highest is the fleet admiral, who commands naval operations in an entire war zone. Lower admirals command squadrons of warships. (For example, a task force of four cruisers and eight destroyers might be headed by an admiral.) Ordinarily, each individual ship is commanded by a captain, and it should be noted that a naval captain is a much higher officer than an army captain.

THE AIR FORCE

The third and newest branch of the American military establishment is the United States Air Force. Aircraft did not come into their own as effective combat weapons until the Second World War. At that time, the air wing was under army command. As the war progressed, the air force grew to undreamed of size. The Eighth Air Force, which operated out of England, eventually numbered 200,000 officers and men. In the Mediterranean, the Seventh and Ninth Air Forces had thousands of planes. The Tenth and Fourteenth Air Forces operated in the China-Burma-India theater. And in the Pacific, the Fifth, Seventh, and Thirteenth Air Forces conducted massive raids that helped to destroy Japanese shipping and devastate the Japanese home islands.

By the end of the war it had become apparent that an independent air command was needed, not only because air activities were so extensive but also because they did not always relate directly to army operations. In 1947, a far-reaching piece of legislation known as the National Security Act created the Department of the Air Force as an equal of the Departments of the Army and the Navy. All three branches were then placed under a new Cabinet officer, the secretary of defense.

Although theoretically the three departments were equal, the army was by far the largest. At the end of World War II, the nation's last full-scale conflict, the numbers in service stood as follows: the army, 8,300,000; the navy, 3,900,000 (including 500,000 marines); and the air force, 2,250,000.

THE DEFENSE ESTABLISHMENT

Chart 3 shows the organization of the U.S. defense establishment under the National Security Act. As the chart makes clear, the president is the commander-in-chief. His orders are transmitted to the military authorities by way of the secretary of defense.

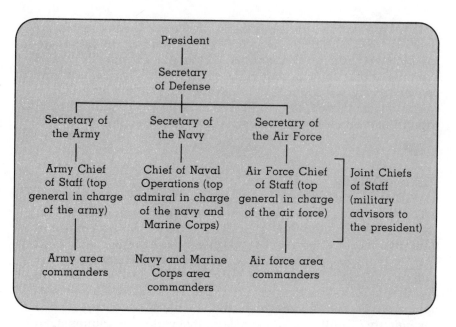

Chart 3. The organization of the United States defense establishment.

The secretary of defense distributes the president's directives to the secretaries of the army, navy, and air force. These secretaries, in turn, communicate with their respective chiefs of staff. The chiefs of staff then activate the orders through their field army, naval fleet, or air fleet commanders.

Perhaps the most important thing to remember about the organization of the American national security system is that even the highest military authorities are subordinated to civilians. Thus the president, with the approval of the Senate, appoints a secretary of defense from the nonmilitary segment of the population. The secretaries of the army, navy, and air force are also appointed by the president, generally after consultation with the secretary of defense. These secretaries are also civilians, not military officers. The top military men—the chiefs of staff—are four rungs down on the ladder of command. Meeting together in a committee known as the Joint Chiefs of Staff, they do have direct access to the president and can often influence his thinking through the advice and information they give him. However, their role is strictly advisory. The decisions are ultimately the president's, and the chiefs of staff must obey his orders whether they agree with him or not. In the American system, there is no tightly knit general staff like that which once played such a decisive role in the affairs of the German nation.

In making sure that the military elements in American life will be firmly under the control of the president—the people's elected representative—the National Security Act was following one of the most basic principles in the United States Constitution. The Constitution, in turn, reflected the deep distrust of militarism that years of domination by British colonial administrators had fostered in the American people. Since independence, that distrust has continued to influence public opinion and thus has had a considerable impact on the conduct of the nation's foreign policy. It has also meant that American draftees have often had more difficulty in adjusting to the demands of war than soldiers in Britain, Germany, and other countries with a stronger military tradition.

A REVERSAL OF VALUES

Many of a person's most deeply cherished values must be suspended when he goes to war. Foremost is the idea that a human life is sacred and that to kill is the most hideous of acts. In war quite the opposite is true, for the greatest heroes are those who have killed the most. America's best-known soldier of the First World War was Sergeant Alvin York, who shot twenty-five Germans to death. The most thrilling moment of the Second World War—from a military point of view—was the explosion of the atomic bomb at Hiroshima, an explosion that killed two hundred thousand Japanese and wounded many more.

Nor is the sending of one's fellow citizens to their deaths any longer viewed as a crime. Thus when General Dwight D. Eisenhower gave the go-ahead for the invasion of Normandy, he knew that tens of thousands of Americans would be killed. Or, lower down the scale, when a platoon lieutenant orders half a dozen men to take out an enemy machine gun, he knows that some, maybe all, will die in the attempt. This is something a commander must learn to live with.

Another concept that must be suspended in wartime is the idea that a person has any individual worth. The platoon, the company, the army, the nation—they are what matter. It is the duty of the citizen—whether that citizen is a soldier on the front line or a woman working in a munitions factory—to give his or her life, if necessary, so that the nation can survive. The individual becomes nothing more than a cog in the gigantic machine of war, to be replaced, if damaged or destroyed, like any other part. Some parts may be difficult to replace, depending on their functions in the machine, but all must be regarded as dispensable. When the life of the nation is at stake, the death of any individual member of it is no longer important.

The concept of democracy must also be discarded by those in the service. One person is no longer as good as another. A sergeant is superior to a private, and a lieutenant is superior to a sergeant. Colonels demand and receive far more respect than lieutenants, while a general has privileges and powers that no colonel can claim. In battle, higher officers are seldom exposed to fire because their lives are worth much more than those of the ordinary enlisted men and the lower officers.

Neither does freedom of choice, that most basic American right, have any place in the armed forces. A man must obey his superior without question; not to do so is an offense that can lead to a court martial. Even wrong orders that may needlessly send people to their deaths must be obeyed, except in the most flagrant of cases.

Nor is the right of privacy respected in the armed forces. Enlisted men live in common barracks. They eat together, use a common latrine, and even dress identically. They march in step and keep their eyes in a forward direction only.

Self-expression is also repressed in the service. Discipline requires the rooting out of all individual desires, emotions, and thoughts that might impair a soldier's obedience to his superiors. This is hard for most people, impossible for a few. Yet iron discipline is the soul of the best armies.

AMERICA'S TWENTIETH-CENTURY WARS

Although all wars make the same basic demands on the soldiers who are required to fight them, the four wars in which the United States has fought during the twentieth century were in many ways quite different from one another. It is difficult to determine which was the most important—each seemed so to those involved. One way to rate the wars is to compare the dollars spent and the numbers of men killed or wounded:

	World War I	World War II	Korea	Vietnam
U.S. dead and wounded	257,000	1,024,000	137,000	350,000
Cost to U.S.	$26 billion	$341 billion	$54 billion	$140 billion

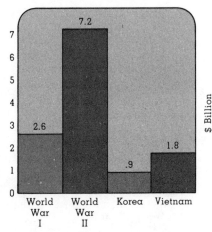

Chart 4. American casualties per 1,000 population.

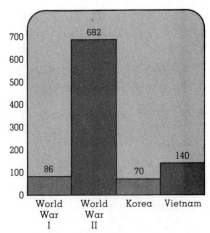

Chart 5. The wars' costs to the United States in Vietnam dollars (1967).

But such statistics can be misleading. For example, although fewer men were killed or wounded in World War I than in Vietnam, the population of the United States during World War I was only half as large as the population during the 1960s. Therefore, when we measure casualties in terms of the total U.S. population in Chart 4, we find that World War I losses were more severe than those suffered in Vietnam. In the same way, the sums spent must be adjusted to reflect the inflation that has occurred since World War I. The Vietnam dollar was worth only thirty percent of the World War I dollar and only fifty percent of the World War II dollar. Chart 5 pictures the relative costs of the four wars adjusted for inflation.

These two charts bring to light several interesting points. First, they reveal the predominance of World War II over the other wars. That war had more casualties per thousand of the American population than the other three wars combined. Its cost was more than twice that of the other three. Second, the charts reveal the relatively high casualty rate of World War I. This rate is especially surprising considering the length of the other wars, for these casualties came in just a year and a quarter of fighting. It is testimony to the peculiar viciousness of the World War I battles. In Chart 6, casualty rates are broken down into yearly averages so that the intensity of the four wars may be compared.

Although U.S. casualty rates during the two world wars were appalling, the numbers of dead and wounded were even greater for the other nations involved—especially for Germany, France,

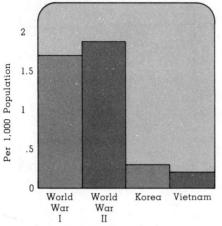

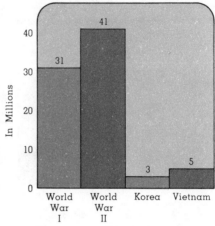

Chart 6. Yearly average of American casualties per 1,000 population.

Chart 7. Total casualties of all nations involved.

and Russia. It must be remembered that these wars were, as their names signify, truly conflicts engulfing the entire world. This was particularly true of World War II. Chart 7 gives the total number of casualties for all nations participating in the four wars. In it, the magnitude of the world wars as compared to Korea and Vietnam is clearly shown.

Chart 7 demonstrates once again that World War II was by far the most lethal of the wars. On a worldwide basis, it resulted in more deaths than the other three wars combined. (The number of Jews slaughtered by Hitler—about six million—accounted for a greater number of deaths than all the fatalities in Vietnam put together.) The chart also reveals that World War I had almost four times as many deaths as Korea and Vietnam combined. Thus there can be no question that, globally at least, the two world wars were far more important than the two later wars.

But casualties and costs are not the only measures of a war's importance to the United States. Chart 8 shows how long each war lasted. The length of the Vietnam War offers a meaningful guide to its effect on American domestic affairs.

The Vietnam experience spanned nineteen years, beginning with President Eisenhower's commitment in 1954 and ending with President Nixon's peace treaty in 1973. This was a longer period of time than all the other wars combined! The young men of an entire generation grew up with the knowledge that they would probably have to fight, and perhaps die, in that distant Asian

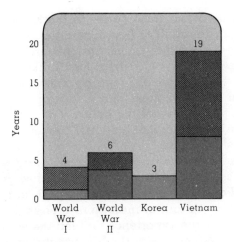

Chart 8. The length of the four twentieth-century wars in which the United States has fought. The dotted portion of the line indicates the period during which the United States government was involved in the war through aid to one or more of the combatants; the solid portion of the line indicates the period during which American troops were engaged in the fighting.

country. Their reluctance to take part in what seemed to many people an unnecessary, immoral war led to riots and to a serious questioning of nearly all American values. Vietnam, in effect, wrenched apart the younger from the older generation. It left the America of the 1970s quite different from what it would have been under more normal circumstances.

As for the other wars, only World War I approached the domestic significance of Vietnam. World War II, for all its casualties, expense, length, and nationwide mobilization, had only minimal effects on the postwar domestic scene. It did, however, have a powerful influence on U.S. foreign policy.

So far, it may appear that there is little to recommend the Korean War as a subject for study. This, however, is not the case. Although Korea turned out to be the least important of the four wars, it *could* have been the most important by far. Had Germany or Japan won the world wars, American security probably would not have been threatened, at least not in the years immediately following the wars. Neither nation had the manpower or the naval resources to mount a full-scale invasion of the continental United States. And obviously little North Vietnam had not the slightest ability to harm the American homeland. But that was not true of our adversaries in the Korean War. In that war, atomic warfare against American cities was a possibility.

There are few episodes in modern history more filled with "what ifs" than the saga of General MacArthur in Korea and his flirtation with the danger of prodding Russia into atomic war. The MacArthur episode offers one of history's most tantalizing and frightening examples of the delicacy of military maneuvers and the precarious hold that national leaders have over their generals in distant lands.

Our study of America's twentieth-century wars will reveal that they were not isolated events erupting in a few years of bombs and bloodshed and then sinking into the past, to be encountered only in history books and grandfathers' stories. Instead, each of the wars was a unique experience that left the world altered in a way that would affect our nation's domestic and international policies far into the future.

In a very real way, we are the products of those wars and the changes they brought about. That is why we should seek to understand them.

THE KOREAN WAR

PART ONE

Scenes of GIs and refugees filing by one another were commonplace during the first year of the seesaw struggle to dominate Korea.

★CHAPTER ONE★

Operation Desperate: June 25 to July 25, 1950

It was quiet and dark within the American Embassy at Tokyo. Suddenly a telephone jangled. Instantly General Douglas MacArthur, commander of the U.S. occupation forces in Japan, was awake. He snatched up the receiver. On the other end of the line was a concerned duty officer: "We have just received a dispatch from Seoul, advising that the North Koreans have struck in great strength south across the 38th Parallel at four o'clock this morning."

MacArthur blinked in astonishment. Was this June 25, 1950? Or was he simply reliving the events of nine years before, when a similar phone call on another Sunday morning had informed him of the Japanese attack on Pearl Harbor? "I had an uncanny feeling of nightmare," he wrote. ". . . It was the same fell note of the war cry that was again ringing in my ears. It couldn't be, I told myself. Not again! I must still be asleep and dreaming."[1] But he was not. War had come once again undeclared, in Asia, with the United States unprepared.

MacArthur winced. Five short years before, the United States had been the most powerful nation on earth. MacArthur then had at his call one thousand warships and several million battle-hardened soldiers. What was left of that force in 1950? Just four undermanned divisions: only a little over sixty thousand men doing occupation duty in Japan. And his strategic reserve? A solitary division in the Pacific, a second division in the United States, and an occupation force in Germany that could not be released.

---

1. Douglas MacArthur, *Reminiscences* (New York: McGraw-Hill, 1964), p. 327.

At that point MacArthur might have made a mental review of Korea's last five years. A temporary partition of the country had been decided by the Allied leaders at Yalta and Potsdam. The purpose of the partition was merely to enable the Russians to disarm the Japanese occupation troops in the north while the Americans did the same in the south. The demarcation line was arbitrarily set at the Thirty-eighth Parallel by MacArthur himself, as supreme commander for the Allied powers.

MacArthur realized that the two Koreas should be reunited— the North depended on the South for its food, and the South depended on the North for its industrial goods. But in May, 1947, the Russians rejected a United Nations resolution calling for a national election. The Russians claimed that the 21 million American-dominated Southerners would overwhelm the 9 million Northerners, who had converted to Communism.

Under the supervision of the United Nations, the United States proceeded to set up a democratic government in their sphere of influence. On May 10, 1948, Syngman Rhee won the presidency of the Republic of Korea, as the South became known. The Russians set up a Communist government in the North shortly thereafter. When the Russian troops pulled out at the end of 1948, followed by the Americans six months later, they left behind a country that was divided by more than a line on a map. Each Korean government had a fierce desire to unify the country under its own rule. And now the North Koreans were attempting to do just that.

To MacArthur's concern, the North Koreans moved rapidly during the next few days. Their 135,000 first-rate soldiers, supplied with Russian-made tanks, artillery, and planes, were ripping apart the 98,000 poorly equipped South Korean troops. The United States had refused to provide the South Koreans with tanks to ensure that they (with their population advantage) would not try to reunite Korea by force. The U.S. advisers had never dreamed that it would be the North Koreans who would attack. But the North Korean leaders had forged a larger and more modern army. And in only four days they had overrun Seoul, the capital of South Korea.

In the meantime, MacArthur followed the events in Washington and New York with keen interest. He firmly approved of President Harry Truman's asking Secretary General Trygve Lie to summon the United Nations Security Council into session. Luckily, the Russian delegate was absent, and an American resolution calling for North Korean withdrawal was passed without a Russian veto. (The Soviets had been boycotting Security Council meetings since early January in order to protest

Korea and its neighbors, 1950.

the exclusion of Communist China from the world organization.)
When the North Koreans continued their drive south, the Security
Council—again upon American urging and again in the absence
of the Russian delegate—called upon member nations to render
military assistance to South Korea. It was the first time in
modern history than an international body had decided to meet
force with force.

On the basis of the UN resolution, Truman wired MacArthur to
back the faltering South Koreans with American planes and

The June 27, 1950, session of the U N Security Council which approved the resolution demanding the withdrawal of North Korean troops from South Korea. Note the vacant chair of the Soviet Union at the table. U N Secretary General Trygve Lie, sitting beside the French representative, is addressing the council.

warships. Convinced that the invasion of South Korea was part of a larger Russian-Chinese play for power throughout Asia, Truman also ordered the Seventh Fleet to protect Chiang Kaishek on Taiwan from a Red Chinese invasion. In addition, he increased financial aid to the French, who were fighting local Communists in Vietnam.

MACARTHUR'S GAMBLE

On June 29, General MacArthur decided to make a personal inspection of the military situation in Korea. He did so in order to determine whether or not the United States could turn back the North Koreans solely by the use of air and sea power, as Truman hoped. Climbing into his private plane, the *Bataan*, he flew to Korea and soon landed twenty miles south of Seoul. Commandeering a jeep, he made a bouncy ride to the Han, a river on Seoul's outskirts. Here he arrived just in time to watch the last survivors of the Republic of Korea (ROK) army retreat from the stricken city. Then he drove to the crest of a low hill. From there he saw a panorama that reminded him of the Philippines during the discouraging days of the Japanese conquest. As he later wrote,

> It was a tragic scene. Across the Han, Seoul burned and smoked in its agony of destruction. There was the constant crump of Red mortar fire as the enemy swooped down toward the bridges. Below me, and streaming by both sides of the hill, were the retreating, panting columns of disorganized troops, the drab color of their weaving lines interspersed here and there with the bright red crosses of ambulances filled with broken, groaning men. The sky was resonant with shrieking missiles of death, and everywhere were the stench and utter desolation of a stricken battlefield. . . . I watched for an hour the pitiful evidence of the disaster I had inherited. In that brief interval on the blood-soaked hill, I formulated my plans. They were desperate plans indeed, but I could see no other way except to accept a defeat which would include not only Korea, but all of continental Asia.[2]

The confusion and despair along the Han convinced MacArthur that the ROK army was not capable of much further resistance. The North Koreans had the war all but won. With more than six divisions pouring southward, they could not be stopped by anything except American ground troops. And MacArthur was not even certain that American soldiers could do the job. Readily available American forces were only about half as numerous as those of North Korea, and there might not be enough time to bring them over from Japan. As MacArthur flew back to his headquarters in Tokyo, he realized that the vital factor was time. With this in mind, he began forming his battle strategy.

He would go against all military teaching: he would throw American troops into the fight piecemeal, not as whole divisions. Small individual units could not hope to blunt the North Korean advance, but the very presence of American troops might be enough to win the time needed to send supplies and additional troops.

MacArthur put himself in the place of the North Korean commanders. When the first American units began showing up on the battlefield, the enemy commanders would become wary. They would ask themselves, "How many divisions are involved?" They then would have to make one of two decisions. First, they could continue their pell-mell drive, hoping to take Pusan—the

---

2. MacArthur, *Reminiscences*, pp. 332—333.

General Douglas MacArthur, Allied supreme
commander of U N forces in Korea, 1950–1951.

only remaining port—before the Americans could supply and
reinforce their troops. Second, they could stop their offensive
momentarily while they reassessed the military situation in light
of the American intervention. MacArthur counted on mystery to
do the job that he was unable to do by might: the mystery of
exactly how many Americans were involved in the initial intervention. If the North Koreans believed that few U.S. troops were
present, they would continue their drive and win the war. If they
believed that the Americans were numerous, they would pause
to bring up reinforcements before continuing. If they did the
latter, they would give MacArthur the time he needed, and they
probably would lose the war. It was as simple as that. MacArthur
called his trick an "arrogant display of strength."

On July 1, units of the Twenty-fourth Division were flown into Korea from Japan and placed astride the main road leading from Seoul to Pusan. However, the American soldiers knew nothing of MacArthur's strategy. They did not know why they had been flown to Korea, what they were fighting for, or even where they were. They were resentful and confused. Marguerite Higgins, a correspondent for the New York *Herald Tribune,* watched as they marched past her. "In the first three weeks of the war," she wrote, "I was filled with pity at the sense of betrayal . . . displayed by our young soldiers who had been plucked so suddenly out of the soft occupation life in Japan and plunged into battle."[3] They were unprepared for fighting. Indeed, it was common knowledge to Higgins and the other correspondents that only a few of the men had ever heard artillery fire before. Worse still, they had no guns that could stop the powerful Russian T-34 tanks.

MacArthur, of course, must shoulder his share of the blame for the unpreparedness of the American troops. Their training in Japan, where MacArthur was in command, had obviously been inferior. But so, too, must President Truman, Secretary of Defense Louis Johnson, and Congress be blamed. They had agreed to cut the armed forces budget to the marrow after World War II. Yet in this action they were only following the wishes of the American public for a quick return to peacetime normalcy. Neither the army nor the people in general were prepared for the brushfire war that had flared so suddenly in Asia.

The first American troops met a series of bloody and humiliating defeats around the city of Taejon. Everything worked against them. Besides being poorly trained, they carried obsolete weapons, were greatly outnumbered, had little tank support, and found it hard to distinguish the South Korean soldiers from those of the North. The Americans did not even have good maps. Marguerite Higgins overheard one frustrated trooper complaining that the only people who knew his whereabouts were the North Koreans.

"In the coming days I saw war turn many of our young soldiers into savagely bitter men," Higgins wrote. "I saw young Americans turn and bolt in battle, or throw down their arms cursing their government for what they thought was embroilment in a

---

3. Marguerite Higgins, *War in Korea: The Report of a Woman Combat Correspondent* (New York: Doubleday, 1951), p. 85.

A grief-stricken American infantryman whose buddy has been killed in action is comforted by another soldier. Nearby, a corpsman methodically fills out casualty tags.

hopeless cause."[4] The correspondent's heart went out to these men, a large percentage of whom were still in their teens. She had her own complaints against the higher-ups who were managing the war. As a woman, she was continually thwarted in her attempts to reach the front lines and to report events as she saw them. She therefore turned a sympathetic ear when one soldier approached "in a fury":

> As his lips trembled with exhaustion and anger, he said, "Are you correspondents telling the people back home the

4. Higgins, War in Korea, p. 83.

truth? Are you telling them that out of one platoon of twenty men, we have three left? Are you telling them that we have nothing to fight with, and that it is an utterly useless war?"[5]

WHY TRUMAN WENT TO WAR

As the Communists chewed up the Twenty-fourth Division during those hectic days of July, 1950, some Americans at home began to share the soldiers' anger at Truman's handling of Korea. Many people were critical of the staggering lack of military preparedness, which hardly matched the president's aggressive stance. Others debated the even more basic question of whether or not the conflict was worth American lives. World Wars I and II were fought because of enemy attacks on American ships and American citizens. But in Korea there had been no American deaths prior to Truman's involvement. Tiny North Korea did not pose the slightest threat to American security. Nor was the possession of Korea by the United States or by a pro–United States government of any real value to American military strategy.

As early as September, 1947, Truman had been told that Korea was useless to American security. At that time four of the leading military men in the nation, including Dwight Eisenhower, had presented Truman with the following analysis of Korea:

> The Joint Chiefs of Staff consider that, from the standpoint of military security, the United States has little strategic interest in maintaining the present troops and bases in Korea for the reasons hereafter stated.
> In the event of hostilities in the Far East, our present forces in Korea would be a military liability. . . . Moreover, any offensive operation the United States might wish to conduct on the Asiatic continent most probably would bypass the Korean peninsula. . . .
> At the present time, the occupation of Korea is requiring very large expenditures . . . with little, if any, lasting benefit to the security of the United States.[6]

It was in response to this report that Truman ultimately had withdrawn the U.S. occupation forces from South Korea.

Truman had obtained more expert analysis of Korea's irrelevancy to U.S. security on January 12, 1950—just six months before

---

5. Higgins, *War in Korea*, p. 83.

6. Quoted in Harry S. Truman, *Memoirs*, vol. 2, *Years of Trial and Hope* (New York: Doubleday, 1956), p. 325.

President Harry S. Truman.

the North Korean attack. At that time Secretary of State Dean Acheson omitted Korea from the Pacific defense perimeter, which included only those areas considered vital to U.S. interests. Attacks on Japan or the Philippines, Acheson declared, would be viewed in a most serious light. But, he continued, "so far as the military security of other areas in the Pacific is concerned, it must be clear that no person can guarantee these areas against military attack."[7] Korea was one of those "other areas."

A secretary of state would seldom, if ever, make such a statement of foreign policy without first discussing it with the president. Therefore, Truman must have been in full agreement with Acheson concerning Korea's unimportance to the security of the United States. Why, then, did he change his mind so radically about Korea six months later?

---

7. Dean Acheson, *The Pattern of Responsibility: From the Record of Secretary of State Dean Acheson*, ed. McGeorge Bundy (Boston: Houghton Mifflin, 1951), p. 185.

The president set forth his reasons for intervention as follows:

> In my generation, this was not the first occasion when the
> strong had attacked the weak. I recalled some earlier
> instances: Manchuria, Ethiopia, Austria. I remembered how
> each time the democracies failed to act it had encouraged the
> aggressors to keep going ahead. Communism was acting in
> Korea just as Hitler, Mussolini, and the Japanese had acted
> ten, fifteen, and twenty years earlier. I felt certain that if
> South Korea was allowed to fall, Communist leaders would
> be emboldened to override nations closer to our own
> shores. . . . If this was allowed to go unchallenged it would
> mean a third world war.[8]

Critics of this view pointed out that it was unrealistic to equate
the 135,000 men of North Korea's army with the 3,000,000 troops
raised by Hitler to terrorize Europe. To such remarks, Truman
had a ready reply. The North Koreans were only a part of a vast
plot of international communism, masterminded by Stalinist
Russia, to dominate the world. Truman was in complete agreement with General Omar Bradley, head of the Joint Chiefs of
Staff, who thought that "Russia was not yet ready for war, but in
Korea they were obviously testing us, and the line ought to be
drawn now."[9] Truman believed that it was Russia's long-term
intention "to take over the free world."[10]

Later events suggested that Truman overestimated Russia's
ability—if not perhaps its desire—to carry out that objective.
Russia had not been able to enlist Communist China in any
effective conspiracy to take over the free world. Quite the
contrary, just as Acheson then believed, Russia and China had a
deep distrust of each other arising from their age-old disputes
over Manchuria and Outer Mongolia. Also, the two nations were
competitors for leadership of Communist parties around the
world. Nor would it matter much to other Asian nations that the
United States had kept communism out of South Korea. For, as
the future would show, American participation in the Korean War
did not discourage the Communist North Vietnamese from attempting to extend their rule over South Vietnam.

It seems probable that the reasons Truman gave for intervention in Korea were, partly at least, justifications for an action on
his part which was more impulsive than rational. Neither the

---

8. Truman, *Memoirs*, 2: 332–333.

9. Truman, *Memoirs*, 2: 335.

10. Truman, *Memoirs*, 2: 212.

Secretary of State Dean Acheson (right) greeting Soviet Minister of Foreign Affairs Andrei Y. Vyshinsky. Acheson was the chief architect of American foreign policy between 1949 and 1953.

president nor the State Department had any coolly thought-out plans to follow in the event that South Korea should be invaded. George Kennan, one of the top men in the State Department, described the confusion that resulted when news of the attack came. As the department tried to set a new course, it was engulfed in a "turmoil of willful personalities and poorly schooled minds." Kennan continued, "The President doesn't understand [Korea]; Congress doesn't understand it; nor does the public, nor does the press. They all wander around in a labyrinth of ignorance and error and conjecture, in which truth is intermingled with fiction at a hundred points."[11]

To understand why Truman decided to send American troops into a land war in Asia requires more than knowledge of the

11. George F. Kennan, *Memoirs, 1925–1950* (Boston: Little, Brown, 1967), p. 500.

president's statements. It also requires a close look at the American attitude toward communism at the time.

AMERICA'S OBSESSION WITH COMMUNISM

Seldom has the United States been so confused and uncertain of itself as during the last half of the 1940s. The fear of communism had become almost a national obsession, an unreasonable fear. Both international and domestic events had helped to create this psychological uneasiness.

Possibly the most shocking event had been Mao Tse-tung's victory in China during 1948 and 1949. The result was the conversion of one-quarter of the world's population from American allies to potential enemies.

Shattering events were also undermining America's position in Europe. Communism had absorbed Rumania, Bulgaria, and Hungary when Russian troops conquered those Axis partners near the end of the war. Bad as that situation was, it was not altogether unexpected. More unexpected were the ruthless Stalinist tactics that had enabled local Reds to take over Poland in 1947 and Czechoslovakia in 1948. Similar takeover bids in Greece and Turkey were blocked only by American aid and the threat of American intervention under the Truman Doctrine—President Truman's announcement that the further expansion of communism by internal subversion or armed force would not be tolerated by the United States. The fact that the Communists had been minority factions in all these countries gave Americans concern. They feared that a coup might also be engineered in the United States.

For these reasons, many Americans became frightened that their own government was being infiltrated by Communists in preparation for a Russian-inspired revolution. In March, 1947, after the discovery of a large Communist spy ring in Canada, Truman ordered the FBI and Civil Service Commission to investigate the 3,000,000 U.S. government employees. The mere fact that the president had ordered an investigation was enough to increase domestic tension.

The gigantic investigation would take four years and ultimately would reveal only 212 persons of questionable loyalties. However, as the investigation proceeded, the House of Representatives' Un-American Activities Committee discovered that an alleged Communist, Alger Hiss, had penetrated the highest stratum of the American government. Hiss had actually been an

Ethel and Julius Rosenberg were convicted of having passed information regarding the U.S.–British atomic bomb project to Soviet agents. They were executed at Sing Sing Prison in New York on June 19, 1953.

adviser to Roosevelt during the "American giveaway" at Yalta! The Hiss hearings before the Un-American Activities Committee were skillfully publicized by a young congressman named Richard Nixon. For months during 1948 and 1949, the nation was chilled as it heard charges that Hiss had delivered sixty-five State Department documents to a Communist agent in 1937 and 1938. The fact that both Truman and Acheson supported Hiss almost to the moment of his conviction for perjury only intensified the public's fears. To many Americans, it appeared that Communists had duped the highest government officials and had wormed their way into places vital to U.S. security.

These fears were heightened still further in February, 1950. At that time the public learned that Klaus Fuchs, a key scientist on the British team working in the United States on the atomic bomb, had been convicted in England for passing nuclear secrets to the Russians. He had managed to elude the security systems of both Britain and the United States long enough to deliver detailed information on the bomb's construction to Russian agents. This information had enabled the Soviet Union to explode its own bomb in September, 1949—far in advance of Western expectations. Two Americans, Julius and Ethel Rosenberg, would later be sentenced to death for their part in the espionage ring.

It was in such an atmosphere that Truman was compelled to decide on the action to be taken in Korea. Truman was a tough politician who had fought his way up the Democratic ranks by way of Kansas City's Pendergast machine. He was a bristling, peppery man who, though very loyal to his friends, was uncompromisingly aggressive toward his enemies. His temper sometimes flared like gunpowder. Even his daughter Margaret admitted that "he could match his sparks against the greatest temper-losers in White House history."[12] It was simply not within Truman's makeup to take lightly a Communist challenge such as that offered in Korea. It was the fact that the Reds had offered the challenge, not the importance of Korea, that mattered.

In addition to his natural combativeness, the president undoubtedly felt that he must demonstrate strength before the American public. It had been during his administration that China had fallen under the rule of Mao Tse-tung, that Eastern Europe had fallen to Russia, and that America's atomic monopoly had vanished. Amid all the domestic hysteria about the administration's being soft on communism, Truman could not back down from a brazen Red offensive in Korea. Thus Truman's need to vindicate himself before the American people, as well as his inborn fighting spirit, played an important role in his Korean decision.

Once Truman had determined a course to follow, he plunged into action. There was no time for the cool-headed members of his administration to point out the evidence which seemed to suggest that Korea was not part of a Russian-inspired plot of world conquest—namely, the indications that Russia had been as much surprised by the Korean offensive as the rest of the world. If the Russians had instigated the attack, was it likely that they would have continued their boycott of the United Nations when by being present they could have vetoed UN aid to South Korea? If the invasion was important to the Russians' interests, would they not be playing a more active role in the fighting? Was it not possible that the North Koreans had acted on their own initiative, and with the limited objective of unifying their country?

---

12. Margaret Truman, *Harry S. Truman* (New York: Simon & Schuster, Pocket Books, 1974), p. 3.

These questions went unanswered, even unconsidered by most. A sense of urgency and crisis prevailed as the Truman administration prepared to meet force with force. Truman did not even take time to ask Congress for a formal declaration of war. Instead, he called the conflict in Korea a "police action" and sent U.S. units there as a sort of constable's force that required no congressional approval. With those who criticized him for bypassing Congress, Truman was short and to the point. He said that he had committed American troops in accordance with a United Nations resolution and that Congress had already approved of American adherence to the UN. Furthermore, he asserted that as commander-in-chief of the armed forces he had the constitutional duty to provide for America's security.

But there were not many critics. Indeed, most Americans approved of Truman's initial handling of Korea. The respected Roper Poll reported a favorable response toward the president from 73 percent of those questioned.

CHAPTER TWO

The Crucial Battles: July 25 to October 7, 1950

By the end of July the crucial stage in MacArthur's strategy had been reached. The Twenty-fourth Division had suffered a series of serious defeats, and the way to Pusan lay open to the North Koreans. Marguerite Higgins, watching the conflict from the front lines, knew that the American and ROK troops were beaten. Yet the North Koreans hesitated to advance. "Why they [the enemy] did not push their tanks straight through to Pusan then and there is one of the war's great mysteries," she wrote. "A hard push would have crumbled our defenses."[1]

Higgins did not know the reason, but wily MacArthur knew. He had correctly gauged the thoughts of the North Korean commanders. Thereby he had gained ten costly but precious days. Once again he had proved himself a master strategist of warfare. During those ten vital days he had managed to scrounge the necessary planes and ships to bring the rest of his soldiers from Japan. Working furiously, the Americans and the regrouped ROK soldiers erected a semicircular line of defense around Pusan. There they awaited the coming Red attack, knowing that even with reinforcements it would be touch and go.

THE FIGHT FOR PUSAN

Could the five ROK and four U.S. divisions (which included the last all-black regiment in the army) hold the Pusan perimeter against thirteen North Korean divisions? The U.S. troops now had heavy Patton tanks that could take the measure of the Russian

---

1. Marguerite Higgins, *War in Korea: The Report of a Woman Combat Correspondent* (New York: Doubleday, 1951), p. 71.

U.S. soldiers moving up to engage North Koreans in battle along the Pusan perimeter.

T-34s. They had the support of the powerful U.S. Air Force, as well as U.S. warships. And soon more men would be joining them, for Truman had called out the reserves for retraining and duty in Korea. But every man at Pusan knew that he and his fellow soldiers had no alternative to withstanding the North Korean attack. To fail would result in being pushed into the sea.

On August 4, the Americans blew up all bridges spanning the Naktong, the river they were using as their line of defense along the most important sector. The 47,000 U.S. troops waited uneasily for the arrival of the 70,000 North Koreans. They did not have to wait long. On the night of August 5, the first North Korean units brushed aside a screen of tired Twenty-fourth Division soldiers to cross the Naktong and occupy Obong-ni Ridge—"Cloverleaf Hill" to the Americans. Quickly, the Communists built an underwater bridge of logs and sandbags over which tanks and artillery rumbled to the American side of the river. By August 11, the town of Yongsan, several miles behind the defensive perimeter, was being infiltrated. Less than fifteen miles beyond lay Miryang, a key town on the railroad between Pusan and the upper two-thirds of the perimeter. If Miryang should fall, the northernmost defending forces would be cut off from their supplies. The result would be disaster and probable collapse.

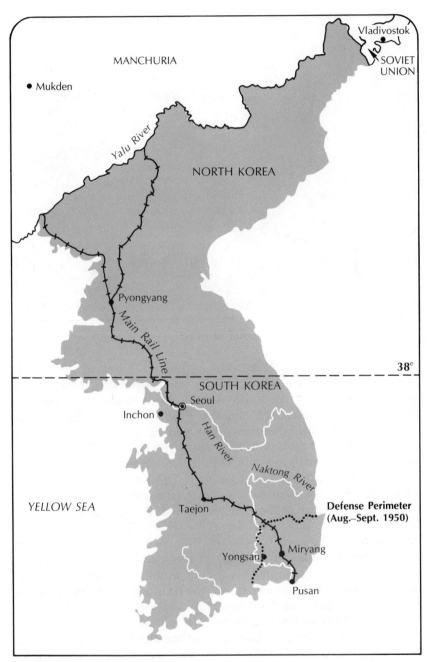

The Korean War, July–August, 1950. The fight to hold the Pusan defense perimeter was desperate. If the North Koreans had broken through, all of Korea would have fallen and probably remained in their possession.

A U.S. gun crew on alert north of Pusan.

The situation was critical. On August 15, General Walton H. Walker, MacArthur's commander of the perimeter, ordered an all-out assault on the North Korean bridgehead at Yongsan. During the ferocious fighting, the North Koreans held on. But when a column of T-34s was destroyed in a pass between two hills, the North Koreans had to retreat. The First Battle of the Naktong ended on August 18 with a U.S. victory.

But the fighting was far from over. The North Koreans rushed up reinforcements to raise their troop strength to 98,000 men by early September. On September 3, the Second Battle of the Naktong began. For four days the North Koreans assaulted various positions near Cloverleaf Hill. Walker skillfully shifted his reserves to meet each attack. Yet the North Koreans pushed on, and at times it seemed as if they would crush the American and ROK defenders. So fierce was the fighting that many veteran soldiers, counting the dead per mile, claimed the battle was as violent as those in Normandy in 1944.

However, the North Koreans lacked the final ounce of strength that might have tilted the battle in their favor. The ten days they lost to MacArthur's ruse had cost them dearly, for American units now were pouring into Pusan from all over the world. By early September, U.S. troop strength had soared to 90,000 men—with nearly as many ROK troops. And the defenders now had an effective force of five hundred topflight tanks—outnumbering the North Koreans' by five to one.

THE INCHON DEBATE

The Second Battle of the Naktong also resulted in a U.S. victory, and the North Koreans once again fell back. American commanders now realized that the time had come to switch from defense to offense. MacArthur, directing the overall strategy from Tokyo, estimated that an attempt to push the enemy back to North Korea mile by arduous mile would cost the ROK and U.S. Eighth Army (as the American force was now called) as many as 100,000 casualties. If, on the other hand, an army corps could be landed at Inchon, it could quickly retake Seoul and cut the North Koreans' supply line. Then, MacArthur reasoned, the North Korean forces in the south would quickly collapse.

As early as July 23, MacArthur had informed Washington of his intention to land forces at Inchon as soon as the Pusan perimeter was stabilized. General Omar Bradley, head of the Joint Chiefs of Staff, was horrified. A few weeks later, when the news from Pusan had improved, Bradley sent the army and navy chiefs of staff to Tokyo to persuade MacArthur to give up the plan. It was, they told him, simply too dangerous.

The chiefs of staff pressed their argument hard. For one thing, they said, MacArthur would be inviting disaster by taking three divisions from the still vulnerable Pusan front to form his proposed Tenth Corps invasion force. If the Inchon landing failed and the Pusan perimeter caved in, Korea would be lost.

Then there were the difficulties of the landing itself, difficulties so great that failure seemed certain. First, there was the tide. The thirty-foot tide at Inchon was one of the world's largest. When the tide went out, it left two miles of mud flats in the harbor. Only when the tide was in, for two hours in the morning and two in the evening, would the harbor be navigable. The main force might manage to strike at the right time, but the ability of backup vessels to deliver supplies and reinforcements would be severely limited. Second, the geography of the harbor would require landing troops in the very heart of Inchon, a city of 250,000 inhabitants. There the buildings would offer every protection to enemy defenders. Third, the high sea wall would prevent rapid disembarcation from landing craft, which would become easy targets. Fourth, it was the typhoon season, and a typhoon could scatter the fleet and leave the invasion troops without the

protection of carrier planes or warships. "If every possible geographical and naval handicap were listed," said Admiral Forrest Sherman to MacArthur, "Inchon had 'em all."[2] General Matthew Ridgway estimated the chances of a successful invasion at five thousand to one.

But MacArthur remained as determined to invade Inchon as Yamamoto had been to strike Pearl Harbor. And like Yamamoto he argued that all the problems were outweighed by the single most important advantage in warfare—surprise. It was precisely

2. Douglas MacArthur, *Reminiscences* (New York: McGraw-Hill, 1964), p. 348.

A South Korean soldier relaxes on a hillside as he watches American troops and supplies being unloaded in Pusan harbor.

the difficulty of the landing that would guarantee its success— the enemy would be totally unprepared. MacArthur was at his eloquent best. "The prestige of the Western world hangs in the balance," he told Bradley's emissaries. "Oriental millions are watching the outcome. . . . Make the wrong decision here—the fatal decision of inertia—and we will be done. I can almost hear the ticking of the second hand of destiny."[3]

The chiefs, both tough military men, fell beneath MacArthur's stronger will. Inchon was on.

---

3. MacArthur, *Reminiscences*, p. 350.

Seated aboard his flagship, the *U.S.S. Mount McKinley*, General Douglas MacArthur and, standing left to right, Generals Courtney Whitney, Edwin K. Wright, and Edward M. Almond watch as the first assault wave establishes a beachhead at Wolmi-do, the fort guarding the entrance to Inchon, Korea.

THE INCHON LANDING

The invasion fleet of 260 ships began assembling off Sasebo, Japan, on September 11. On September 12 MacArthur boarded his flagship, the *U.S.S. Mount McKinley*. Then a typhoon, the very thing Washington had dreaded most, began to roughen the seas. With winds of more than 125 miles per hour at its center, it could have scattered the fleet and wrecked the invasion. But it moved off, and the next day was sunny and clear. MacArthur, full of brass and bluster in front of his subordinates, was nervous as the fleet headed for Korea. As he later admitted, "I had made many landings before, but this was the most intricately complicated amphibious operation I had ever attempted."[4]

---

4. MacArthur, *Reminiscences*, p. 352.

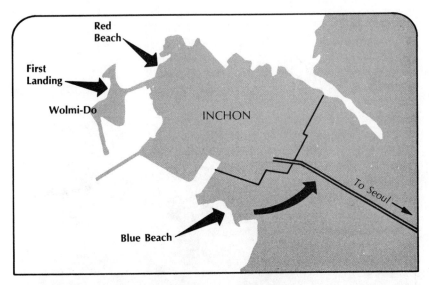

The Inchon invasion, September 15, 1950.

The general found it difficult to sleep the night before the invasion, and at 2:00 A.M. he walked out on deck. The men on duty were tense and silent. MacArthur stood at the ship's bow, listening to the rush of the Yellow Sea under the hull. Now and then he peered over the side to watch the phosphorescent water sparklets that were thrown up as the prow cut through the waves. He told himself, "I alone was responsible for tomorrow, and if I failed, the dreadful results would rest on judgment day against my soul."[5] Still uneasy, he returned to bed.

Before dawn on September 15, MacArthur was awakened by the fleet's thundering guns. They were bombarding Fort Wolmi-do, which guarded Inchon harbor. The plan called for Wolmi-do to be taken by the first assault wave, striking at 6:30 A.M. on high tide. The marines had to be fully landed and supplied before the ebbing tide forced the supporting fleet to retreat back from the emerging mud flats. Then, when the tide rose again late in the afternoon, the main assault teams would strike. One team would land at Red Beach, in the center of the city, and the second would go ashore at Blue Beach, one-half mile south of the city limits. While the Red force drove against the defenders, the Blue would lance across the two-mile-wide peninsula to cut the city off. Then it would strike the defenders from the rear.

The plan worked to perfection. Wolmi-do fell to the marines with a minimum of fighting. Then, while the fleet stood out in the

5. MacArthur, *Reminiscences*, p. 353.

An assault wave of the First Marine Division headed for Inchon's Blue Beach. MacArthur's Tenth Corps quickly captured Inchon and ten days later also took Seoul, the capital of South Korea.

bay awaiting the return of the tide, cruisers and destroyers shelled Inchon and carrier planes smashed it with bombs. As the tide again gurgled across the mud, landing craft carried wave after wave of American soldiers up to the Red and Blue sea walls. Inchon was as severely undermanned as MacArthur had figured. The defenders numbered only about two thousand. They could offer little effective resistance, and the city quickly fell.

MacArthur urged the Tenth Corps on to Seoul, his main objective. The North Koreans, again seriously outnumbered, put up a stiff fight. Nonetheless, the South Korean capital was retaken on September 25, exactly three months after the conflict had begun.

The North Korean troops now were confronted by the ever more powerful Eighth Army to their front at Pusan and by the victorious Tenth Corps to their rear at Seoul. They realized that further resistance was futile. As General Walker blasted out of the Pusan perimeter, the North Koreans broke in panic. Their army ceased to exist. In a matter of days, all that remained was a discouraged mob fleeing northward. Nearly 100,000 North Korean troops and their equipment were captured. The first phase of the Korean War was a complete American victory.

Reinforcements and equipment being brought ashore after In-chon's Red and Blue Beaches had been secured.

But now another question loomed. Should the victors pursue the North Koreans across the Thirty-eighth Parallel into their own country? To this question MacArthur replied with a resounding "Yes!" Somewhat less enthusiastically, President Truman and the United Nations General Assembly (forty-seven ayes to five nays) agreed.

On October 7, 1950, about 200,000 U.S., ROK, and assorted UN troops (including battalion-sized units from Australia, Canada, Britain, France, Thailand, and ten other non-Communist nations) moved across the Thirty-eighth Parallel. Their drive toward the Yalu River, Korea's northern border, began the second phase of the war.

CHAPTER THREE

Thunder out of China: October 8, 1950, to July 10, 1951

> We were moving at quite a clip toward the Yalu, and it was like a shooting gallery at times. Those North Koreans we couldn't catch or kill, we left behind. . . . General Walker had been Patton's right-hand man in Europe, and there we were out ahead of everybody and everything, bypassing enemy pockets, bypassing whole communities. . . . We were riding jeeps and trucks and making forty, fifty, or sixty miles a day, leaving our lines farther and farther behind, and everybody was talking about drinking from the Yalu and going home for Christmas.[1]

It was a heady feeling for nineteen-year-old Anthony Herbert to be sweeping north through Korea just as Patton had swept through France. The American-ROK offensive across the Thirty-eighth Parallel had taken the North Koreans by surprise. The North Koreans melted away in terror as Herbert and his buddies roared northward in a whirlwind of triumph. There seemed to be no stopping the victors of Pusan and Inchon during these early days of October, 1950. MacArthur himself looked forward to a quick end of formal resistance. Once the resistance was broken, the Communist government would be replaced by one chosen in a UN-supervised election. And once the election was held, all Korea would be united under a pro-Western democracy.

THE CHINESE AND KOREA

However, a worried Harry Truman sat in Washington, D.C. The Yalu River was not only the northern border of Korea, but it was

---

1. Anthony Herbert with James T. Wooten, *Soldier* (New York: Dell, 1973), p. 52.

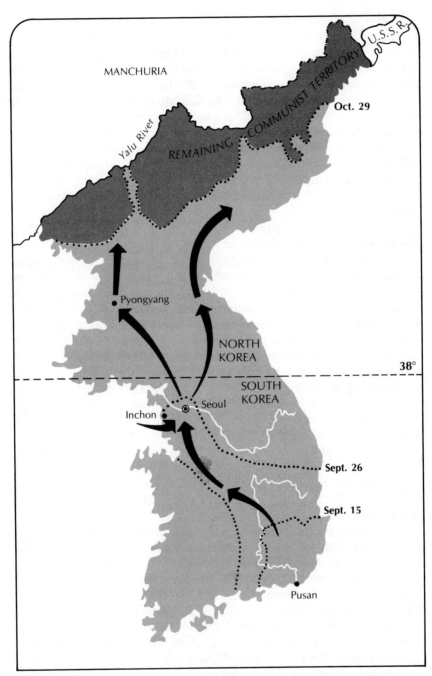

The U N counteroffensive, September–October, 1950. Following
the capture of Inchon and Seoul, the North Korean army became a
disorganized mob falling back before the relentless advance of
U N forces.

also the southern border of Chinese Manchuria. And a short stretch of the border even fronted Russian territory, just eighty air miles from the sensitive base of Vladivostok. Truman knew that the two Communist giants would look as unfavorably at a strong American army on their borders as the United States would upon a Communist army across the Rio Grande in Mexico. Intelligence reports revealed that the Chinese were moving powerful reinforcements to their already impressive army in Manchuria. The total Chinese troop strength in Manchuria was estimated at 300,000. For these reasons the president was concerned about Chinese, and possibly Russian, intervention in Korea.

By the time U.S. troops had reached the Thirty-eighth Parallel, Truman realized that American foreign policy was at a momentous crossroads. As a senator during World War II, he knew that Roosevelt had established a policy of total victory for the United States. This policy required the United States not only to repel aggression, but also to conquer the aggressor. For this reason Truman had permitted MacArthur to cross the Thirty-eighth Parallel into North Korea. But the Cold War, begun around 1948, had given rise to the entirely new policy of containment—a complete break with the Rooseveltian precedent. Containment did not require a fight to the finish. It held that the enemy could exist but should not be allowed to expand its territory at the expense of American security. Thus, Russia could keep its conquests in Eastern Europe. But Russia would not be allowed to absorb West Germany, Japan, or any other nation along its borders or the borders of its satellites.

The policy of containment had been fulfilled once the North Koreans had been driven out of South Korea. Theoretically the fighting could end. On the other hand, to stop now would violate the Rooseveltian policy of total victory. Hence Truman's brief dilemma.

In deciding for total victory, Truman knowingly had risked war with China. But he felt he would be able to play the odds. His instructions to MacArthur stated that U.S. troops were to be pulled back immediately if the Chinese intervened in force. It was a gamble, however, because as early as October 3 the Chinese foreign minister, Chou En-lai, had told the Indian ambassador that if the United States crossed the Thirty-eighth Parallel his government would enter the conflict. Although similar reports had come out of Stockholm and Moscow, Truman continued to be optimistic. He hoped that either the Chinese were bluffing or that he could quell their fears by ordering MacArthur to use only ROK, not U.S., troops to occupy the Yalu area on Manchuria's border.

However, if U.S. leaders had examined Chinese history, they might have guessed that the Chinese were not bluffing. Korea was a highly emotional issue in Chinese foreign policy. Chinese culture had been introduced into Korea more than three thousand years earlier. In 108 B.C., soldiers of the mighty Han dynasty brought Korea into the empire, which matched, and in many ways excelled, the empire being erected by Rome half a world away.

Almost every Chinese dynasty that followed considered Korea as part of its natural area of influence. The Mongols under the Kublai Khan of Marco Polo's time used Korea as a base from which they twice failed in making a sea invasion of Japan. The Ming dynasty had such influence on Korea that Ming manners and dress survived in Korea to modern times. The Yi dynasty introduced Confucianism, a philosophy on which most Koreans have based their way of life down to the present day. When Japanese troops invaded Korea in 1592, it was the Chinese who helped the Koreans expel them. Thereafter the Koreans recognized the loose rule of the Manchu dynasty.

Although the Japanese forced the Chinese out of Korea in 1894, the Chinese still claimed a special relationship with the Koreans. When World War II expelled the Japanese, the Chinese anticipated that Korea would again fall into their orbit. Roosevelt himself had assumed as much, although he had expected the Chinese ruler to be his ally Chiang Kai-shek and not the Communist Mao Tse-tung.

Not only did historical sentiments hint at Chinese intervention in Korea. There was also a very real political need for Mao to assert himself there. Chiang had been driven on to Taiwan only the year before, and Communist supremacy in China was still quite shaky. If Mao proved weak in asserting traditional Chinese rights in Korea, the Chinese people might rise up against him in anger and disgust. Chiang, with half a million troops, would have been only too eager to invade the mainland and gather the malcontents around him. To discourage such an invasion, as well as to cement support for himself among the Chinese by defying the American invaders, Mao probably felt that he had no choice but to intervene.

And so while Truman and MacArthur urged U.S. troops northward, the first Chinese divisions secretly began moving south of the Yalu River.

Truman did not know about this ominous turn of events as the UN forces occupied Pyongyang, North Korea's capital. However, he continued to worry. In mid-October he boarded a plane to fly to Wake Island in the Pacific. There he would discuss with

As U N troops advanced northward, they took prisoner thousands of North Korean soldiers. Above, Marines escort some of the captured defenders of Inchon. At right, the prisoners await the issue of their prisoner-of-war uniforms.

MacArthur the firsthand reports he had received of possible Chinese intervention.

TRUMAN VS. MACARTHUR

General MacArthur and President Truman were as different as two individuals could be. MacArthur was imperious and aristocratic—destined to become a general almost from his birth into a prominent army family. Truman, on the other hand, was a twangy, Missouri-bred politician who had fought at every step on his way to the Senate. Truman's elevation to the vice-presidency and ultimately to the presidency upon the death of Roosevelt had surprised everyone, including himself. MacArthur lived in a world of gold braid, huge air fleets, and thousands of marching soldiers. Truman lived in a world of shirt sleeves, smoke-filled rooms, and small groups of free-wheeling politicians.

The two men were as different in their views on foreign policy as they were in character and background. Whether the North Koreans were crushed or merely contained, Truman was determined that the conflict should not be permitted to grow into a

third world war involving the Russians and the Chinese. It was therefore necessary to limit the scope of the fighting to the Korean peninsula. It was also necessary to limit the purpose of the fighting to one primary objective—the restoration of South Korean sovereignty. The destruction of the Communist regime in North Korea and its replacement by a democratic government was a secondary objective, to be pursued *only* if there were no threat of Russian or Chinese intervention.

This concept of limited warfare was difficult for MacArthur to accept. Indeed, Truman believed that he did not even understand it. Far from cooperating to limit America's military role in the Orient, MacArthur seemed determined to expand it. In a public statement issued in August, two months before the Wake Island meeting, MacArthur had proposed the creation of a Pacific defense line, manned by U.S. air, naval, and ground forces, which would stretch all the way from the Russian port of Vladivostok to the Malay Peninsula—with himself, presumably, in command. Furthermore, he had concluded his statement with ringing praise for Chiang Kai-shek, to whom he swore eternal loyalty.

The statement had infuriated Truman, who was already suspicious of MacArthur's connection with the so-called China Lobby, a powerful political pressure group which sought U.S. military assistance in restoring Chiang's government to the Chinese mainland. With good reason Truman regarded Chiang

General Douglas MacArthur greeting President Truman at Wake Island, October 15, 1950.

as inept and corrupt, unfit even to rule the island of Taiwan. He was unwilling to sacrifice a single American life on Chiang's behalf. Yet to the Russians and the Red Chinese—who would not expect an American general to speak on such important matters without approval from Washington—MacArthur's statement might well appear to be a direct and official challenge.

That statement almost cost MacArthur his job and his history-book fame as leader of the brilliant Inchon invasion, which was still several weeks away. Truman had wanted to fire him immediately, and it was only with difficulty that his military advisers had persuaded him to change his mind on the grounds that morale, both at home and along the embattled Pusan perimeter, would be seriously affected. He did insist that MacArthur repudiate the statement, which had already appeared in newspapers around the world, and with this formality MacArthur complied.

Still, Truman was uneasy. He was not convinced that MacArthur understood—or wanted to understand—why he had been asked to withdraw the statement, why confrontation with Communist China must not be permitted to occur. It was to settle these doubts that he decided to meet with the general face to face.

When Truman landed on Wake Island, MacArthur met his commander-in-chief in a most casual manner. For no apparent reason he kept the president waiting for forty-five minutes. When he finally appeared, wearing an unbuttoned shirt and a battered campaign hat, he offered no salute. Some of the news reporters present thought that his dress and behavior were calculated to show a lack of respect for the president. Truman himself decided to overlook MacArthur's "getup" (which in his opinion looked ridiculous on a man of seventy), but he did comment on the general's "playacting." As Truman later recalled the incident:

> When he walked in, I took one look at him, and I said, "Now you look here. I've come halfway across the world to meet you, but don't worry about that. I just want you to know I don't give a good goddam what you do or think about Harry Truman, but don't you ever again keep your commander-in-chief waiting. Is that clear?"
>
> His face got red as a beet, but he . . . indicated that he understood what I was talking about, and we went on from there.[2]

During the ninety-minute conference that followed, MacArthur strove to deepen what he regarded as Truman's superficial understanding of Asia. MacArthur, after all, had lived in Asia for fourteen years. "Of the Far East," MacArthur wrote, "he [Truman] knew little, presenting a strange combination of distorted history and vague hopes that somehow, some way, we could do something to help those struggling against Communism."[3] Truman, on his part, thought that MacArthur's long association with the East, together with the great power he held there, had blinded him to any viewpoint but his own. Truman therefore discussed the Korean conflict from a worldwide perspective, stressing particularly the threat of the Russians in Europe. If the Chinese became involved in Korea, he said, there was a good possibility that their Soviet ally would come to their aid by engaging U.S. troops on quite a different battleground.

It is in regard to the specifics discussed at the meeting that the historical record becomes cloudy. The two men met alone, and no notes were taken. As Truman remembered the conversation,

> I asked MacArthur point blank if the Chinese would come in, and he said under no circumstances would they come in.

---

2. Quoted in Merle Miller, *Plain Speaking: An Oral Biography of Harry S. Truman* (New York: Berkley, 1974), pp. 294–295.

3. Douglas MacArthur, *Reminiscences* (New York: McGraw-Hill, 1964), p. 361.

> He says, "Mr. President, the war will be over by Thanksgiv-
> ing and I'll have the American troops back in Tokyo by
> Christmas," and he went on like that.
>
> We must've talked for an hour or so, just the two of us, and
> I believe I made it more than abundantly clear to him that I
> was his commander-in-chief and that he was to obey orders
> and . . . not issue any public statements of any kind that
> hadn't been approved by me personally.[4]

Truman also reiterated his standing orders to MacArthur: he was
to use only ROK troops near the Chinese and Russian borders,
and under no circumstances was he to cross those borders by
land or by air.

MacArthur's interpretation of the conversation was quite different. Perhaps this should have been apparent from a comment
he made at another conference later the same day. He said that
"if the Chinese tried to get to Pyongyang [the North Korean
capital], there would be the greatest slaughter."[5] Unfortunately,
the implications of that comment were not explored at the time.
Months afterward, MacArthur claimed that he had *not* assured
Truman that the Chinese would stay out of the war. And he said
he had based his promise of a great slaughter on the belief that
he would be allowed to unleash U.S. bombers against Chinese
supply bases in Manchuria. In fact, MacArthur said he had left
the Wake Island meeting believing that Truman had given him a
blank check in his management of the war.

The exact nature of the misunderstanding between Truman
and MacArthur, and the reasons for it, would eventually be
debated by the American public, investigated by Congress, and
analyzed at length by historians. And by and large the consen-
sus would be that the misunderstanding was chiefly on MacArthur's part and that it was to some degree deliberate. But all that
lay in the future. In October, 1950, the depths of the differences
between Truman and MacArthur had not yet been discovered.
They were differences that would cost the troops dearly.

THE CHINESE DECEPTION

Being an aggressive man and being more confident than ever
of his abilities as a result of the wildly successful Inchon

---

4. Quoted in Miller, *Plain Speaking*, p. 295.

5. Quoted in Harry S. Truman, *Memoirs*, vol. 2, *Years of Trial and Hope* (New
York: Doubleday, 1956), p. 365.

operation, MacArthur took all stops out of his offensive. Little dreaming, or caring, that he was sending his troops directly toward the massing Chinese, he urged the columns on to the Yalu. American spearheads raced northward through Korean towns and villages so fast that many regiments lost contact with divisional headquarters. They shot northward like dozens of lightning bolts. Nothing could stop them.

Yet there was growing evidence that the Chinese meant to fulfill their threat. On October 25 an ROK battalion was destroyed by Chinese who appeared from nowhere. Then, on November 3, a U.S. regiment was overwhelmed by Chinese troops. Two days later a British Commonwealth brigade was forced to withdraw under heavy Chinese fire. Yet the following day the Chinese disappeared. The UN commanders were puzzled. What did it mean? Were the Chinese bluffing? Were they trying to demonstrate their determination to defend their borders before actually committing themselves to full-scale intervention?

Even MacArthur was cautious for a moment. He was confronted by a truly ironic dilemma. Only five months earlier he had tricked his opponent by throwing out a few units in an "arrogant display of strength." By doing so he had gained ten days to bring in reinforcements and to reverse the course of the war. Now what? Were the Chinese doing the same thing to him? Were these troops just token units sent to frighten him at the very moment when complete victory was within his grasp?

"There were but three possible courses," MacArthur recalled. "I could go forward, remain immobile, or withdraw."[6] Withdrawal simply was not in his makeup. To remain immobile was equally impossible—it would have meant erecting defensive positions across territory which in MacArthur's opinion did not lend itself to entrenchment. Also, to remain immobile would be to admit weakness, and that could invite a Chinese attack. MacArthur therefore decided to continue his offensive.

While he waited for supplies to catch up with his forward troops, MacArthur ordered ninety bombers to blast out the China-Korea bridges spanning the Yalu. There was no doubt in his mind that this was necessary to stop the flow of men and material from China. But, just before the planes were scheduled to take off, Truman countermanded the order. In a rage MacArthur obeyed, but it was to him "the most indefensible and ill-conceived decision ever forced on a field commander in our

---

6. MacArthur, *Reminiscences*, p. 371.

The Seventeenth Infantry Regiment of the U.S. Seventh Division advancing on Hyesanjin, a North Korean town near the Manchurian border.

nation's history."[7] His troops were being endangered by the Chinese yet he could not take actions to defend them.

Truman saw matters differently. Bombers could not always pinpoint their targets. Already two confused U.S. jet pilots had flown sixty miles into Russia, where they blasted a Soviet airfield. With planes speeding ten miles per minute, it was almost certain that more bombers would stray over Russian or Manchurian territory. MacArthur would have said: So be it. If war had to come, let it come before Russia had atomic parity with the United States. But Truman was not ready to take America into a third world war. He refused to permit MacArthur to bomb Chinese supply lines in Manchuria. For that refusal MacArthur never forgave him.

THE CHINESE INTERVENE

On November 24, MacArthur launched his "Home by Christmas" offensive. Truman had insisted that MacArthur salve

---

7. MacArthur, *Reminiscences*, p. 372.

Chinese fears by using only South Korean troops near the Yalu. But MacArthur did not want to deny either his men or himself the honor of finishing the war on the Manchurian border. In addition, he did not think the ROKs were capable of a drive to the Yalu. Thus he ordered his Americans forward, once more beyond their supplies and communications. Within a few days scattered units reached the long-sought river. Standing on the snow-frosted hills and gazing on the narrow river and the jagged landscape of China beyond, they enjoyed the finest moment of the war.

Then 300,000 Chinese struck.

The advance American troops first spotted the Chinese on November 26. Tony Herbert, who earlier likened his ride through North Korea to a turkey hunt, was suddenly sobered:

> I walked . . . to the top of the hill, and in the valley below, as far as you could see, were thousands upon thousands of Chinese—a real sea of life. Some were on horseback, some marching in columns. All of them were headed straight for us. Nobody back at headquarters would believe it, and none of us could figure out what to do. By the time they got close enough to fight, it was dark and we were literally pushed off the hill. We fell back because there was no other choice. There was no resupply and there were no reinforcements. . . . We tried to regroup and occasionally did, but

November 21, 1950. U.S. soldiers proudly pose for a photographer on the banks of the Yalu. Note the smoking ruins of the recently bombed bridge.

there were so many of them they just kept pushing us backward.[8]

It was an ill-equipped horde that slugged into Herbert and his fellow troopers. The Chinese had no air support, no tanks, very little artillery, and few mechanized troop carriers. Their supply system was poorly organized and would not have supported a Western army for a week. The Chinese command had no radios and hence no way of communicating with their men except by a clumsy code of flares and bugle calls. Their weapons were a motley assortment of Japanese discards from World War II, some American pieces captured from Chiang Kai-shek, and a few

8. Herbert, *Soldier*, p. 53.

November 28–December 3, 1950. In the face of sub-zero winds and surrounded by three Red Chinese divisions, marines of the Fifth and Seventh Regiments fought to make a five-day, fifteen-mile retreat to the southern end of Chosin Reservoir. There they reorganized to make their epic forty-mile fight to the sea. They brought out their wounded and their equipment.

modern Russian small arms. Yet the Chinese soldiers had been hardened by the battles that had raged over their country during the previous twenty years. And the generals had an expertise that MacArthur gravely underestimated. Both officers and men fervently believed they were fighting to protect their native soil, just a few miles behind them. And at nearly every point of contact they overwhelmingly outnumbered the disorganized U.S. troops.

"It was one of the worst defeats in our history," Herbert wrote about the headlong retreat that followed. Recalling how he and his buddies had stumbled through snow and slush with the Chinese snapping at their heels, he added, "The next few days were a nightmare."[9] Down unfamiliar muddy roads the U.S. soldiers fled, not knowing when the Chinese would swoop upon

---

9. Herbert, *Soldier*, p. 53.

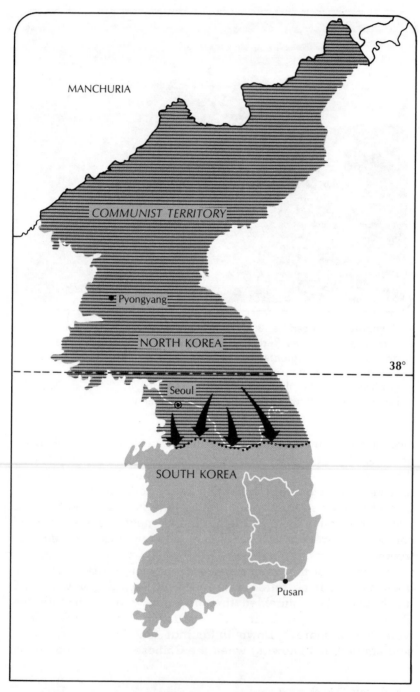

The Chinese offensive, November, 1950–January, 1951.

The rail bridge across the Han River at Seoul, Korea, after being demolished by a U.S. engineer unit during the evacuation of Seoul, January 4, 1951.

them from the bleak hills that hunched close by. The fighting was almost constant. Some regiments were mauled; others were wiped out. Each time the American units managed to regroup they were smaller, and they had become less mobile because of their wounded. Yet the men trudged on through the biting wind and snow, low on ammunition, lower on food, and lowest on morale. They were almost reduced to animals, fighting not for the grand ideal of stemming godless communism but simply to survive.

MacArthur was frantic as there loomed before him a catastrophic defeat. His army seemed to be disintegrating just as the French had during the German breakthrough in 1940. On December 30, MacArthur again begged Washington to permit him massive air strikes against Chinese supply lines in Manchuria and within China itself. He also urged Truman to permit Chiang and his army of 600,000 Nationalist troops invade the Chinese mainland and renew the civil war. To these requests Truman replied that full-scale involvement with China was a "booby trap." Such involvement would benefit only Russia, which was, in his viewpoint, America's chief adversary. General Omar

Operation Meatgrinder. Mounted, self-propelled 155-mm "Long Toms" shelling behind-the-lines Chinese troop concentrations and supply depots. The long-range accuracy and devastating effects of these guns helped greatly to turn back the Red Chinese advance. The tanks (at right) advance to take possession of shelled and bombed out Chinese positions.

Bradley later would summarize the situation even more succinctly. He wrote that to follow MacArthur's inclinations would have brought on "the wrong war, at the wrong place, at the wrong time, and with the wrong enemy."[10]

Meanwhile, the Chinese knifed deeper into Korea. Soon they drove the ROK and UN troops back across the Thirty-eighth Parallel. On January 4, 1951, they recaptured Seoul. Ten days later they had plunged forty miles farther on. Each side was rushing in reinforcements. But the Chinese, with 486,000 troops to the defenders' 365,000, had a thirty percent superiority in manpower. And they apparently were well on their way to forcing UN troops back into the Pusan perimeter and, perhaps, right into the sea.

10. Quoted in David Rees, *Korea: The Limited War* (Baltimore: Penguin Books, 1970), p. 274.

THE UN RESUMES THE OFFENSIVE

Toward the end of January, however, the tide of battle turned rather abruptly. Two months of retreat had brought the UN troops closer to their supplies, and with that their firepower increased. In addition, Matthew Ridgway, who had assumed command of the Eighth Army upon Walker's death in a jeep accident, had rekindled the army's self-confidence. His rugged discipline and inspiring leadership fired the army's morale, again making it a force to be reckoned with. Ridgway also found a tactic to counteract the numerical superiority of the Chinese.

Ridgway's troops grimly called this new tactic "the Meatgrinder." It consisted of making concentrated attacks at points in the front line where the UN's vastly superior firepower could be used to its maximum effectiveness. Heavy artillery would open up first, hurling shells ten miles into the Chinese rear. Then the smaller, more accurate cannons, aided by spotter planes, would blast away at intermediate targets such as ammunition depots and reserve troops.

With the enemy front-line position now isolated and unable to call up supplies or reinforcements, UN tanks and machine guns would begin to rip it apart. And as the chatter of death played over the hills, fighter-bombers would roar in, plastering the

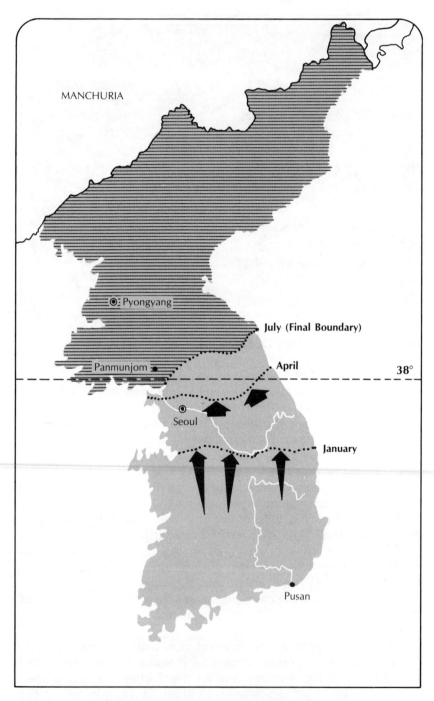

The U N Meatgrinder offensive, January–July, 1951.

Chinese with bombs, rockets, and more machine-gun fire. The fighter-bombers also hurled napalm, a flaming jellied gasoline that penetrated underground bunkers otherwise secure from shelling.

When the front had been thoroughly chewed up, the UN infantry would stalk over the cratered landscape, killing or capturing those frightened, dazed men who had survived. Once the sector was under UN control, the infantry then would lash out laterally to devastate the unprotected flanks of the Chinese in adjoining sectors.

Ridgway, who set the Meatgrinder in motion on January 25, was not trying for a breakthrough in the style of Guderian or Patton. Korea was too mountainous to make the best use of tanks. Neither was Ridgway's Meatgrinder aimed primarily at recovering territory. His main purpose was to inflict heavy casualties on the Chinese. And in this purpose he was tremendously successful. In one battle, for example, the Chinese suffered 4,200 dead and several times that many wounded as compared to UN fatalities of just 70. Not even the Chinese could withstand such lopsided losses. Throughout February and March Ridgway blasted forward, and on March 18 Seoul was retaken. By the end of the month the first American troops had recrossed the Thirty-eighth Parallel.

It soon became apparent that the Chinese were in serious trouble. With very little plane, tank, or artillery support, the Chinese army could not stand against the firepower of the UN forces. And, as a nonindustrial nation, the Chinese were unable to bridge the gap in armaments. Nor was Russian aid effective. The flow of war matériel over the Trans-Siberian Railroad could neither match nor offset the massive flow of material which came across the Pacific from America. The Russians could have flown in enough first-rate planes to cause the U.S. Air Force great concern. However, apparently they did not wish to become too involved because they denied China this important aid.

Another Chinese problem was the complete lack of sea power. And there again Russia, with its powerful navy and submarine fleet, refused to support the Chinese. The lack of warships and submarines required the Chinese to hold back forces from combat in order to protect their flanks and rear from an amphibious attack—they were not likely to forget that just six months earlier the Americans had launched such an attack at Inchon and had broken the North Korean army.

Finally, the farther the Chinese pushed into Korea, the longer and more vulnerable their supply lines became. When the

A U.S. Air Force F–80 Shooting Star participating in the largest single air strike of the Korean War, May 21, 1952. Being napalmed and strafed is a North Korean–Chinese military supply depot, thirty-five miles southeast of Pyongyang. Note the misaimed anti-aircraft shell below the plane.

Meatgrinder began, those supply lines offered three hundred miles of inviting targets to the seemingly all-powerful and ever-present U.S. Air Force.

Yet there was irony about the supply-line situation. The farther the UN pushed northward, the shorter the Chinese supply lines became and, therefore, the more matériel reached the front. Chinese resistance stiffened accordingly. Truman recognized the irony and the alternatives it posed. Either the United States would have to put forth a gigantic, costly effort to drive the Chinese back into Manchuria, or it would have to accept the fact that a stalemate had been reached. Truman reluctantly accepted stalemate and the pursuit of the policy of containment. That is, he decided to settle for freeing South Korea and to give up the idea of controlling the whole peninsula. Toward the end of March, 1951, he prepared an offer to enter into peace negotiations.

THE END OF THE MACARTHUR CONTROVERSY

To Truman's extreme irritation, MacArthur chose to bypass the president's peace offer with his own particular form of militant diplomacy. Before Truman could make his conciliatory offer, MacArthur threatened China with "doom" if its field commander did not meet with him to discuss ending the war. Truman correctly interpreted MacArthur's threat of doom to include the atomic bombing of China. Such a threat would only force the Chinese leaders to continue the war in order to save face. The threat also would require the United States to widen the war. In addition, by issuing his demand, MacArthur had disobeyed Truman's order to secure clearance from the State Department before making public statements. For these reasons Truman was, as he put it, "deeply shocked" at MacArthur's ultimatum to the Chinese.

Truman now felt that he had to take action against MacArthur. To do nothing would be to admit that a general, not the president, was running the nation's foreign policy. Advisers warned Truman that MacArthur had a powerful following in the United States, particularly among Republicans. The advisers also warned Truman that if he removed the general from command, he might not be able to get his military appropriations through Congress. Truman, however, was never one to flinch from a fight with political opponents. Therefore, on April 11, 1951, he relieved MacArthur from command, replacing him with Matthew Ridgway.

The furor in the United States was tremendous. Millions of Americans favored MacArthur's policy of total victory over Truman's policy of containment. MacArthur's homecoming parade through New York City was one of the greatest processions of cheering, confetti, and ticker tape ever seen. More than seven and a half million partisans lined his route. He delivered a speech before a joint meeting of the House and Senate that was heard by untold millions over TV and radio. Republicans all over the nation spoke of MacArthur as the next president of the United States.

General Douglas MacArthur being cheered on the speaker's platform in front of San Francisco's City Hall, April 18, 1951. Note the "MacArthur for President" sign behind the general's right shoulder.

Truman, on the other hand, sank low in public esteem. One poll showed that less than one-third of the people approved of his administration. At least one senator called for his impeachment. And when Truman threw out the first baseball of the 1951 season, the stadium resounded with boos.

However, his action was successful in bringing the Chinese to the conference table. On July 10 the peace talks began.

CHAPTER FOUR

The Deadly Stalemate: July 11, 1951, to July 27, 1953

At a little past eight o'clock on a black night in April, 1953, twenty-one-year-old Martin Russ and thirteen other marines of his squad moved silently into the darkness. Ahead, outlined ominously on the Korean horizon, was a low mound known as Pentagon Hill. The squad's job was to draw close-range fire from the Chinese to determine how well Pentagon was defended. The truce talks that had been droning on for nearly two years meant little to the men on patrol. Tonight those talks meant even less to the men because their lives depended on nothing but the deftness of their movements.

The patrol cautiously moved ahead in a skirmish line: nine men, about ten yards apart. Martin Russ reinforced the right flank, while Sergeant Van Horn brought up the rear. The patrol inched forward, each man carefully testing the ground in front of him with a free foot. When he found a spot with no twigs that might snap or leaves that might rustle, he put his full weight on it. Sometimes the men could take only nine steps a minute. If they were heard before they reached cover, the area would be lit up with star shells and the enemy would plaster them with burp guns.

When the patrol was within two hundred yards of Pentagon, it descended one of the many gulleys. There the men waited for the moon to rise so they could better estimate the number of defenders.

> The sky began to lighten in the west [wrote Martin Russ in his diary] and soon the bright moon appeared, barely peeping over the skyline. This was our signal. We rose and began moving forward, *very* slowly. . . . After creeping twenty or thirty yards toward the Pentagon, we halted. . . .

71

Troop replacements making their way to front-line bunkers.

At this point . . . an enemy mortar tube—startlingly close—
began pooping off a rapid series of rounds. . . . We could
see sparks and a tongue of orange flame from each muzzle
blast. . . . We received small arms fire from the Pentagon at
the same time. . . . It seemed as though the entire skyline of
that knoll was covered with the little sharp white fingers of
light that were the muzzle blasts. It was a good-sized
force. . . . Sgt. Van Horn began pulling out the unit, two or
three men at a time. Pugnacci and I, being the flankers, were
the last to be withdrawn. . . . When the last group of men
disappeared, we rose and sprinted up the slope and tumbled
across the skyline. The Chinese were firing at us from a
distance of about 150 yards, which is damn close on a
moonlit night. That's when I got scared . . . .[1]

WITH THE MARINES IN KOREA

Gunfire in Korea was a long way from New York, where Russ
had begun his travels. But he did not mind being in Asia—his
wanderlust earlier had lured him on four hitchhiking journeys

---

1. Martin Russ, *The Last Parallel: A Marine's War Journal* (New York: Holt,
Rinehart & Winston, 1957), pp. 277–278.

across the United States by the time he was twenty. He had actually wanted to go to Korea, although he had found the voyage on the troopship from San Diego distinctly unpleasant. Thirty-three hundred marines were jammed on the vessel during the two-week sail to Inchon harbor. Their bunks were canvas hammocks hung in tiers of six. The hammocks were so close together that Russ's nose was nearly flattened each time the man above him rolled in his sleep. The Pacific was rough during the early winter crossing, and the hold where the men slept reeked with the odor of vomit. The trip also was boring. The men had little to do except read murder mysteries, write letters home, or gaze at the cold, choppy sea. On several evenings there was a movie. However, since the movie was shown in a cabin with a low ceiling, the top and bottom of the picture were cut off.

When the marines disembarked at Inchon shortly after midnight on December 7, 1952, an equally large group of soldiers was waiting there for transportation home. "You'll be sorry," they yelled, half in jest and half in warning. Above the streets were hung large banners which read, "Welcome Ike." (President-elect Dwight Eisenhower had just fulfilled a campaign promise by visiting Korea.) Russ and his companions were then loaded into an ancient train with straight-backed wooden seats and no toilet. Soon they were rattling down the tracks toward their camp at a snail's speed of twenty miles per hour.

The train chugged through a war-desolated countryside where stony-faced old folk watched the Americans. They passed many tiny villages interspersed between frozen patchworks of stubble fields and rice paddies. After a while they were moving through Seoul. South Korea's capital had changed hands four times by then, and only one-quarter of the original one million inhabitants remained. The homes were heaps of rubble; the streets were littered with gutted tanks, wrecked buses, and thousands of broken mementos of departed or deceased Koreans. By three o'clock that afternoon the marines were at their destination: a tent city atop a hill fifteen miles south of the front.

Early in January the marines moved up to their battle positions. Russ's battalion occupied the right flank of the First Marine Division, with a Canadian infantry brigade, distinguished by natty blue berets, to their right. During this phase of the war, trenches cut across the crests of hills forming a 150-mile battlefront through Korea. The battlefront stretched from the Yellow Sea in the west to the Sea of Japan in the east. On the lee side of Russ's hill were earthen bunkers, reinforced with sandbags. Here Russ's platoon of fifty men slept. They called their abode "Rodent

Riflemen of the Twenty-fourth Infantry Division returning from front-line guard posts to their bunkers on the reverse slope of the ridge line commanding the heights of Kumsong.

City" because rats infested it. In front of the trenches was no-man's-land—a scarred, littered area about eight hundred yards in width. Beyond lay the Chinese lines.

For the men living in the trenches, this phase of the Korean War was eerie and haunting. It was like being caught in an eddy of time, thrown back to the ancient days of the First World War when their fathers and grandfathers had fought without aid of the tank or the divebomber. They lived in trenches and bunkers, strung barbed wire, patrolled no-man's-land, and dared enemy machine gunners.

> Terrible battles have been fought here [Russ wrote], but the armies did not move on: they entrenched themselves in caves, bunkers and trenches which were deepened and strengthened as the months passed. On this same corridor of land, men of many nations have been killed, wounded or captured. Ragged infantry companies were replaced by fresh troops, who were then subjected to the same gruesome adventures until they in turn were replaced. Both sides became so strongly fortified that few men ever ventured out there in daylight and returned.[2]

2. Russ, *The Last Parallel*, p. 304.

A mess crew of the Twenty-fifth Division preparing lunch for soldiers who are not on guard duty just over the hill.

THE PEACE TALKS

It was not technology that had thrown warfare in Korea back thirty-five years. It was the internal and international politics of the United States. As most military experts agree, the United States could have sent a million more men to Korea, could have amassed armored divisions and fighter-bombers, and then could have broken through the Chinese lines. To have done so, however, would have required a tremendous effort at home. The auto industry would have had to retool to manufacture tanks. The shipbuilding industry would have had to convert to warship and transport production. More civilians would have had to be drafted and trained for combat. The government itself would have had to place wartime controls on wages, prices, supplies, and general civilian spending. And the American people, who now suffered only minor inconveniences, would have had to make distasteful sacrifices that most thought not worth the effort. Internationally, the reversion to a fluid, active war might have endangered the United States. If the United States became too involved in Asia, the Russians would have had less restraint in Europe. For these reasons, Truman chose to follow a policy of containment, which now demanded only a holding action. He

Chinese (left) and North Korean (right) negotiators posing for photographers at Kaesong, North Korea, July 16, 1951.

had his army commanders practice limited warfare to spare lives while UN and Chinese negotiators met at the hamlet of Panmunjom, North Korea.

Truman had no idea that the peace talks would drag on for two years. When he opened the talks in July, 1951, he thought that the negotiators could iron out the details in a month. But Truman viewed the talks in a straightforward military manner. He thought that a new boundary would be set between the two Koreas, somewhere around the Thirty-eighth Parallel, and that all foreign troops would leave the peninsula. The Chinese, however, saw things in quite a different light. To them the talks were more political than military. Every little point, no matter how minute, had significance.

To the Chinese, Korea was not a minor little country in some faraway corner of the world. It was in their front yard—just across the Yellow Sea from Peking, their capital. Winning a test of arms here was vital to China's prestige, both abroad and at home. Abroad, it was essential to prove that China now was a power to be reckoned with, a nation that would no longer be bullied by Japan, Europe, or the United States. Even more important was the situation at home, where Mao Tse-tung had just brought China under communism. If he lost face in his first

South Korean and American negotiators posing for photographers at Kaesong, July 17, 1951.

encounter with the West, his hold over the Chinese masses would be seriously weakened. It was vital, therefore, that Mao create a great amount of propaganda out of what was not a victory but a stalemate.

The Chinese tactics at the truce meetings infuriated the Americans. The Americans simply could not understand why the Chinese engaged in such apparent pettiness. For example, the Chinese insisted that the talks be held first at Kaesong and then later at Panmunjom. Both villages lay within the tiny bit of territory held by the Chinese below the Thirty-eighth Parallel. When the U.S. delegates drove to their initial meeting, they had white flags to identify their vehicles, as previously agreed upon. Chinese photographers took pictures of the flags to "prove" to the people back home that the United States was surrendering. When Admiral Turner Joy, the chief U.S. negotiator, sat down at the conference table, he found himself sitting in a low subservient position to General Nam Il. On the green felt conference table the small North Korean flag rose a full six inches above that of the United Nations.

The most serious problem to the Chinese was not the settlement of the boundary line. They early had agreed that the boundary would follow the entrenchment line. To them the real

Chinese prisoners enjoying the spring sunlight in one of the thirty compounds of the United Nations POW Camp, Koje-do, South Korea.

problem was the policy to be followed regarding nearly half of the 132,000 Communist prisoners who did not want to return to Red rule. The leaders of China and North Korea did not want the world to see that many Chinese and Koreans did not view their Communist-ruled homelands as paradise. Therefore, the Communist negotiators insisted that all prisoners be returned, forcibly if necessary.

Truman would not accept such a treaty provision. To have done so would have been "not only inhumane and tragic but dishonorable as well," he thought. Yet neither would Truman agree to suggestions like MacArthur's to compel Chinese assent by threatening to use atomic weapons. The treaty talks, for these reasons, dragged on through the remainder of 1951 and all of 1952. The lengthy negotiations apparently did not bother the Chinese. They seemed content to reap the propaganda advantages of stopping American power. Also the Chinese thought that the 1952 presidential election would remove Truman's Democratic administration and replace it with Republicans who might be easier to deal with.

The Chinese were both right and wrong. The Democrats were toppled, but the new Republican administration was not easier to work with. Dwight Eisenhower won on the pledge to bring a quick end to the war. And there were only two ways for this to come about. Either the Chinese must give in on forced prisoner repatriation, or the United States must bring out the dreaded atomic bombs. Accordingly, Ike ordered the doomsday weapons transported to Okinawa, from where they could easily be carried to Korea by bombers. Eisenhower then gave the Communists an ultimatum. If they refused to conclude the peace treaty, he would not only use atomic weapons on their troops in Korea but would also carry the war into Manchuria and even China proper. He would, in addition, allow Chiang Kai-shek to resume the civil war by transporting Chinese Nationalist troops back to the mainland. "Soon," Ike wrote (no doubt with a smile), "the prospects for armistice negotiations seemed to improve." Yet, although the Chinese began cooperating with the UN negotiators, the talks went slowly. Meanwhile the war continued to drag on.

THE FIGHTING CONTINUES

In a few portions of the front line the battles were fierce. During the two-year stalemate an average of 2,500 Americans were killed or wounded each month. Most of the front-line action was confined to sharp skirmishes that usually occurred during the night when patrols tested the enemy's outer defenses. To move into no-man's-land during daytime was suicidal because snipers covered the area with sharp eyes and high-powered rifles.

In places the two armies were quite close—about one hundred yards along some sectors. Consequently, the men from each side could hear noise and talking from the opposite trenches. Every so often Americans would yell salutes and periodically a few obscenities in Chinese. The enemy soldiers were not permitted to answer back. The Chinese were more interested in pursuing propaganda than in vocal contacts between individuals. Almost every night the Chinese set up amplifiers along these sectors to propagandize the UN troops. Two hours of music and palaver was the usual bill of fare. One such amplifier was set up opposite Martin Russ's position.

Sometimes the Chinese announcer tried to frighten the marines with threats of violence and death. But his heavy Chinese accent and hackneyed phrases only reminded Russ of those "Oriental cats that appear in Hollywood movies screaming things like

T-66 multiple rocket launchers of the Fortieth Infantry Division fire salvos of rockets at Chinese positions.

'Maline! Tonight you die.' " Such threats only provoked laughter. At other times the semicomic man was replaced by a woman. One night she sang "The Last Rose of Summer," which Russ found beautifully moving. Looking at his companions, he saw nostalgia softening their faces. "Did you enjoy my song, marine?" she called out. "If so, then fire your rifles twice and I will sing another." Americans all along the line responded with rifles, artillery, and even flares. In response she only sang a dissonant Chinese classic, which was followed by a horribly out-of-date 1920s jazz record.

In time the men of the two armies developed respect and even an odd kind of friendship for one another. There was, for example, a Chinese sniper whom Russ's buddies named "the Chief." He occupied a position behind some low mounds from which he could command the bleak no-man's-land between himself and the Americans. He remained unseen most of the time, except when, as if by intuition, he sensed there were U.S. scouts nearby. Then he would suddenly hunch up and riddle off a rapid hail of fire. Before Russ or his buddies could shoot back, the Chief was gone.

The platoon tried to pinpoint the Chief's exact location. One marine even sat all night waiting for him to poke up, but he

Two soldiers of the Second U.S. Infantry Division at their guard post overlooking a section of no-man's-land.

didn't. One morning Russ whistled at the Chief, and he whistled back. Several days later an American yelled out the only Chinese phrase he knew—"Gung ho!," which meant "all work together." "Then the wondrous thing occurred. . . . The sound of one clear, evenly pitched voice reached our ears, from the direction of Old Bunker, out of the darkness. One word: 'Okay.' We made a resolution on the spot not to fire at Chief again and to attempt communicating with him at dawn."[3]

It was exciting—like trying to tame a wild animal. Russ grew to think of the Chief as a man who needed only counseling in order to become a friend. Russ wished he would show himself so that he could wave to him.

Russ was so sure the Chief felt the same and would not fire at him that he grew careless. One night around eleven o'clock Russ and three comrades climbed out of their bunker with entrenchment tools. They clanged their tools and needlessly exposed themselves. The Chief, however, did not share Russ's feelings. He directed a mortar crew against them:

> There was a sharp whistle high above us, rapidly increasing in intensity, and then a horrible, hoarse roar as the first

3. Russ, *The Last Parallel*, p. 184.

Signing the armistice agreement formally ending the Korean War are Lieutenant General William K. Harrison, Jr., and General Nam Il.

round plummeted down, exploding ten or fifteen yards to the left of the bunker. Andy was knocked off the bunker by this first round, and received splinters of shrapnel in his arm. . . . I tried to draw my entire body within my helmet, like a fetus, and I was frightened to tears. . . . After each round exploded, I wondered why I was still alive.[4]

Russ found that war, after all, was still a matter of killing. The Americans finally triangulated the Chief's location. And, while a

---

4. Russ, *The Last Parallel*, pp. 186–187.

buddy drew his fire, Russ blasted the Chief's area. After that nothing more was heard from him.

THE WAR ENDS

While the fighting sputtered on and the death rate mounted, the negotiators at Panmunjom finally worked out an agreement. One by one the Communists had conceded all the U.S. demands—including the voluntary repatriation of prisoners. The final armistice was signed on July 27, 1953. The new boundary, which had been settled nearly two years earlier, gave South Korea an impressive slice of North Korea.

Martin Russ was at the front when the war formally ended. It was ten o'clock in the evening. Men from both armies sent flares flashing into the sky—red, yellow, and white fountains of sparks. Then hundreds of soldiers climbed out of the trenches, staring at their former enemies as they all gathered up souvenirs from no-man's-land.

> A beautiful full moon hung low in the sky like a Chinese lantern [Russ scribbled in his diary]. . . . The first sound that we heard was a shrill group of voices, calling from the Chinese positions . . . . A hundred yards or so down the trench, someone began shouting the Marine Corps hymn at the top of his lungs. Others joined in, bellowing the words. Everyone was singing in a different key . . . . Later in the night a group of Chinese strolled over to the base of Ava [bunker] and left candy and handkerchiefs as gifts. . . . So ends the Korean conflict . . . .[5]

5. Russ, *The Last Parallel*, p. 320.

★ CHAPTER FIVE ★

Flames into the Future: Summation of a Forgotten War

Martin Russ, standing in the open vestibule of a troop train puffing slowly toward Inchon, watched the Korean countryside slip away. "This will be the last entry," he wrote in his diary. "We don't do much aboard ship except lie around and dream of the things we will do in San Francisco . . . ."[1]

Russ saw an elderly Korean man in a long white robe and black bird-cage hat walking along a rice paddy. The Korean smiled, bowed, and waved his cane. Then he was gone.

Soon Korea would be gone, too, Russ mused. The hardship, the danger, the night patrols, the snipers—all would begin to fade like memories of a war movie seen long ago. He realized he should be thinking something profound, but nothing came. Had the deaths of more than 54,000 Americans, not to mention the 103,000 wounded, been worth it? And how about the 1,000,000 Chinese casualties and 2,000,000 Koreans (mainly civilians caught between the two armies) who had lost their lives? What had they died for?

Russ wanted so much to discover a meaning for it all—a purpose for the war that, despite all the suffering, death, and devastation, had ended nearly where it had begun. South Korea won only about 1,500 square miles of new territory. Russ simply could not find the words. And yet there was a vague feeling within him that it had somehow been worthwhile. "I dare say most of the men here are glad that they went through the past year, and I dare say that most of them would be at a loss if asked why."[2]

---

1. Martin Russ, *The Last Parallel: A Marine's War Journal* (New York: Holt, Rinehart & Winston, 1957), p. 332.

2. Russ, *The Last Parallel*, p. 332.

Soldiers of the Twenty-fourth Infantry Division at Inchon, Korea, reassembling after debarking from a troop train. The troops are bound for Japan and then home to the United States.

It was a weak way to sum up his experience, but he could think of no other way to put it.

THE WAR'S RESULTS

Back in the United States, Americans shared Russ's inability to determine what purpose the Korean War had served. For the first time in modern American history a clearcut victory had been denied. Communists still leered from North Korea and Red China boasted of its battle prowess against America, the "paper tiger." Truman had said the "police action" was fought to stop the spread of communism. And yet Indochina was gradually falling to Ho Chi Minh, and Red agents were active in Cuba, Guatemala, and throughout Latin America. The war seemed so futile that most Americans did not even want to think about Korea. When the servicemen returned home, they seldom received the heroes' welcomes given the doughboys and GIs, who had fought the Kaiser and Hitler.

Yet, in truth, the Korean conflict, far from being of little consequence, had nearly as profound an effect on history as the

Combatants and adult civilians were not the only casualties of the Korean War. Thousands of children lost their lives, and thousands of others lost their parents and homes amid the seesaw battles to dominate Korea. The orphans above are being cared for by a welfare officer of the United Nations, which was successful in placing many of the children with foster parents.

two world wars. It showed that the United States could not rely solely on the atom bomb to maintain its world interests. Korea also altered the entire pattern of the American defense network. The manpower of the armed forces, which had been allowed to drop to just 1.5 million men, was more than doubled. And a form of military draft was set up that forced most young American men to spend time in one of the armed services. The preparation for war thereby became a prominent feature of post-Korean life.

The readiness of the United States to send troops abroad also gave the United Nations a vitality that the old League of Nations never possessed. Although nearly ninety percent of the UN troops serving in Korea had been American, fifteen other nations also had sent battle units and suffered a total of 17,260 casualties.

Greek Battalion headquarters, March, 1953. From right to left are General Mark W. Clark, U N commander-in-chief, Colonel Coumanakous, and Lieutenant Generals Maxwell D. Taylor and Reuben E. Jenkins. Fourteen other U N members—including Australia, New Zealand, Great Britain, the Philippines, Thailand, and Turkey—supplied combat troops to support the South Korean cause.

This participation showed that under vigorous leadership the UN could act as a force for world stability. Certainly if the League had sent troops to Manchuria in 1931 or to Czechoslovakia in 1938, World War II might have been averted.

The forceful American stance against Communist aggression served also to strengthen NATO, the bulwark of the American–Western European defense against Russia. Not only did NATO nations respond to the United States by beginning programs of rearmament, but West Germany was brought into the pact as a cooperating military power. This recreation of the German army gave NATO a backbone that it had hitherto lacked. The principal reason that Britain and France had accepted German rearmament was that the United States, by its determined action in Korea, had proven it would stand by its allies. The Korean War convinced the two nations that the continued American presence in Europe would more than counterbalance the Germans.

In response to a U.S. veto barring the People's Republic of China from U N membership, Yakov A. Malik (standing), the Soviet representative, walks out of the Security Council after declaring that the Soviet Union could not participate in the work of the Security Council until Chiang Kai-shek's U N membership was revoked.

Thereby French and British fears of German aggression were quieted.

The Korean War also helped to change the role of the president in foreign crises. Before Korea, presidents had not been able to react with the speed that many observers believed was essential. Truman's sending three-fourths of a million men into battle without securing a congressional declaration of war set a precedent for future presidents to follow. Presidents Eisenhower, Kennedy, Johnson, Nixon, and Ford would follow this precedent in hot spots as far apart as Lebanon, Cuba, and Southeast Asia. This new presidential power, when used with wisdom and forethought, could strengthen the stance of the United States in international affairs. But if not used wisely it could expose America to the dangers of unnecessary wars.

The stalemate in Korea disillusioned many Americans who regarded total victory as an integral part of any war. But most Americans came to realize that the policy of containment could maintain U.S. security without taking the nation into a third world war. Indeed, with the advent of nuclear intercontinental ballistic missiles, containment appeared to be the only nonsuicidal manner of dealing with the Communists. Korea demonstrated that this policy could work. South Korea remained outside the Communist orbit, and total war had been avoided.

However, not all of the effects of the Korean War were beneficial. Aside from making containment the central feature of American foreign policy, the Korean War ruptured U.S. relations with Communist China. When Chiang Kai-shek had failed so miserably in 1949 either to win the loyalties of the Chinese masses or to use American aid and weapons effectively, Truman had washed his hands of him. Moreover, the president had all but conceded Chiang's Taiwan to the Communists early in 1950. It was then that Secretary of State Dean Acheson, in a speech which attracted worldwide attention, excluded Taiwan from the U.S. defense perimeter. American foreign policy at that time tended toward a loose sort of cooperation with Red China. The goal of the policy was to exploit the age-old antagonism that existed between China and Russia over Mongolia and Manchuria and the Chinese desire to colonize the unpopulated parts of Siberia.

But the Korean War completely reversed that policy. When Truman ordered the Seventh Fleet to the Formosa Strait, Mao was prevented from seizing Nationalist Taiwan, the last challenge to his rule. China then became an intractable enemy for more than twenty years. In fear of further steps that Truman might take against him, Mao entered the Korean War. To weaken Western power in Asia, Mao also began aiding Ho Chi Minh who was battling the French in Vietman.

Even more important than Taiwan in antagonizing China was the thrust of U.S. troops toward Manchuria. Few observers had disputed that the North Korean aggression justified Truman's involvement in Korea. (Although, even here, some of them wondered if American security was really threatened.) But many Americans, as well as the astute Winston Churchill, questioned the wisdom of allowing U.S. troops to cross the Thirty-eighth Parallel. One study later commissioned by the U.S. Air Force indicated that the Chinese probably would not have entered the war if the Americans had not approached the Yalu. This view conforms with statements made by Premier Chou En-lai at the time. If the Chinese had wanted to insure the North Korean conquest of the South, they would have entered the war when the ROKs and Americans were falling back to Pusan. In this viewpoint, Truman's belief that Korea was part of a cooperative

Russian-Chinese plan for world conquest was radically wrong. If this assessment is true, U.S. involvement in Korea unnecessarily changed China from a potential friend into an active enemy.

The Korean war did more than sour American-Chinese relations. There is evidence that the war also undermined the friendship of China with Russia. It was Russia, after all, which had equipped the North Korean army, and it was Russian advisers who had been active in directing the initial battles. Yet after the Americans had crushed the North Korean army and headed toward Manchuria, it was China, not Russia, that was forced to aid the North. China, not Russia, had to commit its manpower, limited war matériel, and shaky prestige to stop the Americans. And while the Chinese suffered one million casualties, the Russians did little to aid them. Russian air and submarine forces could have created havoc with the U.S. war effort, but the Russians held back. The Russians could have made threatening moves in areas such as Berlin and the Middle East. Such moves probably would have forced Truman, in fear of needing Korean divisions elsewhere, to accept a peace agreement far more favorable to the Chinese. Indeed, Truman fully expected such Russian tactics. But Russia remained quiet.

It would be surprising, therefore, if the Chinese were not irritated with the Soviets. It was Russia which had begun the war, but China which had to fight it. Korea might well have been a major factor in the rift that eventually shattered the relations between the two Communist giants.

The most important effect of the Korean War, at least from the standpoint of America's twentieth-century wars, was that it led almost directly to U.S. involvement in Vietnam. When Truman took Taiwan into the U.S. defense perimeter, he also included Indochina. Under his administration the first American military mission (thirty-five men) was sent to aid the French in their fight with Ho Chi Minh. Truman also gave the hard-pressed French such a great infusion of financial aid that within two years the United States was paying nearly one-half of the war's costs.

Truman had no idea where he was leading the nation when he made the first tentative commitments in Vietnam. Adding Vietnam to the American defense perimeter was an off-handed gesture made to discourage what Truman believed was a Chinese-Russian drive for world conquest. Vietnam did not pose any real threat to American security.

Added support for this interpretation is the fact that Truman and his advisers knew almost nothing about Vietnam. The American consulate in Vietnam employed only seven Americans, none of whom could speak, read, or write the native language. Truman's advisers from the State Department had less than one-half of a file drawer of information about the little country to draw upon. Throughout all the United States there was not one university with an expert on Vietnam with whom the administration could consult. Not one school in America even offered a course in the Vietnamese language. Administration officials who might have wished to examine reports of the conflict from sources other than the French could not do so.

If Truman had known where his actions would lead the United States, he probably would have gasped in disbelief. For the road from Korea led not to Communist containment but into the bloody rice paddies of Vietnam.

THE VIETNAM WAR

PART TWO

A South Vietnamese paratrooper.

★ CHAPTER SIX ★

Toward the Precipice

The country could have been a paradise. The Chinese called it "Viet Nam," or "the distant south." It was dotted with fertile fields, watered by clear streams, and fringed by beautiful mountains that rose gracefully toward the sunset sky. The eastern beaches were abundant with fruitful coconut palms. Natives sailing into the warm surf could net more than enough fish to satisfy their families.

Yet because Vietnam was such a desirable place, it periodically was subjected to warfare and turmoil by those who wished to rule it.

From ancient times the Chinese had coveted "the distant south." As early as 111 B.C. the Han dynasty, which also had eyes on Korea, sent a military force into Vietnam and annexed the country. For a thousand years Chinese governors lorded over the Vietnamese. Only after many revolts were these hated foreigners expelled in A.D. 939.

During the next five hundred years local warlords battled for supremacy. The Chinese, too, made their reappearance and for twenty years held Hanoi. In 1427 the Vietnamese warrior Le Loi threw out the Chinese and proclaimed himself emperor. For the next three centuries weak Le emperors claimed rule over Vietnam. But between 1527 and 1801 the real rulers of Vietnam were the Trinh house in the north and the Nguyen in the south.

The rule of the Trinhs and Nguyens reflected more than the mere rivalry of two factions. The Vietnamese were in reality three distinct groups of people. In the north were the Tonkinese, who were the most aggressive of the three groups. The Cochin Chinese in the south were more easygoing and less apt to press their neighbors. In central Vietnam were the Annamese, who reflected the characteristics of both their northern and southern

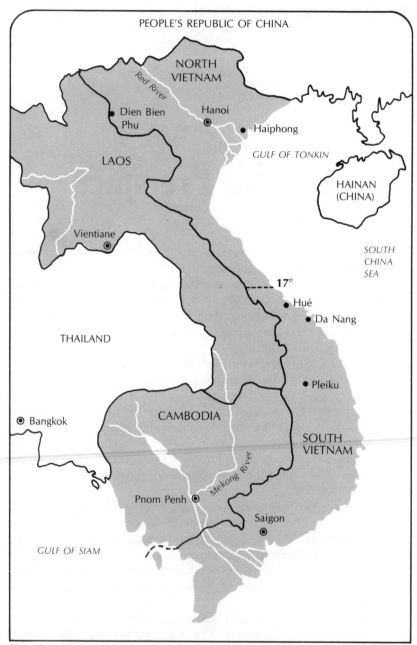

Vietnam and its neighbors, 1954.

neighbors. It could be said that the only element tending to unify
Vietnam was fear and the dislike of the Chinese, who continued
to claim a tributary tie over the country.

THE FRENCH COLONIZE INDOCHINA

By 1802 both the Trinh and the Nguyen houses were in decay, and Gia Long, a new champion, arose. Gia Long raised an army and united the entire country, ruling it from Hue, his capital city on the lovely Perfume River. However, Gia Long had not been strong enough to conquer his enemies alone. He had enlisted the help of the French from their bases in India. In this manner the age of imperialism came to Vietnam.

The expansion of French power was slow but steady. Remaining in Vietnam after the troops left were French Catholic missionaries. These men of peace and gentleness were successful in winning many converts to their faith. In time the Christianized Vietnamese no longer felt the traditional ties of loyalty to the Buddhist rulers at Hue and often took part in revolts. For this reason, some missionaries were imprisoned. To secure their release, the Paris government sent naval vessels storming into Vietnamese ports in the 1840s. Although the missionaries were released, persecution of Christians continued. Therefore in 1859, supposedly to protect the Christians, the French took possession of Saigon, market for the Mekong Delta rice lands, richest in all Vietnam. With the French soldiers came French merchants, who received special privileges from the French colonial government.

The French should have been satisfied with their prize, but imperialism could not remain at ease with hostile peoples on its flanks. Security demanded the conquest of the north. In 1883 six hundred well-armed Frenchmen were able to take Hanoi, so easy was it to seize territory in the heyday of imperialism. From there French expeditions knifed into the interior of Vietnam. The poorly armed warriors of the interior were no match for the French with their rifles and cannons. By 1887 the French had taken not only Vietnam but also Laos and Cambodia. Together the three provinces made up much of Indochina—so called because of its location between India and China. The other countries of Indochina were independent Siam (Thailand) and British-dominated Burma and Malaya.

For half a century the French enjoyed undisputed rule over their part of Indochina. They controlled all the money in the area through the French-owned Bank of Indochina. This bank charged loan rates so high that the Vietnamese farmers fell into debt and had to sell their lands to the French at cut-rate prices. The French landlords let the Vietnamese continue to work the land but charged them high rents—often up to fifty percent of their annual crop. French interests also controlled the opium houses, which increased in number throughout Vietnam. And a

French liquor monopoly forced each Vietnamese adult to pur-
chase a large quota of alcohol imported from France.

HO CHI MINH AND THE FRENCH REGIME

Ho Chi Minh was born around 1890 in the Annam province of
Vietnam. He was a proud youth. He hated the French rulers, who
called the male Vietnamese "boys" and forced them to remove
their hats when a Frenchman approached. By the age of twelve
Ho was carrying revolutionary messages between villages for his
conspiring elders. A year later he was expelled from the local
French-run school because of his nationalist activities.

As a teenager Ho knew the worst aspects of colonial rule.
Although some French colonial administrators and their wives
became very fond of the Vietnamese, other Frenchmen did not.
This was the case with many of the imperial soldiers, whose
"pacifying" missions took them into the villages. Ho described
one such mission:

> On the arrival of the soldiers the population fled; there only
> remained two old men and two women: one maiden, and a
> mother suckling her baby and holding an eight-year old girl
> by the hand. The soldiers asked for money, liquor, and
> opium.
> As they could not make themselves understood, they
> became furious and knocked down one of the old men with
> their rifle butts. Later, two of them, already drunk when they
> arrived, amused themselves for many hours by roasting the
> other old man at a wood fire. Meanwhile, the others raped
> the two women and the eight-year old girl. Then, weary, they
> murdered the girl. The mother was then able to escape with
> her infant, and, from a hundred yards off hidden in a bush,
> she saw . . . the young girl lying on her back, bound and
> gagged, and one of the men many times slowly thrust his
> bayonet into her stomach and, very slowly, draw it out again.
> Then he cut off the dead girl's finger to take a ring, and her
> head to steal a necklace.[1]

In 1911, when Ho was twenty-one, he left Vietnam, having
signed on a French ship as a kitchen hand. He traveled to Africa,
Europe, and the east coast of the United States. During World
War I he was a pastry cook in a London hotel, made a brief visit
to New York, and then migrated to France. There he mingled

---

1. Ho Chi Minh, *Ho Chi Minh on Revolution: Selected Writings, 1920–1966*, ed.
Bernard Fall (New York: Praeger, 1967), p. 29.

The wife of a French government official doing her shopping in Saigon, 1931.

with nearly 100,000 Vietnamese. Most of the men had been dragged from their villages, stamped on the wrist with an indelible chemical, and packed into crowded, foul ships. Once the ships were filled, the impressed Vietnamese were taken to France, where they were sent to the war front to act as forced laborers.

While in France, Ho constantly pondered how to free his country from the French. One day he discovered the writings of the Communist Nikolai Lenin on colonialism. Upon reading Lenin, Ho related, his eyes became flooded with tears. According to his account, he cried out, "This is what we need; this is the path to our liberation!"[2] In 1920 he helped to found the French Communist party. During the 1920s and 1930s he remained an

---

2. Quoted in Marvin Gettleman, ed., *Vietnam: History, Documents, and Opinions* (New York: Fawcett World Library, 1965), p. 31.

active Communist, at one time studying in Moscow, where he took out Russian citizenship.

But Vietnam was always first in Ho's sentiments. He wrote many inspiring pamphlets on resistance to French colonialism, which were circulated widely throughout French Indochina. By 1925 he was a recognized nationalist leader. At this time he organized the League of Oppressed Peoples of Asia and sent two hundred revolutionary agents into Vietnam. But the French quickly nipped the revolt.

In 1939, while Ho was in China, he founded the Vietminh party—a party of nationalist and Communist Vietnamese who would work together for the liberation of their country. With the creation of the Vietminh, the stage was set for the war against the French.

THE FIRST VIETNAM WAR

The strength of the Vietminh grew rapidly. By December, 1940, the French regarded the Vietminh as being a greater menace than the Japanese. French troops conducted extensive operations against the Vietminh. More than six thousand Vietnamese were killed or wounded by the French, but the Vietminh remained unconquered. Although the French themselves soon fell to the Japanese, the new overlords of Vietnam also were unable to put down Ho's guerrilla army. During the week of Japan's surrender to the United States, a Vietminh congress elected Ho Chi Minh the first president of the new Vietnamese republic.

Ho took office in Hanoi on August 19, 1945. His government, obviously seeking American approval, adopted a declaration of independence similar to that of the United States. Indeed, the opening section of the Vietnamese declaration was taken directly from its American model: "All men are created equal . . . ."

Ho was so desirous of American support that he even sent eight letters to President Truman. He hoped that the United States would urge France to grant Vietnam independence as the United States itself intended to do for the Philippines. Ho's appeals were never answered.

France would not accept the loss of its colony, even though as a nation it had received little economic advantage from Vietnam. In fact, France could have obtained the same advantage through free trade. However, the former French landlords, together with influential religious orders, formed strong lobbies demanding

Ho Chi Minh, president of North Vietnam from
1954 to 1969.

resumption of French rule. In addition, the issue of national
honor prompted many legislators to retain Vietnam. To these
Frenchmen and to the people who had elected them, it would
have been a disgrace to French glory to give up any possession
without a struggle. Furthermore, to have done so only would
have encouraged independence movements in other French
colonies around the world. And so, even though France was
trying to recover from German occupation, French leaders
scraped together the funds and the men to ship an army halfway
around the world.

When the French fleet appeared off Haiphong harbor in
February, 1946, Ho decided to negotiate. He agreed to permit the
French to land unopposed. He also agreed that Vietnam would
become part of the French Union, a status to which the French

had already assigned Laos and Cambodia.[3] Under this plan, Vietnam would no longer be classified as a colony. Ho's administration would be independent in domestic matters. Only in international trade and diplomacy would Vietnam be under French guidance. The French and Vietminh also agreed that a referendum would be held to determine whether the people wished to unify their country. Vietnam was still divided into three provinces: Cochin China, Annam, and Tonkin.

It appears that the French had no intention of allowing a referendum, especially in the southern province of Cochin China. This province was the richest part of Vietnam, and it was here that most of the French rice plantations and other commercial interests were concentrated. Thus, with the French entrenched in Saigon, Cochin China's chief city, and Ho ruling the north from Hanoi in Tonkin, the country in effect was split in two. After the French set up a puppet government in Saigon on June 1, 1946, Ho broke off relations with France.

The hostilities growing between Ho and the French soon erupted into violence when the Vietminh killed some French soldiers. In November the French bombarded Haiphong in retaliation. Six thousand Vietnamese, mostly civilians, were killed outright or trampled to death in the panic that followed. Then the Vietminh countered in December with a day of terror. All the French and Eurasian men, women, and children in Hanoi were brutally murdered. With this event the war began in earnest.

The French thought their Foreign Legion of 150,000 battle-hardened troops could easily defeat any rag-tag forces that Ho could muster. The Legion quickly fastened its hold on Saigon and Hue and drove Ho out of Hanoi. But the French had not counted on the great support that Ho had among the villagers, who at that time made up eighty-five percent of Vietnam's population. The motto of the Vietminh was "Victory Is Built with the People As Foundations." The French thought military might alone would win. But Ho knew that as long as the mass of the Vietnamese were with him—gave his troops food, shelter, and information regarding French troop movements—he could not lose.

Ho worked hard in his attempt to gain and hold the favor of his countrymen. His orders to his troops reflected this effort. They must always remember:

---

3. The population of French Indochina in 1946 was 33.5 million. Vietnam had 27 million, with 15 million in the north and 12 million in the south. Cambodia had 5 million persons, and Laos had 1.5 million. The population of France was 40 million.

Bao Dai, the puppet ruler of Vietnam under the
French and Japanese.

1. not to do what is likely to damage the land and crops or
   spoil the houses and belongings of the people.
2. not to insist on buying or borrowing what the people are
   not willing to sell or lend.
3. not to break your word.
4. not to give offense to people's faith and customs.
5. not to do or speak what is likely to make people believe
   we hold them in contempt.[4]

Ho further urged his men to help the peasants with their daily
work, teach them to read, and show them basic hygiene proce-
dures.

---

4. Quoted in Gettleman, *Vietnam*, p. 88.

The French tried to combat Ho's hold over the peasants. They brought large numbers of Vietnamese into their army and tried to persuade the people that they were fighting to protect them from communism. They also set up a Vietnamese leader in competition with Ho. Thus on June 5, 1948, Bao Dai became the French-sponsored ruler of Vietnam.

Bao Dai's royal lineage dated back to 1802, when his ancestor Gia Long had become the emperor of Annam. But Bao Dai was a shy, uninspiring man who preferred night clubs to thrones. He had been a puppet emperor under the French before World War II and then had served in the same capacity under the Japanese. When Ho Chi Minh had proclaimed Vietnam's independence in 1945, Bao Dai recognized that only Ho was capable of leading Vietnam and gladly abdicated. Now he returned unwillingly from the glittering international cafés of Hong Kong and Europe. He had no personal following and was a weak leader. Bao Dai was not to be the only puppet leader that a Western power would install in office with the intent of eroding Ho's popularity.

Nevertheless, Ho found the French Foreign Legion a tough adversary. Until 1950, Ho fought with little if any outside aid, and he made no significant headway. But beginning early in 1950, Mao Tse-tung, fresh from his victory over Chiang Kai-shek, began giving Ho many first-rate American weapons which had been captured from Chiang's Nationalist troops. Then the Vietminh started experiencing some successes.

However, Ho was not the only one to receive aid. President Truman's suspicions were aroused by the Chinese action. Knowing little of China's traditional interest in its southern neighbor, Truman saw Mao's help as part of a Communist plot for world domination. The experience of Korea hardened Truman's belief, and soon massive American funds began reaching the French. To supervise this aid, Truman sent thirty-five U.S. advisers to Vietnam on May 8, 1950. Thus American involvement began.

Meanwhile the French thought they had found the way to bring the war to an end. The key to their plan for victory was to be the astute use of an isolated fortress named Dien Bien Phu.

CHAPTER SEVEN

Exit France: 1954

Fifteen thousand of France's finest troopers hunched behind the brick and earth ramparts of the fortress at Dien Bien Phu. Once they had been self-assured and even cocky, but now they were subdued. General Henri-Eugène Navarre, the French commander in Vietnam, had planned to destroy Vietminh effectiveness in the north, as well as in Laos, from this fortress. The fortress lay astride the only road between North Vietnam and Laos. According to the Navarre Plan, at night squads from Dien Bien Phu would patrol the jungles and shatter all enemy supply and guerrilla units. During the day they would retire into the fort, where they hoped to lure the Vietminh into making a suicidal assault on the battlements. The Vietminh would not be able to stand up to European firepower and would suffer losses that would sap their manpower and morale.

General Navarre had been confident that if he could only draw the Vietminh out of the jungle, he would win a great victory. At Dien Bien Phu the Vietminh were coming out of the jungle, but not as Navarre had planned.

Two things went wrong. First, the French air force was supposed to keep the garrison supplied with the ammunition needed to blast apart the Vietminh. But monsoon rains greatly hindered the airlift. And land support was impossible, because the outpost was located more than two hundred miles away in enemy territory. In addition, Vietminh bombardment eventually made the Dien Bien Phu landing strip unusable.

Second, the French were supposed to have a devastating superiority in firepower. This superiority would enable the French to decimate any Asiatic horde that General Vo Nguyen Giap might throw against them. But Giap had been generously

supplied by the Red Chinese with the finest captured American artillery. He also had been provided with rocket launchers from Russia. Consequently, it was the French, not the Vietminh, who were outgunned.

The French Foreign Legion had taken over Dien Bien Phu on November 20, 1953. It was not until March 13, 1954, that General Giap had brought up the necessary men and guns to open the siege. Then he began subjecting the fortress to a ferocious shelling that would continue for nearly two months.

The French artillery answered Giap round for round at first. But Giap's guns had greater range and the advantage of jungle

French Legionnaires and supplies being parachuted at Dien Bien
Phu to reinforce the garrison against the Vietminh seige.

camouflage. The French, on the other hand, were in the center of
a treeless valley, where the fortress and every battery were
clearly visible. So effective were Giap's gunners that on the very
first day of the siege they reduced to rubble one of the fortress's
strong points. This artillery duel forecast the certain doom of
Dien Bien Phu.

Upon seeing the horrible blunder committed by the French
chiefs of staff in placing the garrison at Dien Bien Phu, the
commander of the fort's artillery committed suicide. Yet the
French fought on. They compared themselves to the Americans at
Bastogne. They would hold out until relief came.

The airlift strove to keep the garrison strong. Two thousand more troops were flown in. But on March 27 Vietminh artillery closed the air field, and no more landings could be made. Yet the airlift continued. A total of eighty-three thousand parachutes brought food and ammunition to the garrison. Nonetheless, day by day, the Vietminh inched forward. Soon most of the parachuted items began drifting into the Vietminh lines. Even a bottle of champagne dropped to the fort commander, General de Castries, was gleefully scooped up by the Vietminh.

French casualties mounted. The hospital, built to serve forty-two patients, was unable to provide care for the wounded and dying who soon topped five thousand. Nevertheless, the Legion held out during the entire month of April. Rumor had it that the United States was about to launch an air armada to wipe out Giap's artillery positions. Day by day the troops gazed longingly at the sky. Airplanes came, but they were pitifully few and bore the circle insignia of France, not the stars of America.

De Castries radioed his superiors in Hanoi. The fort was in desperate condition. Men were dying by the hundreds for lack of medical attention and proper shelter. Food was low. De Castries's artillery could not effectively return the Vietminh fire. Monsoon rains were turning the trenches and dugouts into filthy mires. He would have to surrender.

The reply came back through the static. "What you have done until now surely is magnificent. Don't spoil it by hoisting the white flag. You are going to be submerged [by the enemy], but no surrender, no white flag."[1]

French "honor" had helped to force France into the Vietnam morass. French "honor" had kept the fighting going. Now French "honor" demanded that Dien Bien Phu fight to the last man.

EISENHOWER INCREASES THE AMERICAN ROLE

The long, agonizing death of Dien Bien Phu during the spring of 1954 deeply affected Dwight Eisenhower, who had assumed the presidency in January, 1953. There were many reasons why Ike wished to help the French restore order in Vietnam. First, there was a moral obligation. France had been a traditional ally of the United States from the days of the American Revolution down through World War II. Furthermore, Ike felt a personal attachment to the French from his years as supreme Allied

---

1. Quoted in Marvin Gettleman, ed., *Vietnam: History, Documents, and Opinions* (New York: Fawcett World Library, 1965), p. 107.

President Dwight D. Eisenhower believed in and supported the French cause in Vietnam. By 1954 the United States was paying for more than three-quarters of the war's costs.

commander. He had helped to plan the Normandy invasion and had fought alongside the French and British to crush Nazi Germany. In addition, France was a member of NATO, the Western bulwark against Soviet aggression in Europe. The sooner the Vietminh were defeated, the sooner France could return French soldiers to the weakened NATO force in Europe.

Eisenhower felt that he had a responsibility to continue the foreign policy of Truman, his predecessor. He also had a responsibility to live up to his own campaign promise to resist the spread of communism. Indeed, some thought Ike's landslide victory in 1952 was due as much to his promise to end Communist obstructionism at the Korean peace talks as to his winning smile and immense personal popularity.

Although these reasons help to explain Ike's decision to aid the French, he might also have had a subconscious motive, one of which he was unaware. While there has been no study of Eisenhower like that done on Woodrow Wilson by Sigmund Freud, many observers believed that Ike might subconsciously have been living up to his "father image." Voters in America and people around the world looked up to this good-natured man with something of the awe and respect ordinarily reserved for one's father. Ike, in return, played a paternal role. He kept aloof from the petty bickerings of his subordinates. He settled arguments and soothed hurt feelings as a parent would with squabbling children.

Some observers have suggested that Ike carried this paternal role over into international politics. With the United States being the dominant partner in the Western alliance, it would have been natural for Ike to view other member countries as juniors. Thus, when France became embroiled in Vietnam, Ike may have felt that he had a duty to help France just as a father would try to help a son who was in trouble.

Whether or not this theory is true, Eisenhower believed he had enough reasons to intervene in an area that held no strategic value for U.S. defense. Immediately upon becoming president, Ike increased Truman's military and economic aid to France from $61 million to $446 million. Soon Ike also sent an additional two hundred advisers to augment Truman's thirty-five. Originally the advisers were to remain in Indochina only for four months, but their stay proved to be much longer. By 1954, Ike was deeply involved with supporting the French. By that time American aid had risen to $1 billion, which represented about seventy-eight percent of the war's costs.

While the U.S. government was increasing its aid to the French, Congress and the American people were being kept largely uninformed or misinformed about the true situation in Vietnam. In their 1958 best-seller, *The Ugly American*, William Lederer and Eugene Burdick describe how a not-too-fictional U.S. senator actually was hoodwinked in Vietnam. Their senator, Jonathan Brown, chairman of the Foreign Relations Committee, was making a special inspection trip to Vietnam. The morning after the senator's arrival American advisers escorted him on a preplanned inspection tour designed to permit him to see only what they wished him to see:

> It was a rough ride; the Senator had no way of knowing that Major Cravath had had the shock absorbers on the

weapons-carrier taken up so tight that every bump in the road came through like a blow.

Their first stop was an ammunition depot which they inspected on foot. . . . [Then] they inspected an obstacle course, a tank-training field, a machine-gun range, and a parade field. By 11:30 it was obvious to Major Cravath that the Senator's legs were hurting him. . . .

[That evening there was a diplomatic party for the Senator and his wife.] They took over three hours to eat. Somewhere the assistant to the Commissioner-General had obtained several bottles of Senator Brown's favorite sour-mash whiskey. There were three kinds of wine with the dinner, and they finished up with champagne. Over cigars and cognac the assistant showed Senator Brown a stack of photographs. . . . [The next day] Senator Brown was tired from the food and the exercise and the late hours. . . .

A week later the Senator and his party left Saigon. . . . Just as the Senator was on the edge of falling asleep in his seat on the plane, one of his political reflexes functioned, and his eyes opened with a start. He had just realized that in all of the time in both Saigon and Hanoi, he had talked to only two natives, and to only three military officers below the rank of general.[2]

As the authors point out, congressional visitors were kept under the thumb of the upper military and diplomatic officers in Vietnam. The U.S. advisers told the visitors only that which the army wanted them to learn. Since the visitors could not speak Vietnamese, their only contact with the natives was through French interpreters, and the interpreters' translations often bore no resemblance to the Vietnamese descriptions of conditions. Thus most U.S. congressmen who came to Vietnam could not learn the depth of the Vietnamese hatred of the French. Nor could they learn about the Vietnamese enthusiasm for Ho Chi Minh or about their desire to reunify their country.

Even Eisenhower's officials were not aware of these facts, since they, too, were largely dependent on the French for information. For this reason the administration found itself persuaded that a French defeat in Indochina would be an unthinkable blow to the prestige of all Western nations. To prevent this defeat and loss of prestige, American aid was essential.

As the situation at Dien Bien Phu worsened, Eisenhower and his advisers began to consider even more active U.S. involvement to aid the French in Indochina. During the spring of 1954,

---

2. William J. Lederer and Eugene Burdick, *The Ugly American* (New York: W. W. Norton, 1958), pp. 211–220.

Headquarters of the United States Military Assistance Advisory Group (MAAG), Saigon, South Vietnam.

Secretary of State John Foster Dulles urged President Eisenhower to order massive air strikes from American carriers against Vietminh positions at Dien Bien Phu. Dulles was convinced that such a course of action was necessary. On April 3 the tall, imposing secretary met secretly with eight congressional leaders. He told them that he needed the passage of a joint resolution giving the president power to use air and naval forces in Indochina.

The congressmen were shocked. Lyndon Johnson of Texas voiced the opinion of most congressmen present. He said that they would not push such a resolution unless Dulles first assured them that the United States would not end up fighting the war alone, which had nearly been the case in Korea. As a result of this meeting, Dulles flew to London, where the durable Winston Churchill was once again prime minister. Dulles was informed that the British would give him no support until the results of the upcoming Geneva Conference were known. The conference had been called earlier to seek a negotiated end to the Vietnam war. It was scheduled to open on April 26, 1954.

And so there was nothing Dulles could do for the moment. Two hundred American warplanes stood ready to blast Vietminh positions around Dien Bien Phu, but the word to take off was never flashed from Washington.

Meanwhile the desperate French garrison clung to the smoking fortress.

THE GENEVA CONFERENCE

The Geneva Conference was attended by the top diplomats from Russia, Red China, Britain, France, the United States, Laos, Cambodia, and Vietnam. Representing Vietnam were officials from the Bao Dai and the Ho Chi Minh factions. The Communists wanted to end the war as much as the French, for aside from Ho's strength around Dien Bien Phu his position elsewhere in Vietnam was not strong. At a preparatory meeting in Moscow, Russian leader Nikita Khrushchev learned just how precarious the Vietminh position was:

> After one of these sessions in Catherine Hall at the Kremlin [Khrushchev recalled], Chou En-lai buttonholed me and said "Comrade Ho Chi Minh has told me that the situation in Vietnam is hopeless and that if we don't attain a cease-fire soon, the Vietnamese won't be able to hold out against the French. They want China to be ready to move troops into Vietnam as we did in North Korea. We simply can't. We've already lost too many men in Korea—that war cost us dearly. We're in no condition to get involved in another war at this time."[3]

Yet the Communists were in luck. On May 7 the Geneva Conference learned that Dien Bien Phu had surrendered. It was, in Khrushchev's words, a "miracle." Although the French still had 478,000 Legionnaires and loyal Vietnamese troops to combat 375,000 Vietminh regulars and guerrillas, Dien Bien Phu sapped the will of the French to fight on. They believed that victory could never be theirs, and they wanted out.

Now the negotiations took a new turn. When the Vietminh representative, Pham Van Dong, showed determination to take every advantage from Dien Bien Phu, Dulles stomped out of the

---

3. Nikita Khrushchev, *Khrushchev Remembers* (New York: Little, Brown, 1970), quoted in *Life*, 18 December 1970, p. 23.

Escorted and guarded by Vietminh, French and Vietnamese prisoners of war begin their long trek from Dien Bien Phu to Hanoi. Many of these men died during the long, overland march to the sea.

conference in disgust. Although Russia's V. M. Molotov and China's Chou En-lai persuaded Van Dong to tone down his demands, Dulles would not return. Thus the agreement concluded on July 21 received no official American mark of approval. Undersecretary of State Walter Bedell Smith, however, did voice a conditional American assent.

An understanding of the Geneva Agreements is essential in order to evaluate the subsequent renewal of hostilities. It must be realized that the actual settlement was signed only by France and the Vietminh. The other Geneva participants, except for the United States, indicated by a voice vote their obligation to live by the agreements. However, Bao Dai's representative immediately noted that he had strong reservations about the treaty.

The Geneva Agreements called for a pullback of the Vietminh to the northern portion of Vietnam and of the French to the southern. There would be a demilitarized zone drawn approximately along the Seventeenth Parallel to separate the two sections.

The southern portion of Vietnam would be governed by Bao Dai until elections could be held in two years to determine whether or not the people wished to unite with the north. The French

Vietminh General Quang Buu signing the Geneva Agreements. The document formally ended the French-Vietminh conflict and divided Vietnam between the Communist north and the pro-Western south near the Seventeenth Parallel.

would withdraw their troops from all of Indochina, which included Laos and Cambodia, "at the request of the governments concerned."

The agreements were quite explicit about the future of Vietnam:

> Article 4. The Conference takes note of the clauses in the [French-Vietminh] agreement prohibiting the introduction into Vietnam of foreign troops and military personnel as well as of all kinds of arms and munitions. . . .
>
> Article 6. The Conference recognizes that . . . the military demarcation line [the Seventeenth Parallel] is provisional and should not in any way be interpreted as constituting a political or territorial boundary. . . .
>
> Article 7. . . . In order to ensure that . . . all the necessary conditions are obtained for the free expression of the national will, general elections shall be held in July, 1956. . . .

> Article 12. In their relations with Cambodia, Laos, and Vietnam, each member of the Geneva Conference undertakes . . . to refrain from any interference in their internal affairs.[4]

Thus the matter of Vietnam was apparently settled. The people of South Vietnam would decide themselves in a free election the issue of unification. No foreign nation would interfere with Vietnam's own self-determination.

It seemed firm and final.

---

4. Gettleman, *Vietnam*, pp. 151–154.

CHAPTER EIGHT

Enter America: 1954 to 1960

Secretary of State Dulles was so disgusted by the French surrender at the Geneva Conference that he decided to develop a new American diplomatic strategy for Asia.

In September, 1954, he brought forth the Southeast Asia Treaty Organization (SEATO). Composed of the United States, Thailand, the Philippines, Pakistan, Great Britain, France, Australia, and New Zealand, SEATO was a hodgepodge of nations with little in common. Furthermore, some of the treaty provisions were so vague as to be almost meaningless. For example, in the case of armed attack on a treaty member, each SEATO nation would merely "act to meet the common danger in accordance with its constitutional processes."[1]

Yet, despite its weakness, the SEATO treaty was adequate for Dulles's purposes. He had two objectives. First, he wanted to warn Communist China against any type of Korean-style operation in Southeast Asia. Second, he wished to lay the groundwork for a possible eight-nation intervention in South Vietnam that would satisfy Congress's desire for allies. Congress had refused to intervene at Dien Bien Phu because the United States would have had to act alone, without the support of other nations. It was for this reason that Dulles had a short section added to the treaty which included South Vietnam as part of SEATO's area of concern. The section could be construed to give the United States a right—vague and self-proclaimed though it might be—to intervene in Vietnam.

The SEATO treaty was to play an increasingly important role in America's involvement in Vietnam. For as the years passed

---

1. Marvin Gettleman, ed., *Vietnam: History, Documents, and Opinions* (New York: Fawcett World Library, 1965), p. 93.

U.S. Secretary of State John Foster Dulles signing the SEATO document that he engineered to support his crusade against what he believed to be a Communist conspiracy to dominate the world.

the exact wording of the treaty was forgotten, and all that many people remembered was that SEATO had somehow established Southeast Asia as an essential part of the U.S. security network.

THE FAILURE OF THE GENEVA AGREEMENTS

The formation of SEATO was a clear signal that the United States did not intend to abide by the Geneva Agreements. Indeed, the Eisenhower administration had already demonstrated its dissatisfaction with the agreements when Dulles had walked out of the Geneva Conference. America had just fought a grueling war to prevent South Korea from falling to the Communists. Now South Vietnam was about to fall, and it mattered little to Eisenhower and his advisers that the threat in this case was posed by free elections rather than by armed force.

As a result of the publication of *The Pentagon Papers,* a remarkable series of classified documents that were brought to the public eye in 1971, Americans now know that a full month before the Geneva Conference Eisenhower's military advisers had considered expanding the U.S. role in Vietnam regardless of the outcome of the meeting. A special Pentagon committee had recommended that the United States "actively oppose a negotiated settlement at Geneva." In the event that a settlement was reached, the committee had suggested that the United States "initiate immediate steps" with the governments of Vietnam, Laos, and Cambodia "aimed toward the continuation of the war in Indochina to include active U.S. participation."[2]

The Pentagon Papers indicate that Secretary of State John Foster Dulles, rather than the golf-loving president, was the driving force behind this new foreign policy. Dulles operated mainly through the National Security Council (NSC). Members of the NSC usually are the president, the vice-president, the secretaries of state, defense, and the treasury, the chairman of the Joint Chiefs of Staff, and the head of the Central Intelligence Agency (CIA).

On August 8, 1954, the National Security Council made a crucial decision. The council agreed that the Geneva Agreements were "a disaster." It then approved actions designed to prevent the near-certain Communist takeover of South Vietnam in the promised 1956 election. For the council's purpose, it was fortunate that Emperor Bao Dai had appointed a strong anti-Communist as his premier in June. This premier was Ngo Dinh Diem. Diem was a hitherto little-known person who had spent much of his life outside Vietnam. He was an ardent Catholic who believed that godless communism was an evil to be fought wherever it appeared.

In 1950, Diem had come to the United States as an exile and was given lodging at the Maryknoll seminaries in New Jersey and New York. While there he became good friends with the influential Cardinal Francis Spellman. Through the cardinal Diem was introduced to Supreme Court Justice William O. Douglas. Douglas, in turn, brought Diem to the attention of Senators Mike Mansfield and John F. Kennedy. Mansfield would become one of the Senate's leading authorities on Vietnam, and John Kennedy would in six years become president.

Diem's strong American backing had helped him land the premiership. And his vigorous leadership gave the National

---

2. Neil Sheehan, Hedrick Smith, E. W. Kenworthy, and Fox Butterfield, eds., *The Pentagon Papers* (New York: Bantam Books, 1971), p. 36.

Security Council confidence that he could weld South Vietnam into a bulwark against Ho Chi Minh. For this reason it was agreed to "take the plunge" with Diem—to use Dulles's words.[3]

In December, 1954, General Lawton Collins was sent to Saigon to organize the American effort to make South Vietnam an independent nation. Collins helped pressure the French into turning over to the United States all training and supervision of the emerging security forces of South Vietnam. Under further pressure, in February, 1955, the French agreed to a premature withdrawal from Vietnam. The Geneva Agreements had assumed that the French would remain long enough to oversee the 1956 election, which was an essential article in the document. But once the French were gone, Premier Diem and the Americans felt they were free to arrange the future of South Vietnam to please themselves.

Immediately the American advisory group, which now numbered 342 men, began molding Diem's security forces into a formidible police network. By October, 1955, Diem had such tight control of South Vietnam that he dared to hold a referendum designed to depose Emperor Bao Dai and to name himself as undisputed ruler.

The referendum came out as Diem had planned. He received an obviously fraudulent total of more than ninety-eight percent of the vote. In Saigon he actually gathered an impossible 605,000 ballots from only 450,000 registered voters. By this time it became clear to the world that Diem did not intend to hold the promised 1956 election. Diem justified not holding the election by stating that he had never given his assent to the Geneva Agreements and therefore was not bound by them.

The Eisenhower administration was in complete accord with Diem. The Americans now felt that the time had come to make certain that Diem was able to enforce his decision not to hold the election. Knowing that Diem would encounter opposition in South as well as North Vietnam, the United States bolstered Diem's regime with 350 additional military advisers. The advisers arrived in Saigon during May, 1956. To disguise the stepped-up U.S. involvement, the new advisers were called the Temporary Equipment Recovery Mission. But their mission was not to recover equipment. Instead, they were to help channel new military supplies to Diem's growing armed forces. Funds that Congress had thought were earmarked for South Vietnam's

---

3. Sheehan et al., *The Pentagon Papers*, p. 19.

After rigging South Vietnam's referendum in 1955, President Ngo Vinh Diem reads his own proclamation establishing the Republic of Vietnam.

agricultural and educational programs were spent secretly on weapons and on the construction of military roads.

Thus by mid-1956 the Eisenhower administration—unknown to Congress or the general public—had helped to shatter the Geneva Agreements. It also had led the United States far down the road to war.

THE FIGHTING RESUMES

The North Vietnamese reaction to Diem's refusal to hold the 1956 election was of necessity surprisingly mild. Although Ho Chi Minh was enraged at the rupture of the Geneva Agreements,

From left to right, Secretary of the Treasury George Humphrey, President Eisenhower, Vice-President Richard Nixon, and Secretary of State Dulles emerge from a Camp David meeting where they discussed the budget and cold war strategy.

he was fully occupied putting down a serious anti-Communist revolt in North Vietnam.

The opposition to Diem during 1957 and 1958 arose almost entirely from native Southerners. Diem already had rounded up most of the five thousand former Vietminh that Ho had left as agents in the South. But Diem had not been able to soothe the massive resentment resulting from his interference in village politics. He had deposed the elected village chiefs and replaced them with his own hirelings. These new headmen, while insuring the loyalty of the villages, were usually from outside the village and roused anger from those they ruled. In addition, they were often French-educated Catholics who were out of sympathy with the Buddhist peasants. But for a while Diem's chiefs ruled supreme, being supported by Diem's well-armed security police.

The Eisenhower administration believed its policy in South Vietnam had been very successful in saving the country from communism. Congress was informed that the United States would begin its withdrawal in 1961.

But Ike, Dulles, and their associates had completely under-estimated the hatred that many of the South Vietnamese felt toward Diem. By 1957 the opposition had reached the point that Diem had to throw nearly 100,000 persons into detention camps. Yet the anti-Diem feeling still mounted.

As conditions worsened under Diem, it became almost impossible for Ho Chi Minh not to intervene. Many of the 90,000 troops withdrawn from South Vietnam by Ho to honor the Geneva Agreements were Southerners who wanted to help their country-men depose Diem. And so in 1959, Ho began infiltrating South-erners down what would become known as the Ho Chi Minh Trail. The numbers infiltrated at this time were quite small—only around 4,500 between 1959 and 1960.

The main opposition to Diem continued to come from the South Vietnam villagers. Most of these villagers were united by their hatred of Diem's tactics rather than by any attraction to com-munism. In 1960 this opposition banded together to form the National Liberation Front (NLF). Within a single year the NLF claimed to have 300,000 supporters, though those in actual armed rebellion were a small fraction of this number.

Organized resistance to Diem and his American allies now began to mount.

THE DOMINO THEORY

In 1959 it still was not too late for the Eisenhower administra-tion to pull out of Vietnam without suffering disgrace. Ike and Dulles could truly have claimed they had done their best to support the French and, after the French had failed, to give all possible aid to Diem. Furthermore, there were almost no U.S. economic interests in Vietnam to justify U.S. protection. Nor could observers see any possible threat to American security if a few million people in a minor country adopted communism.

Why, then, did Eisenhower persist in supporting the obviously repressive Diem regime? The answer lies partially in Ike's adherence to what he named the Domino Theory:

> The loss of all Vietnam [Ike wrote], together with Laos on the west and Cambodia in the southwest, would have meant

the surrender to Communist enslavement of millions. . . . It would have meant that Thailand, enjoying buffer territory between itself and Red China, would be exposed on its entire eastern border to infiltration or attack. And if [French] Indochina fell, not only Thailand but Burma and Malaya would be threatened, with added risks to East Pakistan [now Bangladesh] and South Asia as well as to all Indonesia.[4]

The Domino Theory envisioned the free-world countries standing like dominoes. According to this theory, if one domino-country bordering Red China fell to communism, the domino-country next to it would likewise topple. That is, the first domino-country to fall would create a chain reaction that would cause the others also to fall. South Korea had been a domino which, if it had fallen to communism, could have toppled Japan, Taiwan, the Philippines, and other countries beyond. In Vietnam the Communist conspiracy was trying to do what it had failed to do in Korea. In Eisenhower's view, "there was a definite relationship between the fighting in Indochina and that in Korea."[5] Both countries, he believed, were dominoes in the Communist plan for world conquest.

The Domino Theory led to all sorts of speculation. For example, if Southeast Asia became Communist, bigger dominoes might fall: India, the Middle East, and Africa. Thereafter Western Europe itself would become threatened. And if Europe and NATO fell to communism, the United States would stand virtually alone.

The Domino Theory presented a truly frightening prospect. It had its roots in the aggressive strategy followed by Nazi Germany and Japan. The theory first had been introduced by Truman—though he didn't have a name for it—to justify his actions in Korea. Now it would influence the thinking of government leaders in the next four American administrations.

At times, however, Eisenhower seemed to have doubts about the Domino Theory and about the existence of the international Communist conspiracy upon which the theory was based. He later admitted that "there was no incontrovertible evidence of overt Red Chinese participation in the Indochina conflict."[6] Nor had Soviet Russia apparently any thought of using Vietnam as a

---

4. Dwight Eisenhower, *Mandate for Change* (New York: New American Library, Signet Books, 1963), p. 404.

5. Eisenhower, *Mandate for Change*, p. 216.

6. Eisenhower, *Mandate for Change*, p. 412.

domino. In January, 1957, the Soviets had actually suggested that South Vietnam be recognized as an independent country and that North and South Vietnam be admitted to the United Nations as separate nations. Also, Russian aid to Ho Chi Minh had been very small, especially if compared with the American war goods flooding into Saigon.

The unity of the two Communist giants, Russia and Red China, in a conspiracy for world domination was likewise open to question. The most obvious evidence of a rift between them appeared in 1958 when the Russians brusquely ordered several thousand Soviet technicians to leave China. This was a drastic step because these men had been helping Red China to raise its level of technology.

THE ROLE OF JOHN FOSTER DULLES

It is likely that there were other reasons for Eisenhower's determination to increase the U.S. presence in Vietnam besides a blind adherence to the Domino Theory. It is more than probable that Ike was influenced by the magnetic personality of Secretary of State John Foster Dulles. Dulles had had long years of experience in international diplomacy, while Ike's career had almost exclusively been a military one. It would be natural, therefore, for Ike to rely on Dulles. Whatever the reasons, however, it was apparent that Dulles ran the State Department with an iron hand.

John Foster Dulles had a deep hatred of communism. He was a deeply religious Presbyterian who believed that God despised communism with its atheistic teachings. Dulles might have felt that in some manner he was God's agent to combat atheistic communism. As a prominent historian close to the State Department put it, only half in jest, Dulles believed he could "speak for God."[7] He was given to "righteous preachings and diplomatic sermonizing" during NATO meetings, observed Congressman Emanuel Celler.[8] Dulles's crusading spirit was roused by communism, and once he even admitted he had brought the United States to the brink of war three times during his conflict with the

---

7. Arthur Schlesinger, Jr., *A Thousand Days: John F. Kennedy in the White House* (New York: Fawcett World Library, 1967), p. 402.

8. Deane and David Heller, *John Foster Dulles* (New York: Holt, Rinehart & Winston, 1960), p. 277.

Wearing a prisoner-of-war tag around her neck, this nineteen-year-old girl, member of a VC cadre, waits to be interrogated. She was captured with forty-one other Vietcong in a village in the Central Highlands.

Reds. Although critics were horrified by Dulles's "brinkmanship" diplomacy, the secretary of state was convinced that *Right* must never flinch when challenged by *Wrong*. It was a matter of "the good guys against the bad guys," said the press of Dulles's international philosophy.

Because Dulles was convinced that Communists would probably take over the NLF, he decided that Diem's anti-Communist vigor outweighed his dictatorial tendencies. To Dulles, Diem was a necessary force in the battle for good. Therefore, Dulles backed Diem as strongly as possible.

Understandably, it was distressing to Secretary Dulles that Diem began losing ground to the NLF despite American backing. Since Dulles died a lingering, painful death by stomach cancer in 1959, he never learned that by the time John F. Kennedy took office in January, 1961, the NLF controlled about seventy percent of rural South Vietnam.

The new president was shocked when he learned the gravity of the world situation. He later quipped to a reporter that "the only thing that surprised us when we got into office was that things were just as bad as we had been saying they were [in our campaign]." But in a more serious mood, Kennedy quoted to his advisers a warning General MacArthur had given him: "The chickens are coming home to roost, and you happen to have just moved into the chicken house."[9]

And so it was.

---

9. Theodore Sorensen, *Kennedy* (New York: Bantam Books, 1966), p. 329.

CHAPTER NINE

A Challenge That Could Hardly Be Ignored: 1961 to 1963

John Kennedy was not the kind of person who normally would stumble into a trap like Vietnam. He was young and not bound by the aging theories that envisioned an Adolf Hitler behind the move of every leader not allied to the United States. Kennedy had a sympathetic feeling toward all peoples and disapproved of the self-righteousness that many ascribed to Dulles. "There are few things wholly evil or wholly good . . . especially of government policy," he said, quoting Lincoln. He disliked communism, but he did not regard it as Satan's handiwork to destroy the world.

And Kennedy was well aware of the CIA reports describing the unfavorable aspects of Diem's government. For example, there was the report of May, 1959 (brought to light in *The Pentagon Papers*). It warned that Diem "has not generated widespread popular enthusiasm" among the South Vietnamese people; that his government was "essentially authoritarian"; that "no organized opposition, loyal or otherwise, is tolerated, and critics of the regime are often repressed."[1] This repression, as noted in Chapter 8 resulted in about 100,000 persons being put into detention camps.

The CIA reports also revealed that Diem had done little to relieve the peasants from the oppression of the landlords. The landlords owned seventy-five percent of all the farmlands, though they themselves comprised only fifteen percent of the population. The CIA told how Diem had put his family members into positions of power. One such appointment was Diem's

---

1. Neil Sheehan, Hedrick Smith, E. W. Kenworthy, and Fox Butterfield, eds., *The Pentagon Papers* (New York: Bantam Books, 1971), pp. 70–71.

ruthless brother Ngo Dinh Nhu, whom one of Kennedy's closest advisers would soon call "an increasingly unbalanced man."[2] Kennedy also knew that Diem had deposed the traditional village chiefs and forced the predominently Buddhist farmers to submit to his own largely Catholic appointees.

But Kennedy believed in the Domino Theory and could not take time to make a thorough investigation of the problem of Diem. There were so many other difficult situations demanding his attention. Even before he was settled into the White House, a series of international hurricanes struck. It was as if, wrote one reporter, while Kennedy "was still trying to move in the furniture, in effect, he found the roof falling in and the doors blowing off."[3]

The problems were worldwide during the early months of the new administration. In an area of Africa now known as Zaire, domestic turmoil had provided the Russians with the opportunity to intervene and possibly to erect a Communist state in Africa's heartland. Farther north in Africa fighting broke out between France and Tunisia. This event obligated Kennedy to balance U.S. commitments to his European ally against the need for a friend in North Africa. In Laos a Communist offensive threatened to carry all before it. In South Korea a military coup overthrew the government and forced Kennedy to rethink the position of the U.S. troops treaty-bound to remain in that country.

In the space race, the Russians showed the world their rocket superiority over the United States by orbiting the first man in space. Kennedy thereby was spurred to organize greater efforts in this field. Meanwhile, he had to follow the intense negotiations between the United States and the Soviet Union for the banning of nuclear testing. In Berlin the Russians threatened to sign a peace treaty with Communist East Germany. Such a peace treaty would give the East Germans authority to cut off land transportation between the Allied sectors of Berlin and West Germany.

In the Dominican Republic seethed a leftist ferment likely to lead at any moment to a revolt against the dictator Rafael Trujillo. In Brazil the American position was threatened by the resignation of the pro-Western president Janio Quadros. In Cuba, communization under Fidel Castro was proceeding rapidly. Over $1 billion of property owned by U.S. companies was confiscated and nationalized. Meanwhile, Kennedy had to decide whether a group of CIA-trained Cuban nationalists should invade their

---

2. Theodore Sorensen, *Kennedy* (New York: Bantam Books, 1966), p. 741.

3. Sorensen, *Kennedy*, p. 236.

homeland. The invasion plans had proceeded so far that Kennedy was being pressured to approve an operation about which he knew little.

While all these matters clamored for the new president's attention, he had to form his Cabinet, plan his domestic program, prepare his budget, and tend to the many functions that fell to him as head of state. It was a small wonder, then, that Vietnam could not command the attention it deserved.

KENNEDY ENTERS INTERNATIONAL POLITICS

Kennedy's first venture into the international arena ended in disaster. At the urgings of the Joint Chiefs of Staff and CIA director Allen Dulles, Kennedy permitted fifteen hundred anti-Communist Cubans to invade Castro's stronghold on April 17, 1961. The expected popular uprising to support the invaders did not occur. Neither did Kennedy dare permit American warplanes to aid the little army because he feared Russian retaliation against U.S. forces in Berlin. Within three days, twenty thousand of Castro's soldiers had defeated the invading force.

Kennedy admitted he was "aghast at his own stupidity" in permitting such an ill-conceived invasion.[4] Feeling the need for more experience in international dealings, he scheduled a meeting on May 31 in Paris with French President Charles de Gaulle. He also scheduled a second meeting in Vienna with Soviet Premier Nikita Khrushchev.

Charles de Gaulle was a gnarled old fighter who had led the Free French forces against the Germans outside occupied France during the Second World War. Blunt and outspoken, de Gaulle was not one to mince words. Fortunately for historians, de Gaulle left a detailed account of his meeting with Kennedy. From this account comes the following:

> It was above all on the subject of Indochina that I pointed out to Kennedy how far apart our policies were. He made no secret of the fact that the United States was planning to intervene. In Siam [Thailand] . . . they were . . . introducing their "military advisers" in collusion with some local chiefs. . . .
> In South Vietnam, after having encouraged the seizure of dictatorial power by Ngo Dinh Diem and hastened the departure of the French advisers, they were beginning to

---

4. Sorensen, *Kennedy*, p. 330.

The *Cleveland Plain Dealer* headlines the invasion of Cuba, which took place April 18, 1961.

install the first elements of an expeditionary corps under cover of economic aid. . . .

Instead of giving him the approval he wanted, I told the president that he was taking the wrong road.

"You will find," I said to him, "that intervention in this area will be an endless entanglement. . . . Even if you find local leaders who in their own interests are prepared to obey you, the people will not agree to it, and indeed do not want you. The ideology which you invoke will make no difference. Indeed, in the eyes of the masses it will become identified with your will to power [over them]. That is why the more you become involved out there against communism, the more the communists will appear as the champions of national independence. . . . We French have had experience [in Vietnam]. . . . I predict that you will sink step by step into a bottomless military and political quagmire, however much you spend in men and money. . . ."

Kennedy listened to me. But in the end events were to prove that I had failed to convince him.[5]

Why did Kennedy not heed the advice of this forceful French expert on Vietnam? In de Gaulle's viewpoint, "What Kennedy

---

5. *The Intellectual Digest*, May 1972, pp. 35–36.

had set his heart on above all else was the maintenance of his country's dominant situation in the defense of the West."[6] Thus, it was de Gaulle's belief that the president wanted his country to remain Number One in the Western alliance. The way to do this was to take over the defense of Vietnam, thereby showing the superiority of American methods to those of the French.

De Gaulle was in many ways a narrow, jealous individual. He was vying with Kennedy for predominance in Western councils. He took no pains about condemning American influence in Western Europe. Indeed, he eventually would take his country out of NATO and expel NATO troops from France. Yet he was perceptive and highly intelligent. His belief that Kennedy increased the American presence in Indochina in order to maintain America's dominant posture in defense of the West might well have been correct.

After meeting with de Gaulle, Kennedy went to Vienna to confer with Premier Khrushchev. The Vienna conference could have had significant influence on future U.S. actions in Vietnam. Khrushchev seemed little concerned about Indochina, which showed his lack of interest and participation in Eisenhower's Domino Theory. The Soviet premier did not insist on a Communist victory in Laos but, instead, agreed to push for a coalition government. As for Vietnam, Khrushchev cared so little what happened there that the subject was barely discussed. Kennedy, of course, was careful not to disclose that only a few weeks earlier he had raised the number of U.S. advisers from Eisenhower's 685 to 1,085.

At Vienna, Kennedy learned that the Russians' main concern was Germany. Russia was still deeply scarred by the effects of two German invasions within the past half-century. The prime rule in Soviet diplomacy was that Germany must never again be allowed to create the military potential for another invasion of Russia. If the Americans were worried about the Russian use of Vietnam for a domino effect in Asia, the Russians were far more worried about the American creation of NATO and its incorporation of West German armed forces. Russian theorists were firm in their outmoded belief that the Western "imperialists" were planning a military overthrow of communism in the USSR. Khrushchev well remembered Stalin's warning: "You'll see, when I'm gone the imperialistic powers will wring your necks like chickens."[7]

---

6. *The Intellectual Digest*, May 1972, p. 36.

7. Nikita Khrushchev, *Khrushchev Remembers* (New York: Little, Brown, 1970), quoted in *Life*, 18 December 1970, p. 19.

President John F. Kennedy and Premier Nikita S. Khrushchev emerging from their 1961 summit conference held in the Soviet embassy, Vienna, Austria.

The two leaders left Vienna with a mutual respect and even an odd sort of friendship. Upon parting, Khrushchev invited Kennedy to come to Russia to hunt bear with him. Soon Khrushchev opened a private mail correspondence with the president. And later Jacqueline Kennedy, the president's vivacious young wife who had dined with the diplomats in Vienna, received a surprise gift from Khrushchev: a puppy born to a Soviet space dog.

The Vienna talks clearly demonstrated the Russians' primary concern with Germany and their apparent lack of interest in Vietnam. The talks also seemed to disprove the Domino Theory, which held that Russia wanted to incorporate Southeast Asia into an international Communist empire. Since this was so, why would Kennedy six months later agree to increase the number of

U.S. advisers in South Vietnam to nearly seventeen thousand within two years? His doing so altered what *The Pentagon Papers* called Eisenhower's "limited-risk gamble" into a "broad commitment."[8]

WHY KENNEDY UPPED THE U.S. PRESENCE IN VIETNAM

Although de Gaulle believed that Kennedy wanted to maintain U.S. leadership in the Western alliance by taking the reins in Vietnam, this view does not explain the whole matter. Actually the increased involvement was so complex a matter that even Kennedy's secretary of defense, the brilliant Robert McNamara, could not understand how it happened. For this reason McNamara later commissioned the study that became known to the public as *The Pentagon Papers*. *The Pentagon Papers'* thirty-six investigators, being limited primarily to Defense Department documents, were not able to offer a complete story. They did, however, reveal some of the psychology that had lured Kennedy and his predecessors into the quicksands of Vietnam.

One strand that threads its way through *The Pentagon Papers* was the need of U.S. presidents to appear strong and sure of themselves to other world leaders. As the occupant of the nation's highest office, as well as the commander-in-chief of the world's mightiest war machine, an American president had to show his determination to wield this power when necessary. To have done otherwise would have resulted in severe personal, as well as national, humiliation.

Thus, when Kennedy had refused to unleash U.S. air power during the Cuban operation, he felt America had been humiliated. Kennedy also felt that he could not again afford to display weakness before the Communists. Therefore, according to the *New York Times* analysis of *The Pentagon Papers*, "On April 20—the day after the collapse of the Bay of Pigs invasion of Cuba—President Kennedy ordered a quick review of the Vietnam situation." His instructions to McNamara, as quoted from a Pentagon document, were to "appraise . . . the Communist drive to dominate South Vietnam" and to "recommend a series of actions . . . which, in your opinion, will prevent Communist domination of that country." These actions could be either open or secret, economic or military, Kennedy said.[9]

---

8. Sheehan et al., *The Pentagon Papers*, p. 79.

9. Sheehan et al, *The Pentagon Papers*, p. 88.

The report came back seven days later. American efforts, it stated, must be strong enough to impress friends and foes alike that "come what may, the U.S. intends to *win* this battle."[10]

This report had an important effect on Kennedy. He felt that the world was watching. To back away from another Communist threat after his Cuban fiasco might well wreck the vital NATO alliance, which depended on America's willingness to use its power overseas. The writers of *The Pentagon Papers* concluded that, as far as Kennedy was concerned, Vietnam "was a challenge that could hardly be ignored."[11]

Thus the legacy that Dulles had left still influenced U.S. foreign policy. America had created South Vietnam out of its rejection of the Geneva Agreements. To have abandoned the little nation after such encouragement would have been an act of bad faith to the loyal South Vietnamese, as well as to the free world. It would, in the administration's eyes, encourage Communist aggression in trouble spots everywhere. Vietnam then was, in truth, "a challenge that could hardly be ignored."

Such, at least, was the reasoning of the Kennedy people.

THE BUILDUP INCREASES

Despite CIA reports, Kennedy and McNamara refused to admit the strength of the opposition to Diem when they decided to bolster his administration in November, 1961. They could not imagine how they could fail.

How could a rebel faction in a third-rate country stand up to the might of the most powerful nation in the world?

Kennedy's program sent large shipments of American military supplies to the South Vietnamese army. These shipments gave Diem a vast superiority over the force that he called the Vietcong (VC), or Vietnamese Communists. (At this time, however, the VC was mainly manned by land reformers instead of Communists.) Thousands of U.S. advisers arrived to see that the South Vietnamese used the massive U.S. aid in the most effective manner. In addition, the U.S. Navy assumed patrol duty in the many rivers and ocean inlets to intercept infiltrators and supplies being shipped south by Hanoi.

To further assure the supremacy of Diem's army, the U.S. Air Force now provided helicopter reconnaissance to locate VC

---

10. Sheehan et al., *The Pentagon Papers*, p. 89.

11. Sheehan et al., *The Pentagon Papers*, p. 88.

camps. To support reconnaissance, Kennedy began a defoliation program by authorizing the use of six aircraft equipped with defoliants. The defoliants were sprayed over dense forests to strip the trees of leaves that camouflaged VC movements and bases.

Since Diem's force in 1961 outnumbered the NLF by 170,000 to just 17,000, Kennedy was sure he was backing a winner. He believed—and was reassured by McNamara—that the United States could conclude the affair by 1965.

Kennedy, however, was not sure that Congress and the American people could be convinced that South Vietnam was worth the expense. Therefore, the Kennedy administration decided not to lift the veil of secrecy that Dulles first had dropped. To conceal the nature of U.S. involvement, Kennedy called his first contingent of new advisers a "flood relief task force." And the press was told that General Maxwell Taylor, who had been sent to Saigon to determine the exact military role the United States would now play, was merely on an "economic survey" of the country.[12]

During the following year, 1962, Kennedy had many other crises to occupy his mind in addition to Vietnam. Berlin was a far more crucial flash point. Here the Russians had erected a wall to seal off the Russian sector from the Western sectors. The Americans and Russians had become so angry with one another that one night their tanks faced each other with loaded cannons at point blank range! Fortunately, however, no shot was fired.

In the autumn of 1962 an even more serious confrontation arose over Cuba. Here the Russians had begun the construction of an atomic missile system that would have placed every city in the American South within easy range. Kennedy demanded immediate withdrawal of the missiles and threw a naval blockade around Cuba. Once again armed Americans and Russians confronted each other. This time it was a blockade of U.S. warships challenged by Russian submarines protecting the missile-carrying freighters. Until Khrushchev backed down, the prospect for nuclear war had been chillingly real.

Because President Kennedy's attention was spread around the world he was dependent on others for firsthand analyses of Vietnam. But from the experts of the CIA and the Departments of State and Defense came a great many conflicting opinions. What could Kennedy believe? Some praised Diem for his strong

---

12. Sheehan et al., *The Pentagon Papers*, p. 99.

Mariel Naval Port, Cuba. This low-level photograph taken on November 2, 1963, reveals dismantled Russian missiles, which soon were loaded aboard three freighters bound for the Soviet Union.

anti-Communist stance. Others condemned him for the undemocratic tactics that antagonized his countrymen. Some said Diem's military program was driving the Vietcong from the country. Others said the program was a complete failure. Once when Kennedy called upon two of his most trusted advisers to give him an in-depth survey of Vietnam, their reports were so different that the president quipped: "You two did visit the same country, didn't you?"[13]

THE DOWNFALL OF DIEM

The controversy surrounding Diem came to a head during 1963. On May 8, Diem's troops fired into a crowd of Buddhists displaying antigovernment banners. Twenty-three persons were killed or injured. This event triggered a series of ofttimes violent

13. Sheehan et al., *The Pentagon Papers*, p. 175.

Buddhist protests. The climax came when some Buddhists poured gasoline over themselves and committed fiery suicide. Although Madame Nhu, wife of Diem's brother, ridiculed the burnings as "barbecues," they brought shock and indignation to people throughout the world.[14] To many in the Kennedy administration, it now became clear that somehow Diem and the Nhus must be removed from power. If they were not removed, there would never be a South Vietnam government commanding the loyalty of the people.

At this important juncture Kennedy appointed foreign affairs expert Henry Cabot Lodge II as his new ambassador to South Vietnam. Lodge was a well-known and respected figure in American politics. His grandfather had been an influential senator during the Wilson era, and Henry II had recently run for the vice-presidency on the Republican ticket. Although the Nixon-Lodge combination had been defeated, Henry's handsome face and sincere manner had struck a favorable chord among Democrats as well as Republicans. In making Lodge his ambassador, Kennedy had not only brought in a capable man but had cleverly reinvolved the Republican party in the problem of Vietnam.

Lodge arrived in Saigon on August 22, 1963. Almost immediately he was approached by conspirators who sought his reaction to the possible overthrow of Diem. Lodge cabled the information to Washington. On August 24 the answer came back: Lodge should "tell appropriate military commanders we will give them direct support . . . ." This crucial message was signed by Acting Secretary of State George W. Ball. But, according to *The Pentagon Papers*, President Kennedy had seen early drafts of the message and had helped to revise them through telephone conversations. Thus it was Kennedy himself who approved the plot to remove Diem.[15]

Lodge was put in charge of the U.S. role in the revolt. His main contact with General Nguyen Khanh, Colonel Nguyen Van Thieu, and the other conspirators was through Colonel Lucien Conein, a CIA agent. Colonel Conein gave the plotters detailed information about the encampments of the pro-Diem military forces around Saigon. The plotters then moved their own troops into strategic positions.

As the date of the revolt approached, Washington began worrying about the fact that the military balance between the

---

14. Sheehan et al., *The Pentagon Papers*, p. 165.
15. Sheehan et al., *The Pentagon Papers*, p. 167.

Colonel McCown—a U.S. military adviser—and South Vietnamese officials accompanying President Diem (with cane) on a tour of his summer home at Pleiku shortly before he was assassinated and his government overthrown.

two sides was nearly equal. Kennedy cabled Lodge that if the revolt seemed unpromising the U.S. should pull out, for "it will be better to change our minds than fail."[16]

On November 1, 1963, the revolt burst forth. At 1:30 P.M. rebel soldiers seized police headquarters and radio stations. Simultaneously the rebels began attacking the barracks of Nhu's private army. Other rebel groups descended on the presidential palace.

As bullets riddled the palace walls and shattered the windows, Diem made a frantic telephone call to Lodge, who taped the

16. Sheehan et al., *The Pentagon Papers*, p. 161.

conversation. "Some units have made a rebellion, and I want to know what is the attitude of the U.S.," Diem asked nervously. Lodge answered blandly, "I do not feel well enough informed to be able to tell you. I have heard the shooting, but am not acquainted with all the facts. Also it is 4:30 A.M. in Washington and the U.S. Government cannot possibly have a view."[17]

Diem undoubtedly read the meaning that lay behind Lodge's words. Although Lodge urged Diem to call back if his personal safety was threatened, Diem knew that he could expect no help from the Americans in defending his presidency. As the rebels began shooting their way into the palace, Diem and Nhu fled through a secret escape tunnel.

That night the two brothers hid out in the Chinese sector of Saigon. Diem spoke by telephone with the men in charge of the revolt. They promised him safe conduct out of Vietnam. At 6:20 A.M. the following morning Diem agreed to the rebels' terms, but he did not tell them where he was. Before the rebels could make good on their promise, Diem and Nhu were tracked down by an armored unit whose commander hated the president. The two men were shoved into an armored car, where they were shot to death.

Upon the toppling of Diem, Lodge cabled Washington that South Vietnamese morale would undoubtedly improve and the war would be shortened. Such was not the case, however. General Nguyen Khanh, head of the military junta, was unable to direct the war effort with Diem's vigor. Soon Khanh himself was deposed, and for the next two years a series of ineffective military men ruined whatever chance South Vietnam might have had to bring the NLF under control.

The important role played by Kennedy in encouraging the group that overthrew Diem obligated the United States to support the new government, which in many respects was Kennedy's creation. It would have seemed faithless to pull out after these men had risked their lives on the basis of American support.

But the continuing presence of seventeen thousand U.S. advisers was still a long way from full-scale fighting by the U.S. Army. Kennedy had expected to eliminate the major portion of the American effort in Vietnam in two years. In fact, he even planned to withdraw one thousand Americans in a matter of weeks. Whether or not he would have found this plan realistic in view of the deterioration of South Vietnam's military effort will never be known. For on November 22, 1963—just three weeks after Diem's

---

17. Sheehan et al., *The Pentagon Papers*, p. 187.

Under the Kennedy administration U.S. involvement in South Vietnam was stepped up. Above, an explosive ordnance disposal team searches for antipersonnel mines.

murder—President Kennedy was cut down by an assassin's bullet. The problem of Vietnam thereby fell into the lap of Lyndon B. Johnson, Kennedy's vice-president.

But, before we examine the role of Johnson in the war, it will be useful to review the nature of the actual fighting in Vietnam before full-scale American intervention occurred.

CHAPTER TEN

Guerrilla Warfare: 1959 to 1964

It had been a steep, dangerous climb to the crest of the misty peaks that formed South Vietnam's border. Do Luc, a Vietcong volunteer, was glad when his small squad of infiltrators was allowed to rest. As rays from the setting sun lanced into the jungle canyons beneath him, Do Luc began writing in his diary:

> I am sitting on the peak of a high mountain. This is a famous scenic place. This is the highest peak of the whole chain, and it is all covered with mist. All this scenery arouses nostalgia in my heart! I try to recall my life since I was a young boy.[1]

Do Luc remembered many things: the excitement of fighting the French; the joyous welcome in Hanoi after the French had been defeated in 1954. Then he remembered his shock and dismay when Diem had refused to honor the Geneva Agreements' promise of a free election in 1956. Do Luc had wanted to remain in his comfortable life in the North, but as Diem's regime grew more and more intolerable, he again felt the call to duty.

> I joined the ranks of the freedom army in answer to the call of the National Liberation Front of the South. Now my life is full of hardship—not enough rice to eat nor enough salt to give a taste to my tongue, not enough clothing to keep myself warm! But in my heart I keep loyal to the Party and to the people. I am proud and happy. I am writing down this story for my

---

1. Marcus G. Raskin and Bernard B. Fall, eds., "The Diary of a Viet-Cong Soldier, Do Luc," *The Viet-Nam Reader* (New York: Random House, 1965), pp. 226–227.

The Ho Chi Minh Trail, 1959–1964.

sons and my grandsons of the future to know of my life and activities during the revolution . . . .[2]

THE NATIONAL LIBERATION FRONT

Most members of the National Liberation Front (NLF) shared Do Luc's idealism. One was a medical officer named Mai Xuan

2. Raskin and Fall, *The Viet-Nam Reader*, p. 228.

Phong, whose diary also fell into South Vietnamese hands. Phong wrote, "My whole life, my whole strength have been devoted to the most elevated and the most beautiful cause—the struggle for the liberation of mankind."[3] Through these and other captured diaries, the NLF cadre reveal themselves as being idealistic, devoted men. They strongly believed that the overthrow of the Saigon regime was a cause worth their suffering and their possible deaths.

It is difficult to determine the degree to which the National Liberation Front was controlled by the Hanoi Communists. Although the Saigon government called all members of the NLF "Vietcong," many impartial observers estimated that during the early 1960s as many as seventy percent of the NLF were not Communists. They were, instead, South Vietnamese nationalists and land reformers. The official program of the NLF promised to break up the large estates into small private farms. The program did not provide for communal property. The Communist minority, supported by Hanoi, certainly had an influence in the NLF far exceeding its numerical strength. Nonetheless, since the NLF was composed largely of native Southerners, it probably was fairly independent of Hanoi at this stage. Only as the tempo of the conflict increased and the NLF became dependent on Hanoi for supplies and replacements did it lean more towards communism.

Nevertheless, beginning in 1959, Hanoi gave considerable aid to the NFL. Infiltrators were assembled for their journey south at the town of Dong Hoi. From there North Vietnamese trucks took them to the Laotian border and the famous Ho Chi Minh Trail. The infiltrators traveled in groups of thirty to forty men. They marched more than 120 miles along steep jungle paths guided by local people and quartered and fed at waystations set up a day's march apart. The exact route they followed through the myriad paths that made up the Ho Chi Minh Trail was a secret kept even from the local guides, who each knew only a single section.

It took as long as a month and a half for the infiltrators to tramp through the tropical undergrowth and over the mountainous terrain. Sometimes the waystations were low on supplies of salt, which the sweating men needed almost as much as food. For those men who fell ill from diseases spawned in the heat and humidity or carried by the ever-present swarms of mosquitoes, little, if any, medical relief was available. Neither was their thin

---

3. Raskin and Fall, eds., "Excerpts from the Diary of a Viet-Cong Medical Officer, Mai Xuan Phong," *The Viet-Nam Reader*, p. 229.

clothing adequate to protect them from the misty chill of the lofty mountain passes. Also, enemy planes frequently sped overhead at low altitudes, hoping to spot infiltrators through the canopy of branches and hit them with bombs.

In view of the arduous nature of the Ho Chi Minh Trail, it is little wonder that the numbers of Vietcong making the grueling trek southward were small. During 1959 and 1960 only 4,500 infiltrators journeyed into the South, where Vietcong troop strength was only 17,000 by 1961. Against this pitiful few Diem could muster an army of more than 170,000. To enhance Diem's strength, the Army of the Republic of Vietnam (ARVN) was firmly in control of the South's largest cities, including Saigon, Hue, and Da Nang. In such cities the recruitment of soldiers was easy, and good port facilities permitted the unloading of vast quantities of war goods from the United States. American supplies, such as tanks and troop carriers, gave the ARVN superior firepower and mobility over VC foot soldiers armed mainly with rifles and homemade grenades. American fighter-bombers and helicopter gunships often acted in concert with ARVN, striking the VC with blinding speed.

VIETCONG TACTICS

The Vietcong adopted guerrilla tactics to cope with the American-supported ARVN. Fortunately for the VC, they had an admirable operational handbook in the writings of Mao Tse-tung. Mao had to overcome similar problems during his long struggle with Chiang Kai-shek.

Mao envisioned guerrilla warfare as a three-stage conflict. The first stage dealt with setting up the movement among the rural people. In the first stage Mao viewed the masses as a sea and the guerrillas as fish. Thus the guerrillas should "swim" through the hamlets winning the loyalties of the peasants, upon whom the VC were dependent for food and new recruits. When the sharks came—the heavily armed government troops—the guerrillas either should merge with the villagers or hide in the jungle until the troops had left. The guerrillas were to avoid all contact with government forces and to return to the village only after they were gone.

The second stage would begin when the guerrillas were established among the peasants. The guerrillas now should begin fighting the government troops, but only in the artful method devised by Mao in China. Thus, when the enemy attacked, the

Marines examine a Vietcong's gun and personal effects following a brief skirmish. The Vietcong usually avoided fire fights, especially when they were outmanned and outgunned.

guerrillas—who nearly always would be vastly outnumbered and outgunned—should retreat. When the enemy halted, the guerrillas should regroup. And when the enemy moved back toward its supply base, the guerrillas should fall upon their rear guard and flanking units. By hitting small exposed units, the guerrillas would be able to achieve momentary numerical superiority. But when the main enemy force turned to engage them, the guerrillas once more should disappear into the jungle. Never should the guerrillas enter open battle with the enemy's main force. By using these tactics, a guerrilla force could successfully hold its own against an enemy five or even ten times larger than itself.

The third stage should begin after the enemy was weakened and demoralized by the stage-two tactics. By this time the guerrillas also should have bolstered their forces with village recruits and captured enemy weapons. The third stage was a frontal attack on the enemy. The war should now be carried right into the cities to defeat the enemy in its own strongholds.

The Vietcong followed Mao's system faithfully when the first stage of guerrilla warfare began in 1949–1950. The Vietcong courted the hearts of the peasant-farmer population with sincerity and vigor.

> Revitalize agriculture [ran the official program of the NLF]; modernize production [in village industries], fishing, and cattle raising; help the farmers in putting to the plow unused land and in developing better production . . . . Institute a just and rational system of taxation . . . . Organize social welfare: find work for jobless persons; assume the support and protection of orphans, old people, invalids . . . improve their working and living conditions. . . . Increase the number of schools . . . watch over public health; develop sports . . . establish equality between the two sexes . . . .[4]

Ideally, the first Vietcong to approach a village should be men and women from the area itself. They should talk to the villagers about the injustices of the Saigon regime: the absentee landlords who controlled much of the land, the too-heavy taxation, the lack of educational facilities, the unconcern of the rich Saigonese for the hard-pressed people of the provinces. While the VC representatives flooded the peasant-farmers with NLF propaganda, they should work with them in the fields. When the VC attracted enough village men to join their ranks, they then should abolish the landlord system. For this action alone the VC would win the loyalty of other villages in the vicinity.

Theoretically, all the villagers should willingly endorse the VC. But such was not always the case. Many of the peasants— who at this time made up perhaps eighty percent of South Vietnam's total population—did not find the Saigon government as bad as the VC claimed. Although the villagers might have preferred to see their nation united under Ho Chi Minh, they were not prepared to risk a destructive civil war to achieve this goal. Neither could they dismiss their suspicions of communism with its communal, rather than individual, land ownership. So even though the VC often were received with mild goodwill, the villagers did not always flock to their standard with the eagerness that the VC idealists had hoped. Therefore, the VC sometimes had to resort to terror to maintain their hold on the villagers.

---

4. Bernard B. Fall, trans., "Program of the National Liberation Front of South Viet-Nam," *The Two Viet-Nams* (New York: Praeger, 1963), quoted in Raskin and Fall, *The Viet-Nam Reader*, pp. 217–220.

Once the VC had taken control of a village, they
dug tunnels to provide storage areas for their
weapons and escape routes to use when U.S. or
ARVN troops were conducting one of their many
search-and-destroy missions. The marine above
has just finished inspecting one of these tunnels.
The VC living in this village had already fled.

The VC terror tactics first were directed against the village
chiefs. These men were more often than not political appointees
from Saigon—not elected heads of the villages as had been the
case before Diem abolished rural democracy. Although the chiefs
were supported by the local police, as well as by whatever army
units might be in the vicinity, the VC found it fairly easy to strike
down the chiefs at night. The effectiveness of this assassination
campaign was startling: between 1959 and 1965 the VC killed
more than fifteen thousand chiefs, most of whom were Catholic.
This figure meant that each village had more than one chief.

Although at first most of the assassinated chiefs were replaced, eventually they were not. And when they were not, the VC were able to move in and live and work with the villagers.

The VC used many tactics to extend their hold over the villagers. By inducing certain young men of the village to join their cause (sometimes with a pistol against the temple), they had hostages to hold over the rest of the villagers. "And once some village men come over to us," said a VC deserter to reporter Marguerite Higgins (as active in Vietnam as she had been in Korea), "they can no longer get away. If they tried, then we would kill them or their families. And one or two deaths are usually enough to keep the rest terrorized into obedience."[5]

With the villagers now at least partially in their grasp, the Vietcong pushed them into planting land mines and setting up ambushes against the government troops. Thereupon, continued the former VC to Higgins, "They are on the Viet Cong side, because having attacked the government, there is no going back. They have become, so to speak, our partners in crime."[6]

Higgins pursued the matter further. "How do the people feel about the Viet Cong?" The answer did not surprise her. "The villagers hate the Viet Cong. But they know that we hold life and death in our hands. So they do what we say. We infiltrate gradually, and at first in small numbers, to avoid alarming the people. By the time our power base is built and we come out in the open, it is too late."[7]

However, *The Pentagon Papers* do not support Marguerite Higgins's report that most of the villagers hated the VC. By the time her report was published in 1965, the VC had 100,000 South Vietnamese villagers in their ranks, and those villagers fought hard and rarely deserted.

SAIGON'S STRATEGIC HAMLET PROGRAM

Saigon did not sit idly by while the countryside was coming under Vietcong control. Diem and his successors adopted a tactic of their own that might well have defeated the VC. This tactic was the Strategic Hamlet Program. Begun with great fanfare in the spring of 1962, the Strategic Hamlet Program required the

---

5. Marguerite Higgins, *Our Vietnam Nightmare* (New York: Harper & Row, 1965), p. 141.

6. Higgins, *Our Vietnam Nightmare*, pp. 141–142.

7. Higgins, *Our Vietnam Nightmare*, p. 142.

Some South Vietnamese soldiers, their families, and personal belongings being transferred to remote army posts. At these army posts ARVN units were on call night and day to defend the strategic hamlets against the Vietcong.

villagers to move to central locations. This gave the villages greater numbers of people with which to resist the VC. Around these "new-life hamlets," as they were called, moats were dug and walls of bamboo and barbed wire were constructed. Before any inhabitant could live in a strategic hamlet, he was thoroughly checked by Saigon for loyalty. If he passed his loyalty check, he was issued an identification card, which he had to present to the guards before being admitted into the stockade. Strong militia units were formed with male members of the strategic hamlets. These local troops were armed by Saigon. They also were equipped with radios and flares, with which they were to signal nearby regular army units for help if the VC tried to reassert its domination.

The program started off extremely well. More than five million peasants moved into the new-life hamlets. Soon the countryside was dotted with stockaded outposts similar to those that had proved so effective on the American frontier. Marguerite Higgins, inspecting a new-life hamlet, found the villagers free from VC terror. They recently had actually beaten back VC infiltrators in a pitched battle. And with the fear of nightly VC visits gone, some

ARVN soldiers prepare to clear a proposed strategic-hamlet site of VC so that a palm-cutting crew can safely follow to erect fortifications and a moat.

villagers began informing government officials about the location of VC hideouts.

The VC admitted that 1962 was Diem's year. In Washington, officials of the Kennedy administration beamed broadly. The president had taken a chance on Vietnam, and now he apparently was proven right. The war would be won soon.

Yet the next few years saw the Strategic Hamlet Program fall apart. Within two years only about one thousand of the original eight thousand hamlets still resisted the VC.

One reason for the catastrophic decline of the program was the succession of weak leaders that followed Diem, who was assassinated in November, 1963. Another reason was the inability of government troops to aid the village militias when they were needed. The VC found that they could draw off large numbers of government troops with a fake attack on one village, and then overrun their target village. There were just too many hamlets for the government to protect, and the hamlets could not be combined into fewer, larger units because then the peasants would be too far from their fields. Also, as the VC guerrilla tactics neared stage two, the Vietcong had armed themselves with mortars, rocket launchers, and even some artillery, which had been dragged down the rugged Ho Chi Minh Trail. With such weapons the VC had the firepower to flatten even the most sturdy bamboo walls.

In most cases the peasants were happy to leave the strategic hamlets, because they had come to hate the program. The Strategic Hamlet Program prevented them from living on their beloved ancestral lands. It also provided Diem and his successors with the means for establishing dictatorial rule over them. Thus by the end of 1963 the peasants were trooping out of the government stockades and back to their villages. Quickly the VC reestablished their influence, and soon about seventy percent of the villages were in the NLF camp.

THE GREEN BERETS

President Kennedy and his staff did not wish to see South Vietnam slip into the Vietcong orbit. As noted earlier, Kennedy increased the number of American advisers to nearly seventeen thousand. Many of these "advisers" were not just consultants and coordinators for American military aid. Soon members of an elite unit called the "Green Berets" began to arrive in Saigon. The Green Berets actually were known in military circles as the Special Forces. They received their nickname from their colorful headgear.

The Green Berets originally had been organized to carry out guerrilla warfare behind Russian lines if the Soviet Union ever invaded Western Europe. Now their training had been expanded to include antiguerrilla warfare against the Vietcong.

The theory behind the Green Beret antiguerrilla training was simple. Since the VC had been successful because they moved secretly at night in small, mobile units living off the land, government forces led by Green Berets could do the same. Therefore special antiguerrilla teams were formed. The teams were each composed of six South Vietnamese led by two American Green Berets. Those units then were flown into VC territory by helicopters. They hid by day, then emerged at night to shoot up VC supply lines, ambush any VC troops they found, and awe the villagers by their presence into remaining independent of the NLF. When the VC began concentrating against a unit, choppers were radioed in to carry the men off to safety. After a brief rest, the unit was flown into a new area, where the unsuspecting VC again were subjected to ambush.

Since the teams were composed of so few men, their success depended on being highly mobile. And to a certain degree their

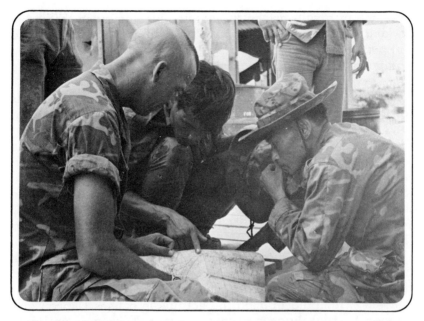

The marine lieutenant and members of his Vietnamese squad study a map to pinpoint an area of reported Vietcong activity. Shortly the squad was flown out and deposited by helicopter to carry out its search-and-destroy mission.

success depended on the farmers' not giving information of their whereabouts to the VC in the area.

One former Green Beret, Donald Duncan, wrote a vivid account of his part in one of these dangerous missions. At nightfall he and his team were deposited by a chopper in a jungle clearing:

> Holding on to each other's pack, we move a short distance into the trees and stop. The blackness is complete; so is the silence roaring in our straining ears. The hand holding on to a buddy's back is as invisible as the pack and the man carrying it. Hearts beat fast. This is the critical period.[8]

Although the sound of the departing chopper reverberates through the jungle, no VC scouts have located the team. Using luminous compasses and pencil flashlights held over maps, the team moves toward the area where it will spend the night before setting up tomorrow's ambushes.

But the hunters become the hunted. One of the men dropped his map at the landing zone. A VC scout has found it. There is

---

8. Donald Duncan, *The New Legions* (New York: Random House, 1967), p. 14.

the crack of a rifle as the VC notifies his comrades that he is tracking Duncan's team. Although it is too dark for Duncan and his men to try forcing their way very far through the jungle matting of thorns and thick vines, neither can the VC locate them.

The team radios its position to the air contact and then beds down in black nylon parkas. Duncan falls asleep with his right hand clutching a handgun.

At dawn he is awakened by the clamor of jungle birds and the chatter of squirrels. The eight men eat a breakfast of precooked rice mixed with water from their canteens. Then they take two salt tablets to protect themselves from heat exhaustion and move off on a course that they hope will enable them to elude their VC trackers. Soon they hear the fateful crack of a rifle to their rear. The VC are still on their trail.

The VC are intent upon preventing the team from slipping from their grasp and setting up ambushes. They send squads to guard the streams where the team must, sooner or later, refill their canteens. Tramping through the hot jungle causes Duncan and his men to drink large amounts of water. They are constantly perspiring. Duncan wrote, "My clothes are heavy with sweat, salt burns my eyes, and as usual the humidity is a smothering blanket."[9]

As they flee from their pursuers, the jungle growth becomes thicker. But the team carries no machetes to cut through it because the noise would give away their position. Duncan continues:

> Now we're getting into real thick stuff: dense, bushy thorn trees with branches almost to the ground joined together in a tangle of vines. We duck-walk and crawl more than walk now. Damn! Even the vines have small grabber thorns on them. . . . We stop frequently. This is exhausting work. . . . Crawling bugs and flying insects of every variety are around us; the hot air is heavy with moisture.[10]

Leeches cling to their bodies, and toward evening swarms of mosquitoes zero in on them. They douse themselves with repellent, and that helps a little.

They manage to stay ahead of the VC that day, but throughout the night they hear an hourly rifle shot as their trailers notify other VC that they are on the scent.

---

9. Duncan, The New Legions, p. 23.

10. Duncan, The New Legions, pp. 23–25.

Early the next morning the unit again is on its way. Duncan knows the mission has been a failure. Now he must locate an area in the jungle where a chopper can pick up the team. But even more urgently, he must find an unguarded stream where the team can refill the canteens. Their water supply now is so low that they do not even have enough water to wash down their much needed salt tablets.

They push on through the barrier of vines and thorns. In the distance they hear the muted sounds of a pitched battle. They sense that another Green Beret team is in trouble. "The men exchange glances. The volume of the fire says it must be a hell of a fight. Long, too: the firing continues for at least five minutes—too long not to take hits."[11]

They spend the night with no water.

The third day of their ordeal begins. They locate a stream, but it is guarded by several VC. With great stealth Duncan and his men slip to the enemy's rear. As the men silently and slowly let the precious water trickle into their canteens, Duncan continues, "I try to avoid looking directly at the man [VC] whose back is toward me. The man changes position, there is a murmur of voices and a rustling of twigs and leaves. I freeze. They resettle."[12]

With full canteens, the team moves on. But the rifle shots tell them that the VC are following ever more closely. Making their way quietly through the jungle, they suddenly see figures through the underbrush before them:

> . . . Then a dark-blue movement to the side—a man stooping and weaving, searching. My feet are in a boxer's stance, weapon ready, my thumb having already moved the selector off "safe."
>
> A face. The eyes lock onto my own. A look of absurd shock. Whatever [the VC] expected to see, it certainly wasn't a bearded "round-eye." For him it is the split-second hesitation that always proves fatal in a war, for in that fine second I fire: two at the dark blue. . . . It disappears. By the time my third shot is on its way the whole jungle is in [a] crescendo [of shooting]. The familiar sound of the three team weapons on my side. *Thunk*—one [bullet] in the tree behind me. The acrid smell of the gunpowder. *Snick, snick*—brush being sliced with bullets. The peculiar *crack* of one close by which seems to create a vacuum in the ear. I'm still firing; how many rounds now? The laborious heavy banging of a sub-machine gun firing in bursts. The adrenalin is pumping, the

11. Duncan, *The New Legions*, p. 30.
12. Duncan, *The New Legions*, p. 36.

eyes are clear, the mind works with fantastic speed and great clarity. An involuntary scream . . . .

An ejected casing hits the left side of my face. It's hard to pick targets through the brush, even harder to judge results. How long have we been shooting? Hope nobody's hit. . . . Keep firing even if there is no target. Fire is still coming at us but it is not aimed; most of it is high. The sound of a magazine being changed on my right. I think I still have two rounds left but change it now. A yell from the other side. The fire slackens.

I wave my arm. We start moving back, crouching, firing. Grady falls . . . . Hit? Son of a bitch! Now I'm down.[13]

Duncan is lucky. None of his team members has been hit. They only tripped over vines. The team flees fast. Duncan spots two VC running toward him. He fires a burst at them and they "are hurled back, broken at the waist like rag dolls."[14]

But now the rest of their pursuers close in. "We can hear voices on all sides. . . . We are desperate."[15] Then through the gathering dusk they spot a large pile of cut up limbs. They locate an opening and crawl in. The VC are shouting all around them. The team members are closely packed in their sweaty little cave of prickly branches.

Fear gnaws at their stomachs. Suddenly a South Vietnamese next to Duncan vomits. The stench is horrible. "Gagging, I turn my head and strain for clear air, breathing through my mouth. Again [he vomits]. And the noise. It can't be helped but it seems that even if the [VC] can't smell this putrid mess, they surely must be able to hear."[16]

But the VC do not find Duncan and his men. Duncan then uses his portable radio to call his air contact. Earlier in the day he had spotted a chopper-sized clearing. Now he gives the location coordinates and orders a chopper to pick them up at dawn. It will be tight, he knows, because the VC certainly will see the chopper making its descent.

Before dawn the next morning the team files silently through the jungle, fearing every moment to be ambushed by the VC. They make it to the landing site safely. In the distance they see two choppers. One peels off to make a fake landing sweep toward another zone, hoping to draw the VC away from the pickup area. The other chopper heads toward Duncan and his

---

13. Duncan, *The New Legions*, pp. 38–39.

14. Duncan, *The New Legions*, p. 46.

15. Duncan, *The New Legions*, p. 46.

16. Duncan, *The New Legions*, p. 46.

A marine squad filing aboard a helicopter after having made a fruitless sweep of the area for Vietcong. Most of these missions were unsuccessful because the Vietcong would hide or avoid detection by posing as Vietnamese farmers in a nearby village.

men. The motor roar is loud. Duncan knows the VC in the area are hurrying to intercept them.

The chopper inches earthward—a perfect target for enemy gunners. The team members dash toward the chopper. Duncan is the last. Out of the jungle emerge black-clad Vietcong. Duncan lunges to the chopper hatch. "Hands grab for me . . . the chopper is up and turning. Ragged rifle fire follows—and then there is only the noise of the motor. We made it."[17]

As Duncan heads toward his base, he sees a fleet of gunship choppers racing toward the landing site. Their rocket launchers are uncovered and will momentarily be hurling high explosives into the area.

---

17. Duncan, *The New Legions*, p. 59.

Duncan reflects over the mission. They killed three VC, maybe more. But it was only by sheer luck that the eight team members were not killed or captured. All in all, the mission was not effective. The VC were not very badly hurt, and certainly no villagers will be tempted to come over to Saigon's side.

If this example was representative, the Green Beret adviser program could hardly be called a success. "As we've learned the hard way," Duncan concluded, "nobody living in the area will help us. The VC have the people, [and all] we have [are] our helicopters."[18]

---

18. Duncan, *The New Legions*, p. 69.

★CHAPTER ELEVEN★

President Johnson's War: 1964 to 1968

On August 4, 1964, two American destroyers knifed through the Gulf of Tonkin. The sailors on board were tense because one of the warships, the *U.S.S. Maddox*, had been attacked by three North Vietnamese patrol-torpedo boats just two days earlier. The *Maddox*, aided by jets from a carrier not far away, had sunk one PT and damaged the others. Nevertheless, the skipper, Captain John Herrick, and his crew knew North Vietnam had many more PTs. These little boats were fast, difficult targets, and just one of their torpedoes could easily sink a destroyer.

Even though there were no American combat troops in South Vietnam, Captain Herrick was aware that the United States had heavy commitments there in war matériel and military advisers. The North Vietnamese, then, had ample reason to be antagonistic to American warships patrolling within the twelve-mile limit that they claimed as their territorial waters. To further provoke the North Vietnamese, the South Vietnamese were conducting seaborne commando raids along the Tonkin coast. The raids were being made while the *Maddox* and her companion destroyer, the *U.S.S. Turner Joy*, were cruising through the gulf. Although it was kept secret at the time, *The Pentagon Papers* reveal that American advisers in Saigon had helped to plan these commando raids. The advisers used data gathered in part by the U.S. destroyers patrolling the North Vietnam coast.

The destroyers moved slowly northward toward the Red River delta. The *Maddox*, equipped with electronic gear to ferret out potential bombing and commando targets, picked up indications that the American ships were being tracked by North Vietnamese radar. Herrick radioed the aircraft carrier that he wanted overhead air protection. But his superiors did not wish to provoke the North Vietnamese needlessly and replied that the planes would

161

The *U.S.S. Turner Joy* on patrol duty off the Vietnam coast, May, 1964.

remain on the carrier, fifteen minutes' flying time away. With that reply Captain Herrick grew even more uneasy. "We were beginning to feel the pressure," he later confided. "There's no use pretending we weren't pretty excited and concerned for the safety of the ships and their crews."[1]

By noon the destroyers had reached the northern limit of their patrol and turned about to retrace their route. Once more they moved nervously past the suspected PT bases. Dark clouds moved turbulently overhead, reminding the sailors that the worst part of the typhoon season was upon them. The *Maddox*'s radar detected a vessel shadowing them at a distance of fifteen miles. A short time later Herrick intercepted a North Vietnamese message ordering some units to make ready for military operations. Feeling the danger mount, at 5:30 P.M. Herrick headed out to sea.

It grew very black, with storm clouds billowing close overhead. When the two destroyers were about sixty miles at sea, the *Maddox*'s radar picked up blips that could have been ships—four

1. Quoted in Anthony Austin, *The President's War* (Philadelphia: J. B. Lippincott, 1971), p. 276.

or five of them. The blips were large and fat, yet suddenly they would disappear and then mysteriously reappear. The radar operator believed that the low storm clouds were interfering with radar reception, and the *Turner Joy*'s radar was not picking up anything at all. Nevertheless, Captain Herrick could not take chances. When the blips followed him as he made a sharp turn southeast, he ordered all men to battle stations.

Herrick knew this was a perfect time for the PTs to attack—at night when they could make their runs without being seen. Herrick radioed frantically for planes. When eight aircraft arrived, they dropped flares and scoured the area for enemy PTs. But they could find none in the swelling, boiling waves.

No sooner had the planes left than the blips on the *Maddox*'s radar began closing in at high speeds. The *Turner Joy* began to get contact, too. As the blips approached within eight thousand yards, both destroyers shot star shells. But the shells' light was lost in the hovering clouds. When the blips reached four thousand yards, the *Turner Joy* opened fire at the yet unseen enemy. Rain was falling and the sea was pitching. Nonetheless, four men on the *Turner Joy* believed they saw a torpedo churn past the port side. At nearly the same moment the *Maddox*'s sonarman, listening with his underwater device, reported torpedo sounds.

But there was doubt. The *Maddox*'s sonar had not been working well, and the *Turner Joy*'s sonar, much better situated to hear the torpedo, reported nothing. The condition of the sea and the darkness of the night made the visual torpedo sightings questionable.

The action continued. The *Turner Joy*, though still not sighting the PTs, deluged shells in the area directed by radar. At 10:24 P.M., the *Turner Joy*'s captain thought he saw a thick column of smoke rise from four thousand yards. At this time one of the blips, then another, disappeared from the radar screen. Although the *Turner Joy*'s crew believed they had sunk two PTs, the *Maddox*'s radar could not confirm either sinking. And, indeed, while the *Turner Joy* was shooting up the ocean for two and a half hours, the *Maddox* could find no targets at all to fire at. Her guns, accordingly, were silent. Nevertheless, the *Maddox*'s sonarman kept reporting torpedo sounds. The ship zigged and zagged to dodge the perhaps nonexistent torpedoes. Since no torpedoes actually were sighted in the stormy blackness, Captain Herrick eventually concluded that the sonar operator might have been picking up the rumble of his own ship's propellers as the noise deflected off the rudder during the full zigzag turns.

The *U.S.S. Ticonderoga*. During the Vietnamese War the fighter-bombers of the *Ticonderoga* and other aircraft carriers provided air support for ground troops and made air strikes against enemy PT-boats, strongholds, and supply depots.

When it was all over around midnight, the Americans claimed between two and four PT-boats sunk or damaged. Nevertheless, an element of doubt played in Captain Herrick's mind, and he sent the following top-priority message to his superiors:

> Review of action makes many reported contacts and torpedoes fired appear doubtful. Freak weather effects and overeager sonarman may have accounted for many reports. No actual visual sightings by *Maddox*. Suggest complete evaluation before any further action.[2]

THE TONKIN GULF RESOLUTION

Reports of the "battles" in the Gulf of Tonkin struck Washington, D.C., with stunning reverberations. President Johnson and his advisers regarded the PT "attack" as an outright act of war because the American ships had been sixty miles at

---

2. Quoted in Austin, *The President's War*, p. 293.

sea—unquestioned international waters. Johnson was then in a presidential election contest with the hawkish Republican candidate Barry Goldwater, and he did not wish to give his opponent any basis for saying that the president was soft on communism. When the first attack on the *Maddox* had occurred two days earlier, Johnson had refused to heed the outcries to retaliate.

In addition to the Tonkin Gulf engagement, the situation in South Vietnam had grown steadily more grave. The worst development was the failure of the Strategic Hamlet Program. It had become clear, too, that the Green Berets and other advisers were not capable of helping Saigon turn back the NLF. And the government of General Nguyen Khanh was given only a fifty-fifty chance of surviving for as long as half a year.

President Johnson now felt compelled to take some sort of action. After conferring with his National Security Council and sixteen respected congressional leaders, Johnson ordered an air strike against the North Vietnamese PT bases. At 10:43 P.M. that very evening fighter-bombers roared off U.S. carriers to targets that had been selected three months earlier. With that air strike the first U.S. bombs of the war hurtled down on North Vietnam. Within hours twenty-five North Vietnamese patrol boats had been damaged or destroyed, as well as ninety percent of the oil storage tanks in the target areas.

Johnson immediately took steps to secure congressional approval for further action against North Vietnam should it be required. He sought approval because he regarded Truman's taking action in Korea without congressional support a serious error. Thus on August 6, 1964, Senator J. William Fulbright introduced a resolution in the Senate. The resolution authorized the president "to take all necessary measures to repel any armed attack against the forces of the United States . . . ."

The resolution gave as one of the main legal justifications for American action against North Vietnam the United States' "obligations under the Southeast Asia Collective Defense Treaty." Thus Dulles' SEATO pact finally bore its bitter fruit. Presumably, the haste with which Congress was forced to act prevented the legislators from examining the SEATO treaty to discover that action in Vietnam was *not* required under the treaty's terms.

During the debate, Senator Gaylord Nelson, a Democrat from Wisconsin, questioned whether the North Vietnamese were not justified in attacking the U.S. destroyers. The warships, after all, were in the proximity of the South Vietnamese raids along the coast. "It would be mighty risky," he said, "if Cuban PT-boats were firing on Florida, for Russian armed ships or destroyers to be patrolling between us and Cuba [only] eleven miles out."[3] Furthermore, there was even at this time some doubt about whether or not the attack had actually taken place. But under pressure to present American solidarity before the Communist world, the congressmen did not have time to conduct their own investigation of the incident.

Administration officials were not above deceit in their attempt to place all the blame on North Vietnam for the incident. Thus, when Senator Wayne Morse asked Defense Secretary McNamara if it wasn't possible that the destroyers were helping South Vietnam commando operations, the answer was "No." The warships were on "routine patrol" and the navy "was not associated with, [and] was not aware of, any South Vietnamese actions." But this statement was clearly untrue, for the secretary knew that elements of the U.S. Navy had been in on South Vietnamese plans for at least three months—so The Pentagon Papers reveal.

After a hurried debate, Congress passed what became known as the Gulf of Tonkin Resolution by an overwhelming vote of 504 to 2.

Although Johnson now had the power to escalate the war ("as the President determines" ran the resolution wording), few dreamed of the extent to which he would do so. Few believed that Johnson would, for example, send American combat troops to fight the North Vietnamese because he was the "nonescalation" candidate in the 1964 presidential contest. During the campaign he was quite explicit. "We are not about to send American boys nine or ten thousand miles away from home to do what Asian boys ought to be doing for themselves," he told audiences. Yet The Pentagon Papers indicate that two months before the 1964 elections Johnson and his associates had decided that they would probably have to use the U.S. Air Force against North Vietnam.[4]

Fortunately for Johnson, this decision was kept from public knowledge, and on election day he won by a gigantic landslide that topped the records set by all former presidents, including his idol, Franklin D. Roosevelt. Now, with the American people solidly behind him and with the Gulf of Tonkin Resolution safely in his pocket, President Johnson felt free to deal with North Vietnam.

---

3. Neil Sheehan, Hedrick Smith, E. W. Kenworthy, and Fox Butterfield, eds., The Pentagon Papers (New York: Bantam Books, 1971), p. 265.

4. Sheehan et al., The Pentagon Papers, p. 265.

The president, however, still was reluctant to open an air offensive, even though his military advisers assured him that Hanoi would certainly yield within two to six months. It would be a cheap, relatively easy victory. Furthermore, it was the only way out—aside from the introduction of U.S. combat troops.

While Johnson hesitated, the Khanh government fell to a civilian clique, and South Vietnam seemed on the verge of complete dissolution. Still Johnson could not bring himself to start full-scale bombing. The year 1964 slipped by, and 1965 began. The South Vietnamese crisis deepened. The United States must act soon or share the humiliation of an ally's defeat.

Yet Johnson remained poised on the fence of indecision.

JOHNSON MAKES HIS DECISION

The situation came to a head on February 6, 1965. At this time a small unit of about one hundred Vietcong launched a surprise attack against the American air base at Pleiku, South Vietnam. While some VC directed shell fire that destroyed five American planes and seriously damaged fifteen more, other VC lobbed homemade beer-can grenades into the American barracks. Explosions ripped through the buildings, and eight Americans were pulled dead from the flaming ruins. One hundred and eight more were injured.

When Johnson received news of the Pleiku attack, he angrily called the National Security Council into session. The council agreed that Johnson should retaliate by bombing North Vietnamese barracks in the region from which the VC had infiltrated south. The danger of this move was most grave, however, for at this time Russian Premier Aleksei N. Kosygin was visiting Hanoi. Of this consideration Johnson wrote the following:

> As we talked, there was an electric tension in the air. Everyone in the room was deadly serious as he considered the possible consequences of this decision. Each man around that table knew how crucial such action could be. How would Hanoi react? Would the Chinese Communists use it as a pretext for involving themselves? What about Kosygin and the Russians in Hanoi? . . .
> "We have kept our gun over the mantel and our shells in the cupboard for a long time now," I said [in response to Montana Senator Mike Mansfield, the lone doubter of the dozen men present]. "And what was the result? They are killing our men while they sleep in the night. I can't ask our

Following President Johnson's escalation of U.S. involvement in
Vietnam, the Vietcong also stepped up their military activities.
Above, the VC have scored a mortar hit on Tan Son Nhut Air Base,
and fire fighters spray foam on nearby fuel tanks to prevent the
fire from spreading.

American soldiers out there to continue to fight with one
hand tied behind their backs."[5]

Twelve hours later forty-nine U.S. fighter-bombers soared off
carriers in the South China Sea and hit North Vietnamese
barracks. Two days later the VC retaliated by blowing up
another U.S. barracks—killing or wounding 44 servicemen.

The president now believed he had no choice except to send
the first U.S. combat troops to Vietnam in order to protect the U.S.
airmen. Thus on March 7, 3,500 marines arrived at the Da Nang
air base. But the VC once more retaliated with terror—this time
blowing up the U.S. Embassy in Saigon, killing 20 and injuring
175 persons.

It rather quickly became apparent that the bombing of North
Vietnam was having little, if any, effect on the Vietcong in South
Vietnam. Therefore, on April 1, Johnson and the National Security

5. Lyndon Baines Johnson, *The Vantage Point: Perspectives of the Presidency,
1963–1969* (New York: Holt, Rinehart & Winston, 1971), pp. 124–125.

Council secretly agreed that they must escalate the war once more. Six days later the order was sent out for 20,000 more U.S. soldiers to go to Vietnam.

But this was only the beginning, for the administration now had decided that the mere protection of air bases was not going to win the war. American combat troops would have to search out and destroy the VC in their jungle hideouts and in the Vietnamese villages. By the beginning of June, 1965, U.S. troop strength had soared to 70,000, and by the end of the month it was nearing 125,000.

The president was now at the point of full-scale involvement. A Gallup poll taken just after Pleiku encouraged him. It showed that sixty percent of the nation favored the type of U.S. intervention in South Vietnam that had taken place fifteen years earlier in Korea. In order to reinforce the beliefs of this majority and also to bring around the other forty percent to his way of thinking, Johnson made an important speech:

> Why must this nation hazard its ease, its interest, and its power for the sake of a people so far away?
> We fight because we must fight if we are to live in a world where every country can shape its own destiny, and only in such a world will our own freedom be finally secure. . . .
> Over this war—and all Asia—is . . . the deepening shadow of Communist China. . . . This is a regime which . . . had been condemned by the United Nations for aggression in Korea. It is a nation which is helping the forces of violence in almost every continent. The contest in Vietnam is part of a wider pattern of aggressive purposes. . . .
> We are there because we have a promise to keep. Since 1954 every American President has offered support to the people of South Vietnam. . . . We have made a national pledge to help South Vietnam defend its independence. . . .
> We are also there to strengthen world order. Around the globe from Berlin to Thailand are people whose well being rests in part on the belief that they can count on us if they are attacked. . . .
> We are also there because there are great stakes in balance. Let no one think for a moment that retreat from Vietnam would bring an end to conflict. . . . The central lesson of our time is that the appetite of aggression is never satisfied. To withdraw from one battlefield means only to prepare for the next. . . .
> . . . We fight for principle, rather than territory or colonies . . . peace demands an independent South Vietnam . . . tied to no alliance—a military base for no country.[6]

6. Lyndon B. Johnson, "American Policy in Viet-Nam," quoted in Marcus G. Raskin and Bernard B. Fall, eds., *The Viet-Nam Reader* (New York: Random House, 1965), pp. 344–347.

President Johnson addressing the nation from
Johns Hopkins University explaining America's
willingness to discuss a peaceful solution to the
Vietnam War.

Although Johnson said the United States was fighting exclusively for "principle," at least one member of his inner circle saw
the matter in a less idealistic light. Assistant Secretary of
Defense John McNaughton gave his own estimation of why
America was in Vietnam as follows:

> 70% to avoid a humiliating U.S. defeat. . . .
> 20% to keep South Vietnam . . . from Chinese hands. . . .
> 10% to permit the people of South Vietnam to enjoy a better,
> freer way of life.[7]

---

7. Sheehan et al., *The Pentagon Papers*, p. 255.

An impartial view of the upcoming U.S. tactics in Vietnam gives support to McNaughton's contention that fear of humiliation rather than any love of the South Vietnamese was an important motive in the president's increasing commitment to Vietnam.

Johnson, of course, could not admit this motive in public. But there is no doubt that he would have withdrawn gladly if he could have done so gracefully. For this purpose he offered North Vietnam and the Vietcong an alternative to war. In a speech on April 7, 1965, he announced willingness to embark on a $1 billion dam-building and agricultural improvement program in the Mekong valley. The project would have been so vast that it would have dwarfed even the Tennessee Valley Authority (TVA) in the American South.

Hanoi's answer to Johnson's idealistic Mekong project was to denounce it as a ploy to justify the U.S. takeover of South Vietnam. Furthermore, the project would not help North Vietnam, since the Mekong did not flow through it.

Johnson was angered by this condemnation of his peace offer. He thereupon ordered more U.S. troops to Vietnam. By early 1966 the total was 180,000 and still climbing. Despite growing discontentment on the campuses, as well as in the Senate Foreign Relations Committee, Johnson kept pouring troops into the country. By January, 1968, the total had soared to 550,000. William Fulbright, chairman of the Senate Foreign Relations Committee, referred to this escalation as a mistaken "commitment to American pride."

America now had unwittingly stumbled into a major war.

CHAPTER TWELVE

The Hawks and the Sharks: 1966 to 1968

Three American F-4 fighter-bombers sped down the runway of the huge Chu Lai air base. In a matter of seconds they were airborne hawks. Soaring over the beach where GIs were sunning themselves, the hawks turned inland.

The flight commander radioed ahead to Major Billings, who was flying reconnaissance over the target area in a small Forward Air Control plane. The commander told Billings that he had 750-pound bombs, rockets, and 20-mm cannon available for the operation. "We can use all that good stuff," Billings radioed back.

Billings dipped his observation plane close to the suspected VC area. Beneath him were two churches surrounded by thirty or more dwellings—mostly huts or "hooches" made of clay and bamboo, with thatched roofs. He saw flower gardens in bright bloom and plots of vegetables reaching through palm glades to rice paddies. Scrutinizing the churches, Billings radioed down to the officer in charge of American ground troops on the village outskirts. "Do you want them taken out?" he queried.

"Roger," came the reply.

"There seems to be a white flag out front," Billings cautioned.

"Yeah, beats me what it means," the officer said with a tinge of sarcasm.

Billings shrugged. The ground unit had received some sniper fire; it might well have come from the churches, which were the tallest and sturdiest structures in the little village. He relayed the information to the F-4 flight commander, who was still a few miles distant. "Believe it or not, two of those big stone buildings down there are churches."

Heavily armed Intruders from the *U.S.S. Constellation* flying toward Vietnam on a combat mission. Such missions were commonplace and were flown in response to calls for assistance made by ground troops in combat situations.

"No kidding," came the light reply.

The major fired a phosphorus rocket toward the church. "Do you see my smoke?" he asked the flight commander, whose squadron was making its approach.

"Yeah, I got you," came the answer. "I'll make a dry run then come in with the 750-pounders." The lead plane roared in from the south and dove low over the churches. The pilot called back technical information to his wingmen. The second F-4 dove and released one of its bombs. But it only succeeded in demolishing a portion of the vegetable garden that was providing a Vietnamese family with its sustenance.

"That's about a hundred meters off," Billings said in a gentle voice.

"O.K. Sorry," the flight commander apologized. On the planes' second pass a bomb exploded against the church's back wall.

"Oh, that's nice, baby, real nice," Billings congratulated. "You're alyin' those goodies right in there!"

The planes continued their runs. Soon both churches were in ruins. But the F-4s still had rockets and cannon shells left. No sense in wasting them. Major Billings sent the planes straffing the thatched homes. The 20-mm cannons could fire a hundred explosive shells per second. Quickly they riddled the flimsy structures and flames began to break out. When the planes' ammunition was finally used up, they arched back toward Chu Lai.

But the major's day was not over. The ground commander radioed that his men had seen VC trenches on a hillside in their path. "We'd like to get an air strike put in down there," he said courteously.

Billings flew over the area and spotted some bunker entrances. "I've got you," he said, and then he radioed Chu Lai. Twenty minutes later three more F-4s winged in. The flight carried 1,000-pound bombs, the largest used in Vietnam, and canisters of fiery napalm. Under the major's direction the bombs ripped into the bunkers, sending earth and trees high into the air. The napalm was dropped over some hooches that might possibly have been VC headquarters. The jellied gasoline engulfed the houses with flame. "Beautiful!" Billings shouted. "You guys are right on target today!"

When the bombing and straffing were over, Billings radioed the flight commander how pleased he was with his execution of the strike. "It's been a pleasure to work with you," he told him. "See you another day."

The commander, in turn, was happy with Billings's efficient spotting. "Thank you," he answered politely as he sped back to Chu Lai.

When his three hours of observation duty were over, Major Billings and reporter Jonathan Schell, who accompanied Billings and kept notes of the conversations, returned to Chu Lai. That evening the pilots' conversation covered the day's activities. There was good humor, lots of joking, and much laughter. The funniest thing of all to Billings was that the white flag was still flying over the church even after all the bombs and shells had plastered the hamlet. Another pilot told about shooting a pregnant woman. "We count that as two VC," he chuckled loudly.

Yet writer Schell sensed the underlying tension as the men talked. They tried to dissociate themselves from the terrible destruction that was turning parts of Vietnam into deserts. Everyone in the target area was supposedly VC, for American leaflets and helicopter loudspeakers had warned the civilians to leave. The churches, therefore, were obviously VC strongholds. The pregnant woman's baby would have grown up to be a VC. "It gets completely impersonal," Billings told the reporter. The VC were simply the enemy, not human beings. "After you've done it for a while, you forget that there are people down there."[1]

THE FAILURE OF U.S. AIR POWER

Despite unchallenged control of the air and overwhelming superiority in infantry firepower, the Americans were faced with stupendous problems in Vietnam. If the VC had been willing to risk outright battle, like the Germans, Japanese, and North Koreans of prior wars, the Americans could have blasted them apart. But the VC continued their Mao-style guerrilla warfare. When the American troops came, the VC disappeared into the dense jungle, where intricate networks of tunnels protected them from air bombardment, as well as from being located by ground pursuit. Even if the American infantry should discover a tunnel entrance, there were dozens of other openings from which the VC could exit. When the Americans moved on, the VC emerged to shoot stragglers and to mine the route the Americans were taking.

American strategy centered on two means of combatting the VC. The first was to end the infiltration of reinforcements and supplies from the North. The second was to separate the peasants from the VC, thereby depriving the VC of food and recruits.

To accomplish the first goal, President Johnson embarked on a carefully orchestrated bombing of North Vietnam. Since the United States was not officially at war with Hanoi, the bombing seemed to many an incredible stretching of the Gulf of Tonkin Resolution. Nonetheless, the Johnson-instituted air campaign, called "Rolling Thunder," opened on March 2, 1965, with air strikes against barracks, bridges, and supply dumps in the lower North Vietnam provinces. When Ho Chi Minh made no favorable response, the bombing moved another notch north. As the months passed, Rolling Thunder inched toward Hanoi, the capital and heart of North Vietnam.

Johnson wanted to force Ho to withdraw his ten thousand troops aiding the VC and begin truce talks. But the tough-minded Vietnamese leader remained as determined as ever to reunite the

---

1. Jonathan Schell, *The Military Half: An Account of Destruction in Quang Ngai and Quang Tin* (New York: Alfred A. Knopf, 1968), pp. 132–139.

Operation "Rolling Thunder." Air force B-52s releasing their bombs over North Vietnamese military targets.

two portions of the country under Communist rule. During the winter of 1965–1966 the president ordered the bombing stopped for thirty-seven days and sent his top diplomats around the world to try to discover a basis for negotiations. In Russia they found a favorable atmosphere. But the Soviets had little influence over Ho Chi Minh, to whom they had given only $100 million in aid, an amount that was dwarfed by America's massive multibillion-dollar-a-year Vietnamese effort. Ho refused to budge from his position that the United States had no right to be in Vietnam. Before negotiations could begin, Ho insisted, the bombing must be permanently ended and all U.S. soldiers must be withdrawn. This demand, if complied with, would have been a tremendous

North Vietnamese victory and so was unacceptable to Johnson. Johnson's "Peace Offensive," as he called it, was a failure. He resumed the bombing.

By now, however, it had become obvious that North Vietnam presented almost no vital targets. Even the transportation system was nearly indestructible. Within North Vietnam supplies were moved at night in small boats and barges, on the backs of laborers, in carts, or on the frames of bikes. If the Americans bombed out a bridge, workmen would build log rafts or simply wade across. Most roads were narrow dirt trails where bomb craters were skirted with little inconvenience. And there were almost no warehouses to bomb—war matériel was stored under the thick canopy of jungle trees.

The bombing actually spurred the North Vietnamese to greater war efforts. "Thanks to your raids," a North Vietnamese official told an American reporter touring the country by invitation of the Communist government, "we have accomplished in two years what it might have taken twenty years to do in peace." And as bomb craters began dotting the countryside, the North Vietnamese farmers jokingly referred to them as part of the "American Fishpond and Well-Digging Program."[2]

While the bombing continued in the North, the Americans in the South tried to implement their second goal: to separate the civilian population from the Vietcong. U.S. planners thought the Strategic Hamlet Program had been a good idea but had not been carried far enough. Now, instead of having isolated hamlet-outposts in VC country, the Americans decided to relocate the peasant-farmers in refugee centers near the coast. Here they could be much more easily protected by Saigonese and American troops. The evacuated areas could then be designated "free-fire zones." Any human being—man, woman, or child—remaining in a free-fire zone could then be regarded as a VC and could be fired upon at will and without warning.

THE RELOCATION PROGRAM

In theory the Relocation Program was nearly perfect, though chillingly ruthless. American and ARVN troops swept through the provinces, forcing four million inhabitants to relocate. These

---

2. David Schoenbrun, "Journey to North Vietnam," *Saturday Evening Post*, 12 December 1967, p. 7.

A U.S. marine assists a Vietnamese family as
they arrive at one of the coastal camps set up to
implement the relocation program.

Vietnamese had to abandon their homes, their rice paddies, and
all their possessions except those that they could pack on their
aching shoulders. They were herded to coastal camps where they
were housed in quickly constructed barracks consisting of corru-
gated steel-sheet roofs supported by wooden poles. There were
no barrack walls to protect them from the monsoon rains or to
keep out the swarms of mosquitoes and other insects.

Most of these relocation camps had no schools and made no
provision for the employment of the adults. And since the
refugees had been forced to leave their farms, all food had to be
imported. Sometimes the supply system broke down, and
Jonathan Schell found one camp where the inhabitants had gone
four days without anything to eat. Corrupt Saigon officials

sometimes confiscated huge amounts of food from U.S. supplies to sell on the black market for their own profit.

So hateful did the Relocation Program become that many peasants hid from the U.S. and ARVN troops coming to relocate them. Then, after the troops passed by, the peasants would return to their villages, even though these villages were in a free-fire area. A village in a free-fire area was totally at the mercy of fighter-bombers from air bases such as Chu Lai.

As the Relocation Program moved into high gear, the American military conducted search-and-destroy missions against the VC in the vast areas outside the refugee centers. American aircraft pounced upon slow-moving VC soldiers with napalm, with cluster bombs that devastated three acres of ground almost instantly, and with gas that left its victims violently nauseous and helpless. Scout planes constantly droned over VC country calling in air strikes or helicopter-carried troops for ambushes. In order to deny the VC jungle cover, U.S. planes applied defoliation sprays that denuded a quarter of South Vietnam's forested areas of leaves and undergrowth.

The VC could expect to be hit anywhere. Heavy-duty choppers, called "Chinooks," freighted long-range artillery to vantage points over suspected VC supply routes. Here U.S. artillerymen conducted surprise bombardments, and then had the choppers evacuate them before the VC could mount a counterattack. And at night American ambush teams carrying starlight scopes, which multiplied starlight fifty thousand times, shot up VC patrols attempting to gather food from the free-fire villages.

Yet for all their advantages, the Americans could not win the war. Although the United States had complete mastery of the air, the VC in their tunnel mazes were fairly safe from the 1,000-pound bombs and napalm canisters. Vietcong agents were always in the villages. American patrols searched for them during the daytime, but they blended in with the villagers, and the Americans could not identify them. This was a most exasperating experience for the U.S. soldiers.

> At seven each day [wrote Lieutenant William Calley], we would start out through the villages to reconnoiter them: and . . . we were sniped at. We never learned who by, though. Of the infantry's mission here, we didn't get to part one: to *find*, to close with, and to destroy the VC. We never knew who the snipers were, and the Vietnamese told us, "We don't know, either." It frustrated us. It hurt our morale. My soldiers said, "God, am I dreaming? Or going mad?" We had been in Vietnam three months: we were losing men, we were being

nickled-and-dimed away, we were being picked off. We were
in Vietnamese villages daily, and we still hadn't seen one
VC.[3]

The daytime belonged largely to the Americans, for they, like
hawks, were usually far too strong for the Vietcong to meet in
open battle. Yet despite all American efforts, nighttime belonged
largely to the Vietcong. Like sharks swimming through the jungle
depths, hidden from U.S. air power, they were free to prey on
their quarry at night. They fastened their hold ever more firmly
over the villagers, who became drawn even closer to the NLF by
the arrival of the feared and, frequently, ruthless "round-eyed"
Americans.

The Americans fought few big battles. The VC were nowhere
yet everywhere. They sniped at the Americans, planted land
mines that blew off legs, and made hit-and-run night attacks on
U.S. bases. But when the American patrols sought them out, the
VC vanished into their caves or merged with the populations of
the villages.

WAR CRITICS

There were many critics of American war tactics. One of the
most knowledgable was Lieutenant Colonel Anthony Herbert.
Herbert had fought in Korea, where he became that war's most
decorated American. Now he was in command of a front-line
battalion in Vietnam. Colonel Herbert believed the weakness of
the American war effort lay with the leadership. Herbert asked,
"Where were the Pattons or the Eisenhowers . . . or the MacAr-
thurs?"[4] The top command lacked the imagination that had made
these men great.

In Herbert's view nearly everything was wrong. The U.S.
armed forces had the greatest destructive capability of any in the
world. But the generals did not use it to best advantage.
American bombing and artillery had a minimal effect on the
tunnel strongholds—everyone knew that. The only result of the
bombing and shelling was the destruction of the homes and
fields of the Vietnamese villagers, who consequently became
ever more firmly attached to the VC cause.

---

3. William Calley and John Sack, *Lieutenant Calley: His Own Story* (New York:
Grosset & Dunlap, 1970), p. 57.

4. Anthony B. Herbert with James T. Wooten, *Soldier* (New York: Dell, 1973), p.
258.

Marines from the rest-and-relaxation center at Da Nang, Vietnam, climb into the center's newest addition. The marine-green dune buggy was used for entertainment, transportation for a nearby orphanage, and rescue-and-recovery missions along the beach.

What was needed, in Colonel Herbert's view, were more aggressive offensive tactics on the ground. Night operations were of special importance, for it was then that the VC was most active. Starlight scopes gave U.S. troops a tremendous advantage in night ambushes. Herbert himself had had so much success with the starlight scopes that the VC were forced almost entirely out of the area where his battalion was operating.

Furthermore, according to Herbert, although the VC tunnels were too narrow for the average U.S. soldier, they were not impervious to the American daredevils called "tunnel rats." These men blasted their way through tunnels, forcing the VC to flee through escape exits where U.S. infantrymen waiting outside picked them off.

The American troops should have been always on the move, Herbert felt. Officers should have taken fullest advantage of the helicopters, which could have dropped troops directly on unprepared VC units or across portions of the vital Ho Chi Minh Trail. By using helicopters and infantry troops in this manner, the Americans could have forced the VC to fight. And man for man, U.S. troops were superior.

But the generals did not do this. They were beguiled by the explosive power of bombs and artillery. Instead of using ground troops to force the VC to fight, the generals permitted their troops to call in fighter-bombers and artillery barrages. The VC simply darted to the safety of their tunnels. That was how barely two hundred thousand Vietcong, North Vietnamese, and peasant irregulars successfully withstood the ineffective onslaughts of half a million U.S. troops aided by a million ARVNs. Such, at least, was Herbert's opinion.

Just as harmful as the generals' battle tactics was their mistaken (in Herbert's eyes) preoccupation with making GIs comfortable instead of preparing them to fight. Herbert's own battalion was part of a brigade of ten thousand men. Yet, out of this number, seven thousand were assigned to pizza huts, clubs, recreation activities, desk jobs, mess halls, post exchanges, swimming pool supervision, and so forth. Even the three thousand remaining combat troops spent most of their time in activities other than fighting. They performed guard duty, took sick leave, worked with company supply, or simply goofed off. Thus Herbert calculated that out of the entire ten-thousand-man brigade, only about eight hundred soldiers were fighting at any given time! "In any other war, it would have been ridiculous," he complained. ". . . We had a 500,000 man army fielding less than any one infantry division did in World War II or Korea."[5]

Neither were the higher-ups able to instill in the men any sense of why they were fighting, any lofty goals, any purpose, any mission. "We didn't have [a mission] before I got there, we didn't have one while I was there, and we never had one after I left. But an army requires a mission; it desperately needs some direction toward a specific goal." As a result, "pound for pound, the brigade was garbage. Discipline was lax, the troops were slovenly, disrespectful, and sluggish." In short, Herbert concluded, the army as it was then was not worth a damn.[6]

THE VC TET OFFENSIVE

Vietcong chieftains had excellent pipelines into the American camps. Agents posing as laborers, suppliers, and B-girls easily learned of the supposedly sad condition of the American army. This encouraged the VC leaders in January, 1968, to swing into

---

5. Herbert, *Soldier*, pp. 140–141.
6. Herbert, *Soldier*, pp. 287, 139.

U.S. marines fighting a fierce house-to-house battle to retake the city of Hue from the Vietcong during the Tet offensive, February 1, 1968.

After several days of intensive streetfighting, Hue belonged to the U.S. marines. On February 5, 1968, they ripped down the North Vietnamese flag and hoisted the Stars and Stripes over the ancient, embattled royal capital.

Following the U.S. and ARVN successes in retaking Hue and other strategic sites from the Vietcong, the VC still had enough troop strength to mount attacks against U.S. military installations. Here, in March, a U.S. marine post is under VC mortar fire.

their third stage of guerrilla warfare: the all-out offensive to overthrow the enemy in the cities.

The frontal attacks of the Tet Offensive, named for the Vietnamese New Year upon which it began, seemed to come within a whisper of defeating not only the government of newly elected President Nguyen Van Thieu but the Americans as well! Large formations of VC, marshaled for the first time into battalions and full regiments, fought their way into five of the six major South Vietnamese cities. Pleiku and Da Nang, sites of some of the largest U.S. air bases, were heavily hit. The defenses of Hue, second only to Saigon in importance, were breached, and for several days the fate of the ancient capital seemed uncertain.

Most striking of all, the VC penetrated Saigon itself. The American public was dumbstruck when news broadcasts told that the American embassy was being riddled by VC gunners.

But now the U.S. troops showed their mettle. American soldiers not only stood their ground but struck back with a devastating

By April, 1968, the Tet offensive had wound down but the danger was far from over. In the pictures above, one U.S. military base is being shelled by the Vietcong and another is being reinforced with fresh troops and supplies.

firepower that killed more than half of the eighty-four thousand enemy soldiers taking part in the Tet operation. The success of the U.S. and ARVN troops in resisting the VC encouraged the inhabitants of the cities to remain loyal to President Thieu. When the VC finally retreated, Johnson justly called Tet a "debacle" for the VC: their most disastrous defeat of the war.[7]

Yet to the American public Tet was a horrendous experience. After three long years, billions of dollars, and thirty thousand deaths (a third of them in the Tet Offensive), the VC was as far from being defeated as ever. How long would this war go on? How many more Americans would be killed? Was it all worth it?

In no other American twentieth-century war was the disenchantment of the home front to play such a significant role.

7. Lyndon Baines Johnson, *The Vantage Point: Perspectives of the Presidency, 1963–1969* (New York: Holt, Rinehart & Winston, 1971), p. 383.

CHAPTER THIRTEEN

The War in America's Streets: 1966 to 1968

The home front in October, 1967, was in an uproar. Soldiers stood ready, bayonets poised, in Washington, D.C. More than a hundred thousand young men and women—mainly university students—cheered and sang antiwar songs during a huge rally near the nation's Capitol. After the rally, large numbers of students marched toward the Pentagon, headquarters of the Department of Defense. Here the military establishment was directing the nation's war effort in Vietnam.

The students paused before a line of soldiers barring their way. Suddenly a group from the radical Students for a Democratic Society (SDS) broke through the soldiers, leaped a weather fence, and ran toward the Pentagon. Quickly thousands more surged through the breach. The troops hit the students with rifle butts, and federal marshals flailed with clubs. Tear gas was fired. But still the students thundered forward until ten thousand had rushed through the barrier.

As Secretary of Defense Robert McNamara and other top officials watched from upper windows, the SDS and other students raised the Vietcong flag on a Pentagon flagstaff. The demonstrators made violent speeches against the Vietnam War. Then ten thousand voices shouted approval as some men of military age burned their draft cards. The crowd chanted antiwar slogans, openly smoked marijuana, and some even urinated on the Pentagon walls. When evening came, they ripped apart the weather fences to build bonfires.

At midnight the soldiers were given orders to drive the students away. As the soldiers advanced, the students called to the officers over bullhorns: "The troops you employ belong to us

Military police confronting anti–Vietnam War demonstrators in front of the Pentagon, October 21, 1967. In spite of the presence of troops, the demonstrators succeeded briefly in storming the doors of the Pentagon.

and not to you." The officers consulted and ordered the soldiers to fall back, fearful, perhaps, that some young troopers might actually join the students. Demonstrators on the fringes, over seven hundred of them, were arrested and hauled off. But the mass of students would not budge, and the Pentagon officials decided not to direct the troops against them. If they had, the repercussions across the nation might have been grave in the extreme.

When dawn came, the students and other demonstrators began to disperse—the siege of the Pentagon had been held to catch the public eye, and there were no plans for further action. But they had made their point. If Johnson and the Pentagon continued the war, they could expect growing opposition from a formidable army recruited from nearly eight million college students. Although a majority of these students were not at present concerned with the antiwar actions of the SDS and other groups, the campuses were potential seedbeds of opposition. In fact, the campuses might even erupt in violence if the Selective Service System began drafting college men into the war.

THE RISE OF THE ANTIWAR FACTION

The war had caused a deep split between the generations. To many older Americans, it seemed almost beyond belief that their children would demonstrate against the government. Members of the older generation had seen the catastrophies that had followed appeasement in Czechoslovakia and Manchuria. To them, retreat from Vietnam would be another Munich that would encourage the Communists in their drive toward world conquest. To many of these people, it seemed better to fight in distant Asia than on the shores of California.

But the young men and women in their late teens and early twenties had not experienced the woes of the 1930s and 1940s. They knew only that, historically, the older generation started wars while the younger generation had to fight them. If they were required to risk their lives for a cause, they wanted a cause that they could believe in. Soon after Johnson's escalation in 1965, university students across the country took part in a series of what they called "teach-ins." After much study, many students concluded that neither the SEATO pact nor the low quality of Saigon's military-dominated government required American intervention. They also disagreed with the Domino Theory and its contention that Russia and China were fast friends conspiring to take South Vietnam in their pursuit of world conquest.

Once these conclusions had been reached, some students began organizing with the purpose of forcing the government to alter its foreign policy. This was a unique goal, for, while European and Latin American students had always been involved in politics, young Americans had traditionally been preoccupied with grades, parties, and sporting events. But the war issue caused American youth to reorder their values, and organizations, such as the SDS, rapidly attracted new membership.

Nonstudents, too, joined in speaking out against the war. Martin Luther King, Jr., and other black leaders resented the billions of dollars being spent on a war in Vietnam that could be better spent on antipoverty programs at home. But the antiwar campaign did not join forces with the civil rights movement. Each group was sympathetic to the other, but each went its own way, one predominantly white, the other predominantly black.

As the number of American troops in Vietnam rose toward its peak of 550,000, the SDS and other antiwar organizations held many protest demonstrations that sent thousands of students into the streets. During "Vietnam Summer," 1967, the SDS was particularly active. Gradually the demonstrations, as well as the sincerity of the students, caused older Americans also to question why the United States was fighting in Vietnam. By January, 1968, only forty-eight percent of the general public was in the pro-Johnson camp. The president began receiving about one thousand letters each month threatening his life. Student leaders vowed never to let him speak again in public, and hooting demonstrators tried to make good this threat.

While radical students carried their "Stop the War" banners through the streets, large numbers of the more conservative students adopted a different tactic. These students cut their hair, put on dress clothes, and flocked into the political arena to try to unseat Johnson during the upcoming Democratic primaries. Many of these students volunteered to work for Senator Eugene McCarthy of Minnesota, who advocated immediate withdrawal from Vietnam.

THE FALL OF PRESIDENT JOHNSON

The first primary of 1968 was in New Hampshire shortly after the shocking VC Tet Offensive. Students working for McCarthy tirelessly canvassed throughout the state. Their effectiveness was startling. An early Gallup poll had given McCarthy a modest twelve percent of the vote. But when the final returns came in on March 12, McCarthy and his student legions had scored a most stunning victory. The Minnesota senator had captured forty-two percent of the vote—almost four times more than anticipated. And he even came within a mere 230 votes of actually defeating the president! Thus it was clear that the antiwar movement was beginning to attract popular support.

Lyndon Johnson was extremely disturbed by the results of the New Hampshire primary. With other primaries rapidly approaching, particularly the one in Wisconsin where McCarthy's student campaigners were already hard at work, Johnson urgently needed a victory in Vietnam. He felt that he had to justify his enormous commitment of men and money. But the victory was not immediately forthcoming. Far from it. The seriousness of the Tet Offensive had revealed to General Westmoreland, the commander in Vietnam, that a far greater effort was needed if the United States were to win the war. Westmoreland urged the president to send an additional quarter of a million soldiers to South Vietnam to fight the VC. He also urged the president to invade North Vietnam and neighboring Cambodia and Laos, which served as sanctuaries for the Communists.

Lyndon B. Johnson dropping his televised political bombshell as he announces that he neither will run nor accept renomination for the Presidency.

Johnson was aghast. Such an escalation, aside from possibly provoking Chinese and Russian intervention, would rocket war costs from $17 billion to around $27 billion yearly. It also would necessitate a major mobilization, as well as require a huge increase in taxes. The first measure would affect the student population and would undoubtedly result in even larger demonstrations. The second measure would strike the conservative older generation, which had hitherto been Johnson's main support. The president could see disaster looming ahead.

On March 31, 1968, Johnson went on national television. He looked weary. His face sagged. Through his long political career, Johnson, the tall Texan, had always been a fighter. Now, for the first time in a long while, he had to face stark, outright defeat.

But he had no choice. Thus he told the people: "I shall not seek, and I will not accept, the nomination of my party for another term." With his withdrawal from politics and his order to halt the bombing of North Vietnam above the Nineteenth Parallel, Johnson said he hoped immediate talks leading to peace would be opened. Ho Chi Minh agreed, and negotiators began talks in Paris on May 13.

But the negotiations quickly revealed the extreme difficulty of working out a peace that would satisfy both the United States and Hanoi. The United States insisted on a free South Vietnam, but Hanoi refused to acknowledge the legality of President Thieu's government. Almost as sticky was the question of when the Americans should stop bombing the North. Immediately, said Hanoi. Only when Hanoi stopped sending troops into South Vietnam, replied Washington. But, Hanoi objected, if we stopped sending supplies and reinforcements the VC would eventually be chewed to pieces. While these points were hashed and rehashed, the Americans continued their bombing and Hanoi continued to build up its seventy-five-thousand-man army in the South.

The war continued just as ferociously as it had for the past three and a half years, and the students continued campaigning for McCarthy. Now, however, McCarthy had to overcome Vice-President Hubert H. Humphrey, Jr., Johnson's man for the Democratic nomination. The students believed that Humphrey was committed to continuing Johnson's policies in Vietnam. If he were president, they said, the negotiations might drag on for years.

The student supporters of McCarthy knew that even though they were winning primaries they would have an uphill fight at the Democratic convention, to be held in Chicago in late August. Their chief problem was that most states did not hold primaries. The convention delegates from these states would be selected from small councils of party regulars. Most of these regulars would be pledged to support Humphrey. The interests of the two student groups—those working within the Democratic party and those, like the SDS, working in the streets—now combined. They realized that they had to apply pressure tactics on what would probably be a pro-Humphrey majority. When convention time arrived, great numbers of students and other antiwar supporters flocked to Chicago, where they camped in the spacious lake-front parks. They swarmed around like angry hornets, taunting the police and haranguing delegates, reporters, and passersby about the evils of the war. In picking up more McCarthy support the students were not successful. This fact became painfully apparent during the afternoon of August 28, when the convention voted on a peace plank resolution. The pro-McCarthy delegates had so little support from the other delegates that the peace plank resolution was defeated. They could muster only about one thousand votes to the Johnson-Humphrey faction's total of about fifteen hundred. Seeing the need to convince the Johnson-Humphrey delegates of their determination to end the war, the students sprang into action.

THE CHICAGO RIOTS

The students' intention was to march west out of Grant Park early that evening to Michigan Boulevard. From there they would march south down the boulevard and file past the Hilton Hotel, where most of the delegates, then on a dinner break, would be certain to see and hear them. They then would continue south three and one-half miles down the boulevard to the International Ampitheater, where the convention soon would be nominating the presidential candidate. There they would demonstrate in sound and fury until the delegates responded to their wishes.

But Chicago's stocky Mayor Richard Daley had long foreseen such an eventuality. The police and National Guard had formed a line across Michigan Boulevard. There they awaited the student mob.

The students were not intimidated. They marched slowly toward Daley's men, Vietcong flags flying and chants of "Ho, Ho, Ho Chi Minh" on their lips. In the rear they had their own hospital corps of medical students. There was a moment's hesitation when the two forces confronted each other. Then Daley's men struck with startling ferocity. Norman Mailer, watching from a window in the Hilton Hotel, described the scene:

> The police attacked with tear gas, with Mace, and with clubs, they attacked like a chain saw cutting into wood, the teeth of the saw the edge of their clubs, they attacked like a scythe through grass, lines of twenty and thirty policemen striking out in an arc, their clubs beating, demonstrators fleeing. . . . The police cut through the crowd one way, then cut through them another. They chased people into the park, ran them down, beat them up . . . .[1]

It was close to actual warfare. The police had been spat on and pelted with bricks, bottles, and balloons filled with urine. They had been called "pigs," and their squad cars had been smashed. For two days bearded boys and long-haired girls had taunted

---

1. Norman Mailer, *Miami and the Siege of Chicago* (New York: New American Library, Signet Books, 1968), p. 169.

Police attacking demonstrators on Michigan Avenue near the Conrad Hilton Hotel during the Democratic National Convention in Chicago, August, 1968.

them, had insulted the American flag, and had ridiculed the president of the United States. Now, at last, the police would even the score—and with a vengeance.

Television cameras carried pictures of the conflict into homes across the nation. Viewers saw police, guardsmen, SDS, and innocent bystanders flash across their screens in wild, bloody melees. It was deeply distressing. How, wondered many Americans, had the Democratic convention fallen into such a lowly, lawless state: "It is a scene from a movie of the Russian revolution," wrote political analyst Theodore White as the riots were going on. "The Democrats are finished," he noted bluntly.[2]

RICHARD NIXON'S VICTORY

Richard Nixon, the Republican candidate, was quick to take advantage of the chaos in Democratic ranks. As the representative of the minority party, he knew he had to run a masterful

---

2. Theodore H. White, *The Making of the President: 1968* (New York: Simon & Schuster, Pocket Books, 1970), p. 335.

campaign to attract voters from the independent and Democratic ranks. Except for the blurtings of vice-presidential candidate Spiro Agnew, who called Polish-Americans "Polacks" and a Japanese correspondent "the fat Jap," Nixon's campaign team performed almost perfectly.[3]

Nixon stressed the loss of purpose and self-respect that had come to plague America during the Johnson war years. To support his view, he cited the student riots, the increase in crimes of violence, and the endless fighting in Vietnam that never gained victories. He promised to lead the nation on a fresh path to law and order at home and to peace with honor in Vietnam. "The real crisis of America today is a crisis of the spirit," Nixon told audiences. "What America needs most today is what it once had, but has lost: the lift of a driving dream."[4]

With regard to Vietnam, Nixon was purposefully vague. But he had two reasons for being so. First, he did not want to hamper the peace negotiations, and, second, he wished to be unencumbered by campaign promises when he tackled the problem as president. His slogan was "End the War and Win the Peace."[5] Beyond that he would say nothing concrete. The advocates of harsh peace conditions could interpret Nixon's statement to mean one thing, and the advocates of a quick, easy peace could take the statement to mean quite another thing. All Nixon promised was that the voters in choosing him were "going to determine whether America again is respected in the world."[6]

As election day approached, it became clear that Nixon had made great inroads into the Democratic ranks. Hubert Humphrey could not overcome the bitterness that had torn the Democrats apart. A banner at a Nixon rally summed up the expectations of Americans who voted for Nixon: "BRING US TOGETHER."

When the votes were tallied, Nixon won over Humphrey by a hairline plurality of .68 percentage points.

With Nixon's victory, the war entered a new phase.

---

3. White, *The Making of the President: 1968*, p. 460.

4. White, *The Making of the President: 1968*, pp. 161–162.

5. White, *The Making of the President: 1968*, p. 162.

6. White, *The Making of the President: 1968*, p. 464.

CHAPTER FOURTEEN

The Year of the Great Disillusionment: 1970

On April 30, 1970, Richard Nixon, president for a little over a year, appeared on a special television broadcast. His manner and voice were grave. He was about to announce unpleasant news to the nation. Earlier, he had spent a tense session with the head of the CIA, the chairman of the Joint Chiefs of Staff, and his national security adviser, Henry Kissinger. Then he had walked alone through the woods near his Camp David retreat, pondering over his latest crisis. What should he do in response to the plea for help from Lon Nol, head of the Cambodian clique that had just ousted Prince Norodom Sihanouk? This clique was now being threatened by North Vietnamese Communists. President Nixon, who had been withdrawing U.S. troops from South Vietnam at the rate of around 12,500 per month, now felt that further withdrawals would be impractical. He believed that if the Communists took Cambodia, thus securing the port of Sihanoukville, they would be able to ship greater quantities of supplies to their forces in southern South Vietnam.

Nixon felt that he must strike the Communists in Cambodia while he still had the strength to do so. Therefore he had ordered General Creighton Abrams, commander in Vietnam, to ready 31,000 troops for combat. These troops represented nearly all the United States had available out of its diminished 429,000-man force. With this combat force, Abrams was to push into the Cambodian region known as the "Fishhook," a Communist supply center.

Nixon, preparing his TV address, knew the foray into Cambodia was a dangerous gamble. The North Vietnamese, despite Ho Chi Minh's death eight months earlier, remained strongly united and determined to resist the Americans wherever they

President Richard Nixon announcing on television his decision to send several thousand American combat troops into Cambodia to destroy a Vietcong stronghold, supply depot, and staging area.

were encountered. Furthermore, the American public was sick of the war. Everywhere people complained that the South Vietnamese army of 1,100,000 men should be able to tend to the 150,000 Vietcong and the 120,000 North Vietnamese if it had the will. Congress, too, was questioning the continuation of hostilities. It might well adopt stern measures against the president for crossing Cambodia's border when the United States was not at war with that country. (Little did the congressmen know that Nixon already had been secretly bombing enemy positions in Cambodia for fourteen months.) Nixon was wary of the American people and their legislators' reaction. In fact, he was so wary that he had not even dared to inform Congress of his move until minutes before his TV appearance.

True to his prediction, the address brought extremely unfavorable responses. Senator Edward Kennedy raged that the Cambodian venture was "madness." Senator Vance Hartke fumed that by going into Cambodia without securing congressional approval, "the President's action . . . amounts to a declaration of war against the Senate."

Meanwhile, on campuses across the nation, students gathered in angry protests. The demonstrating sometimes turned into

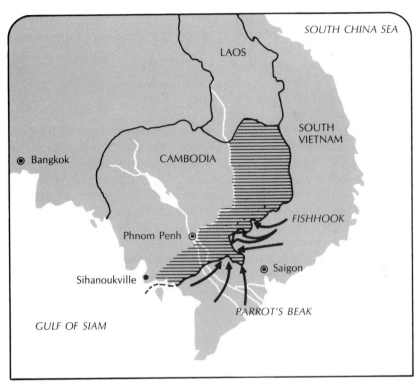

U.S.–ARVN Cambodian offensive, April–May, 1970.

rioting, accompanied by the burning of buildings and the wrecking of other property. State governors were forced to call out National Guard units in Illinois, Maryland, New Mexico, Wisconsin, Kentucky, and Ohio. Across the country more than two hundred colleges and universities were shut down for at least one day. Washington, D.C., was besieged by 100,000 enraged students, some of whom were courageously met by President Nixon for a dialogue on the steps of the Lincoln Memorial. The protests and violence peaked on Monday morning, May 4, when a National Guard unit collided with students at Kent State University.

THE KENT STATE KILLINGS

Kent State, located in the rolling hills of northeastern Ohio, had a student population of 19,000. Most of the students were not particularly political, and only a small number attended the antiwar rallies that had been held periodically during the Vietnam conflict. The Cambodia invasion prompted more students to attend the rally held on May 1, but it was still peaceful until a few students decided to hurl empty beer bottles at some squad cars. When Kent's twenty-nine-man police department tried to clear the streets of students later that night, the students began smashing windows in defiance.

The next day the mood of violence increased. After an antiwar rally, the students marched to the Reserve Officers' Training Corps (ROTC) building—symbol of the army's influence on the campus—and burnt it to the ground. With the police unable to control the students, Kent's mayor made a frantic appeal for help to Ohio's Governor James Rhodes. Rhodes immediately declared martial law in Kent and sent in National Guard units. Rhodes also made an appearance in Kent to deliver a strong speech, during which he called the more radical student demonstrators "the worst type of people that we harbor in America." If the radicals succeed in taking over Kent State, commented a Kent resident, "no campus in the country is safe."

Throughout Sunday, May 3, the campus simmered as soldiers were stationed at strategic locations. Some of the guardsmen came from low-income families and resented wealthy collegians who scoffed at the president while enjoying the finest education in the world. Other guardsmen were out of sorts from five days' duty near Cleveland during a wildcat Teamsters strike.

The student radical leaders staged a rally the next day, May 4, at noon. Campus police called on the demonstrators to break up, fearing that the radicals would incite another wave of violence and destruction. After five successive attempts to disband the rally, campus officials turned the matter over to the National Guard.

The guardsmen moved toward the demonstrators and, with rifles loaded and bayonets leveled, pressed them up Blanket Hill. The student mob threw rocks and chunks of concrete at the guardsmen. The guardsmen lobbed tear gas in return. But the tear gas was ineffective. "Pigs! Pigs!" the students yelled at the oncoming troops, who steadily grew more angry. A few guardsmen knelt as if to shoot, but the students jeered. They believed the guardsmen had only blank cartridges.

Suddenly some of the guardsmen thought they heard a sniper's shot. Quickly, sixteen or seventeen guardsmen aimed their rifles at the crowd. Then they fired. Fourteen students fell to the ground—four of them dead!

The "butchery" at Kent State—as one campus radio commentator called it—jarred the nation like few other events in the war

Kent State students falling back before the advancing National Guardsmen, who supposedly have only fired a barrage of tear gas into the mass of demonstrators. When the smoke cleared, however, fourteen students lay on the ground—four of them dead. Some guardsmen had loaded their rifles with live ammunition.

years. "Have we come to such a state in this country," mourned the father of dead student Allison Krause, "that a young girl has to be shot because she disagrees deeply with the actions of her government?" President Nixon himself met with six Kent State students, at which time he agreed that there must be a quick termination to Vietnam, as well as to the drafting of young men for the armed forces. The next day Nixon held a conference with eight respected university presidents. He appointed one of them, Dr. Alexander Heard of Vanderbilt University, to be his goodwill ambassador to the campuses. He also promised an early withdrawal of U.S. troops from Cambodia.

Nixon kept his promise. By the end of June all U.S. troops had left Cambodia. The government reported that the operation had been a success. The army had captured enough rifles to arm 35,000 enemy soldiers and enough shells, rockets, and bullets for two years of combat. In addition, the enemy had lost 7,000 men, while the ARVN and U.S. forces lost 400 and 125, respectively. Skeptics, though, were quick to question the figures and the government's claim that the Communists would no longer be able to mount a first-class offensive in southern South Vietnam.

There was, however, no VC offensive the next year, and the offensive of the following year fizzled for lack of supplies and men.

Nixon's invasion of Cambodia had aroused deep resentment in Congress, which had been completely bypassed in the war-making decision. In response, Congress passed the Defense Appropriation Act, the first serious attempt to reestablish congressional control over the right to declare war. The Defense Appropriations Act forbade the use of federal funds for military action in foreign countries without congressional approval.

THE MY LAI MASSACRE

As serious as Kent had been, the year 1970 was to bring the American people an even greater shock. Through news reports, they learned that American troops were responsible for a massacre at the village of My Lai. The incident had occurred on March 16, 1968, but it had been covered up until the press got hold of the story a year and a half later. Then sensational headlines revealed the killing of as many as 130 South Vietnamese civilians by a platoon of U.S. soldiers. With that the army was forced to take action, and in November, 1970, the court-martial trial of platoon leader Lieutenant William Calley began.

The half-dozen villages that made up the My Lai complex sat on low knolls surrounded by rice paddies. To the west was a long line of hills and beyond them was Highway 1, South Vietnam's main transportation artery, which connected Saigon with Da Nang and Hue. The Vietcong had found My Lai to be of strategic value as a base from which to cut Highway 1. Reports placed the elite VC Forty-eighth Battalion within the village complex, which had been declared a free-fire zone.

In order to rid the area of the Vietcong, Lieutenant Colonel Frank Barker was given a task force, in which was Company C—"Charlie Company." Commanding the 130 men of Company C was Captain Ernest Medina, a tough, professional soldier. Medina gave Company C a skull-and-crossbones arm patch and told his men that they would be known as "The Death Dealers." Under Medina was Lieutenant William Calley, heading one of the company's three platoons. Twenty-four year-old Calley was a cocky little man with a baby face, which prompted Medina jokingly to call him "Young Thing." Calley was a complex

The lead ship of a helicopter squadron carrying U.S. troops on a search-and-destroy mission.

personality: gentle with animals, devoted to his mother, shy with strangers, but fiercely loyal to the army, for which he would kill without question.

Each platoon was given an objective in the operation. Calley's orders were to end all enemy resistance in the district known as My Lai Four.

At 7:30 A.M., Calley's platoon was carried by choppers to a landing area a short distance from My Lai Four. As soon as the men had checked over their guns and ammunition, Calley marched them down the narrow dirt road toward the village.

Lieutenant Colonel Barker, Captain Medina, and the other officers were in choppers circling over the general area. They had radio contact with their subordinate officers in charge of ground operations. The first reports coming from Charlie Company were good: the platoons were reporting considerable killing of VC. In a little more than an hour eighty-four VC were confirmed as dead, and VC hooches in several of the My Lai villages were being burned.

But, as more reports came in, an ominous undertone developed. Charlie Company was making many kills, but it was taking very few weapons. Could this mean that the dead were

One of many armed sweeps through Vietcong-occupied territory. The goal of such missions was to seize and destroy VC arms and supplies and, if possible, to confront the VC in combat. The marines above were not involved in the tragic My Lai massacre.

actually unarmed civilians? Helicopter pilots sent radio messages about senseless shootings, and one of them, Hugh Thompson, even landed his chopper at My Lai Four. Here the chopper's machine gunners trained their weapons on Lieutenant Calley while Thompson evacuated some of the wounded civilians. These were only rumors, however, until the court-martial made them facts.

The trial brought out the shocking truth. Calley's men revealed they had met no resistance by the VC at My Lai Four. Whatever VC troops had been there had long since pulled out. As the Americans entered the village, they began shooting at dogs and farm animals. Then the soldiers rounded up many of the inhabitants. "Most of them were women, children, and old men trying to hide," testified Rennard Doines. The villagers thus captured were herded into the center of the village.

Q. "How many people did you have at this time?" asked the prosecutor of Paul Meadlo [another of Calley's men].
A. "Oh, about 35 or 40."
Q. "What did you do when you got there? . . ."

A. "[Calley] came up to me and said, 'You know what to do with them . . . . I want them dead.' . . ."
Q. "What did you do?"
A. "I helped him shoot them."

Soon the killing became infectious:

A. "[There were] some old women and some little children—in a group around a temple where some incense was burning [ran another account]. They were kneeling and crying and praying, and various soldiers . . . walked by and executed women and children by shooting them in the head with their rifles. The soldiers killed all . . . ."[1]

From the village center, Calley's platoon moved eastward into the rice field. There they came upon a man in monk's robes. He was brought to Calley for questioning.

A. "The priest would say, 'No Viet,' and he held his hands in this [prayer] shape [testified Charles Sledge]. Calley asked him a few more questions and he bowed his head and he still said, 'No Viet.' Then [Calley] hit him with the butt of his rifle in the mouth."
Q. "What did the priest do?" asked the prosecutor.
A. "He didn't do nothing but fall back, doing this with his hands again, sort of like pleading. Lt. Calley took his rifle at point blank and pulled the trigger in the priest's face. Half his head was blown off."[2]

At 10:30 A.M. Captain Medina, alarmed over reports of civilian slaughter, radioed Calley: "That's enough for today." Although it was a direct order, the killings went on.

At a drainage ditch just beyond the eastern edge of the village, the platoon rounded up seventy-five to one hundred terrified persons.

A. "Lt. Calley started shoving them off and shooting them in the ravine [Meadlo testified]. . . . He ordered me to help him kill the people, so I started shoving them off and shooting them, too."[3]
A. "A lot of them were trying to get up [Dennis Conti added]; most were just screaming. I looked down and seen a

---

1. Quoted in Wayne Greenhaw, *The Making of a Hero: The Story of Lieutenant William Calley* (Louisville, Ky.: Touchstone, 1971), pp. 129–131.
2. Quoted in Greenhaw, *The Making of a Hero*, p. 133.
3. Quoted in Greenhaw, *The Making of a Hero*, p. 131.

1st Photos of Viet Mass Slaying

WEATHER
Snow flurries and
colder today.
High in the upper 20s.
Details on Page 34.

THE PLAIN DEALER

FINAL
Stocks & Races
Dow-Jones off 5.21

OHIO'S LARGEST NEWSPAPER

128TH YEAR—NO. 324 • • • •   CLEVELAND, THURSDAY, NOVEMBER 20, 1969   96 PAGES   10 CENTS

Exclusive

This photograph will shock Americans as it shocked the editors and the staff of The Plain Dealer. It was taken by a young Cleveland area man while serving as a photographer with the U.S. Army in South Vietnam.

It was taken during the attack by American soldiers on the South Vietnamese village My Lai, an attack which has made world headlines in recent days with disclosures of mass killings allegedly at the hands of American soldiers.

This photograph and others on two special pages are the first to be published anywhere of the killings.

This particular picture shows a clump of bodies of South Vietnamese civilians which include, women and children. Why they were killed raises one of the most momentous questions of the war in Vietnam.

A clump of bodies on a road in South Vietnam.

Cameraman Saw GIs Slay 100 Villagers

By JOSEPH ESZTERHAS
(c) 1969, The Plain Dealer

U.S. Army troops "indiscriminately and wantonly mowed down" civilian residents of a tiny South Vietnamese hamlet on March 16, 1968, a former Army photographer has told The Plain Dealer.

Along with his eye-witness account, the former photographer has made available to The Plain Dealer a set of photographs taken at the village. They are being reproduced today on two pages of the Plain Dealer. This is the first publication of the photos, which also are in

Senate OK's Draft Reform;
Lottery Eyed for January

woman try to get up. I seen Lt. Calley fire and blow the side of her head off."[4]

As the testimony continued for four long months, My Lai began to take on a wider aspect. It soon became evident that My Lai was not the only occasion on which the American military had killed large numbers of civilians. "There was not a commander in Vietnam," admitted one officer, "that did not have a My Lai on his conscience." How could it be helped, asked Calley's defenders, when women and children were known to hurl grenades at soldiers or to shoot them from ambush? The villagers also planted mines, which caused more deaths than VC snipers.

The American troops had no way of telling which villagers were friends and which were foes. Soon this frustration turned to anger at all the villagers. "If you're a GI," wrote Calley, "who has lost eighteen friends in a minefield with a Vietnamese

---

4. Quoted in Greenhaw, *The Making of a Hero*, p. 136.

village a few hundred meters away—well. You think, 'Why didn't the Vietnamese signal us?' 'Hey there's a minefield there.' . . . Never: they sat in front of their hooches talking, twiddling thumbs, and all saying, 'Gee, I see an American unit,' 'I wonder what it is doing.' . . . 'hahaha.' "[5]

Was Calley's crime so great, many wondered? Throughout the Vietnam conflict, fighter-bombers laid carpets of explosives over suspected VC villages, killing many times the number of people that Calley had at My Lai. Calley himself maintained that he was merely following orders. "I never . . . wantonly kill[ed] a human being in my entire life," he maintained just before his sentence. He was ordered to fight communism and that was what he was doing. "They didn't give Communism a race; they didn't give it a sex; they didn't give it an age . . . ."[6] The Vietnamese he murdered were Communists, the enemy of America—not actual people.

The army court-martial board found Calley guilty of murder. The board maintained that even though Calley might have thought his orders were to kill civilians, he should have realized that such orders were illegal. Consequently, he should not have obeyed such orders. Calley was sentenced to life imprisonment, but the sentence was soon reduced to ten years at hard labor.

The outcry against the verdict was immense. "There have been My Lais in every war," roared the national commander of the Veterans of Foreign Wars (VFW), and "Now for the first time in our history we have tried a soldier for performing his duty." A sign went up in Houston, FREE CALLEY OR TRY TRUMAN— referring to the atom bomb attacks on the predominantly civilian targets at Hiroshima and Nagasaki. Some observers pointed out that since 325,000 South Vietnamese civilians already had been killed, most of them by U.S. tactics, it seemed unjust to sentence Calley while permitting the others to go free.[7]

Among those others sometimes singled out as being responsible for the deaths of innocent Vietnamese civilians was General William Westmoreland, commander of U.S. forces in Vietnam. Japanese observers claimed that Westmoreland's role in Vietnam was very similar to that of their own general, Tomoyuki Yamashita, in the Philippines over twenty-five years earlier

---

5. William Calley and John Sack, *Lieutenant Calley: His Own Story* (New York: Grosset & Dunlap, 1970), p. 74.

6. "Who Else Is Guilty?" *Newsweek*, 12 April 1971, p. 34.

7. "Who Else Is Guilty?" p. 34.

during World War II. Editors of the respected Tokyo newspaper *Asahi Evening News* pointed out the fact that Yamashita had been held accountable and sentenced to death for war crimes committed by his men. No evidence whatsoever had been presented to the U.S. military commission that Yamashita either knew of or ordered the massacre of the thousands of prisoners of war and civilians. Nonetheless, the U.S. military commission in Manila sentenced Yamashita to hang because he "failed to provide effective control of his troops as required by the circumstances." Yamashita was hanged on February 23, 1946. "In light of standards invoked [in Yamashita's trial]," *Asahi* asked, ". . . how can Westmoreland . . . be considered free from accountability for the crime [of My Lai]?"[8]

But in the United States the demand was for more leniency, not less, in the prosecution of the men involved at My Lai. A Gallup poll found that eighty-one percent of the American public thought that Calley's sentence was too harsh. Within a few days of the verdict, President Nixon received almost a hundred thousand letters and telegrams protesting the sentence. The president, too, believed that Calley was being treated with undue severity. Nixon ordered that Calley be released from the Fort Benning stockade and given complete freedom of the base until his appeals were completed.

Lieutenant Calley's appeals continued for a long time. In September, 1974, a federal judge overturned Calley's sentence and ordered him set free. The judge based his action on the fact that Calley's attorneys had been prevented from calling to the witness stand General William Westmoreland, whose policies, they maintained, Calley had been following. Thus Calley's right to a fair trial was denied, because as a defendant in a criminal proceeding he had the right to call witnesses on his own behalf. A year later, the appeal court reversed this decision. Finally, in April, 1976, the case reached the Supreme Court. There it was ruled that the ten-year sentence should stand. The army, however, put Calley on parole.

Long before Calley's conviction was upheld, many people had complained that My Lai was only the tip of the iceberg. They felt that the punishment of one lieutenant was not sufficient to right the wrongs being committed by Americans in Vietnam. To these people, the immensity of American destruction in Vietnam was horrifying.

---

8. *The Pacific Rivals* (New York: Weatherhill/Asahi, 1972), p. 181.

President Nixon's withdrawal of American troops caused a change in strategy that partly accounted for the increase in destruction. The strategic shift began to restrict the search-and-destroy missions of Calley-style infantry and to expand the vastly more destructive missions of the U.S. Air Force. While the new emphasis on air war brought about a decline in American deaths, it did result in a gigantic upsurge of Vietnamese casualties.

American planes showered a deadly rain of explosives on all areas of South Vietnam suspected of harboring Vietcong. The bomb tonnage was simply staggering. By the end of 1970 a total of nearly 6 million tons of explosives had shattered rural Vietnam. This tonnage was almost three times as much as the United States had dropped during World War II on Europe and Japan combined! There were few areas of rural South Vietnam which were not pitted with bomb craters or strewn with bomb shrapnel.

The bombing wiped out thousands of villages, killing many of the inhabitants and forcing others to trudge to the hated relocation camps. Besides the cost in human life and suffering, the bombing destroyed many of the intricate irrigation systems upon which the Vietnamese peasants depended to water their precious rice paddies. In addition, the bombs devasted many of the coconut palm groves from which the Vietnamese gathered fruit for food, oil for cooking, and fiber for nets, baskets, ropes, and brooms. From the palms, too, the Vietnamese made their furniture, the walls of their huts, and their thatched roofs. Rice and coconut palms were the Vietnamese staffs of life.

Just as destructive as the bombs were the herbicides sprayed over the countryside from low-flying planes. Although the object of using herbicides was to deny the VC food crops, as well as jungle hideaways, the effect was to leave large areas of South Vietnam barren. By the end of 1970 over twelve percent of South Vietnam's crop and grazing lands had been hit by chemical warfare. If similar tactics had been used by the VC against twelve percent of the United States, most of the vegetation from Maine through New York and Pennsylvania to Florida would have been damaged or destroyed.

The result of U.S. war tactics on the Vietnamese way of life was almost catastrophic. South Vietnam suddenly was reduced from a land of surplus rice to one where food had to be imported. The village system, which had been the mainspring of traditional Vietnam, was largely destroyed. Before the war eighty percent of the people had lived in these villages. The villages

Herbicides being sprayed over rice paddies and forests along the South Vietnam–Cambodia border. The object of such missions was to deprive the Vietcong of food supplies and forest hideouts.

were composed of tightly knit families. Local chiefs were elected by their neighbors. Most villagers spent their lives within a small radius of their clustered homes and outlying rice fields. The village was everything to them.

But by 1970 most villages were in decay. Their inhabitants had been either killed or forced into relocation camps or into the cities. Saigon's crowded population soared from 300,000 to 3,000,000. Da Nang's population rose from 25,000 to 300,000. In total, approximately 7,000,000 South Vietnamese—nearly half the entire population—had become refugees!

In fairness, however, it must be pointed out that the American presence also had good effects on the lives of some South

The U.S. influence in South Vietnam was present in most of the cities: modern office buildings, stores, businesses, restaurants, cocktail lounges, neon lights, automobiles, motor scooters, toys, and clothing styles. Especially noticeable was the growth of a middle class made up largely of Vietnamese employed by American business firms or by the armed forces.

Vietnamese. The Americans were influential in prodding President Thieu to return democracy to the villages that remained, and by early 1970 nearly all these villages once again were electing their own chiefs. Americans, too, played an important part in ridding the country of the evils of absentee landlords by encouraging Saigon's sweeping "Land to the Tiller" program. In addition, American farm machinery was given to the villagers. One such machine was the Rototiller, which replaced the inefficient water buffalo and wooden plow. American fertilizers and irrigation pumps also were great aids to the farmers. The United States helped to bring electricity into the countryside, where by 1970 television had become so popular that even the VC did not dare tamper with the broadcasts coming out of Saigon. Thus, for many farm families, American intervention resulted in larger incomes, as well as the opportunity to enjoy luxuries never before imagined.

In the cities the effects of the American presence were even greater. Many Vietnamese grew wealthy running restaurants, night clubs, gift shops, and services that catered to American GIs. Signs of the new affluence were everywhere. Parts of once drab Saigon blossomed into swank business areas with neon lights rivaling those of California's glittering strips. Many people adopted American clothing fashions and roared about on new motorbikes. Wages of the Vietnamese working for the Americans soared. One Vietnamese raised his wages from $25 to $300 a month when he quit his job as a policeman and signed on with a U.S. construction company. To many inhabitants of Saigon, Hue, Da Nang, and the other cities in which more than half the South Vietnamese lived by 1970, the American presence was highly valued.

In spite of these beneficial effects of the U.S. presence in Vietnam, as reports of destructive tactics reached the American public growing numbers of people began to regret and then despise the nation's role in Vietnam. Yet President Nixon would not be swayed from what he believed were his obligations to keep the Communists from taking over South Vietnam. And so he not only maintained his leisurely withdrawal rate of 12,500 men per month, but he even dared another escalation.

Thus, in the spring of 1971, American warplanes were flying over Laos. The war would not end.

★ CHAPTER FIFTEEN ★

The Fighting Withdrawal: 1971 and 1972

When the year 1971 opened, 310,000 U.S. troops still were stationed in Vietnam. But President Nixon was conducting his steady withdrawal, the fighting was diminishing, and the peace talks in Paris showed signs of slight progress. The war seemed to be drawing to a close.

Suddenly the situation changed.

Japanese and Russian newspapers broke the news first: At dawn on February 8, ARVN troops, supported by nearly a thousand U.S. bombers and helicopters, invaded Laos. The invasion had a twofold objective. First, the United States wanted to cut the Ho Chi Minh Trail until fall, when the monsoon rains would prevent the southward movement of men and supplies from North Vietnam. Second, the United States wanted to take Communist pressure off the shaky pro-American government of Laos. Nixon had clamped a complete censorship on news coming out of Vietnam in order to surprise the enemy and to quiet congressional debate. As before, he had not informed the legislators of his decision.

The Laos invasion was a sister of the Cambodian adventure of 1970. The long-term intention of both operations was to throw the delicate Communist supply system out of balance and, thereby, to insure the diminishing of hostilities while the United States withdrew. Just as important was the Pentagon's desire to gain more time to strengthen the ARVN before all U.S. troops were removed. The main difference between the Cambodia and Laos invasions was that in the latter offensive no American ground troops were used. To have used U.S. troops without prior congressional approval would have violated the Defense Appropriations Act.

213

Billed as the greatest peace rally ever held, the
May Day, 1971, march and rally attracted half a
million demonstrators. Nearly twelve thousand
demonstrators were arrested and jailed.

The Laotian campaign did not go as well as the one in
Cambodia. North Vietnamese resistance was ferocious. Some
ARVN units fought well; others did not. Both armies suffered high
casualties, but the ARVN accomplished its purpose of delaying
an enemy offensive for another year.

At first, Nixon also seemed to have won his gamble on the
domestic front in spite of congressional criticism. Senator Ed-
mund Muskie of Maine complained, "We were not consulted . . .
it is an outrage," and Senator Hubert Humphrey grumbled, "The
shortest distance between peace and war is not through Cambodia and Laos." Although these and other critics reacted with
varying degrees of intensity, students across the country did not
resort to the kind of demonstrations that triggered the Kent State

disaster. One reason for this mild reaction was that there were
no U.S. ground troops involved. Another reason was that this
operation was clearly the last action in which U.S. combat troops
could be readied even for a back-up role. Nixon had upped the
withdrawal rate to 15,000 men per month. By the end of the year
only about 175,000 U.S. troops would remain in Vietnam, and
these troops largely would be support, not combat, troops.

Despite the lack of immediate country-wide campus demonstrations, militant antiwar groups announced their intention to
gather in Washington, D.C., on May Day, 1971, to hold the
greatest peace rally ever. And, indeed, the capital would be
invaded by half a million people. But because the more militant
groups billed the rally as the occasion to bring the Pentagon war
machine to a standstill, the Nixon administration grew fearful of
another Siege of the Pentagon or, perhaps, something worse. The
prospect triggered yet other fears. Nixon felt that if he did not
deal firmly with the demonstrators, other demonstrations might
be held across the nation. Such demonstrations might cause him
to lose popular support for reelection in 1972.

Because of these fears, Nixon and his associates took strong
action against the demonstrators. Seven thousand people were
arrested—the most ever jailed in a single day in the nation's
history. Later five thousand more were arrested. Though all but
two dozen or so cases eventually were thrown out of court, the
back of the peace rally had been broken and Nixon won a rather
spectacular victory.

THE PENTAGON PAPERS BOMBSHELL

As a result of Nixon's May Day success, the administration felt
itself "drenched with power"—to use the words of Barry
Sussman, an editor of the *Washington Post*. In Sussman's view,
Nixon now decided "to turn Mayday to his own advantage, using
it as a means of furthering the message that antiwar sentiment
was disloyal [and] that Americans should be alarmed at the
conduct of those who opposed the war and not at the government's handling of the war itself." The victory over the demonstrators, as well as that over Congress in his Cambodia and Laos
operations, indicated to Nixon that he had the strength to do
almost whatever he wished.[1]

1. Barry Sussman, *The Great Cover-Up: Nixon and the Scandal of Watergate*
(New York: New American Library, Signet Books, 1974), p. 211.

On June 13, 1971, President Nixon, now at the crest of his power, decided to accept and take on what he considered a personal challenge. It was on this date that the *New York Times* and the *Washington Post* began printing segments of *The Pentagon Papers* given them by Daniel Ellsberg. Ellsberg, a highly placed government researcher, felt that the American public had been deceived about U.S. involvement in Vietnam. Consequently, he made copies of the papers from classified Defense Department files and passed them on to the *Times*, the *Post*, and the *Boston Globe*.

The papers had been commissioned by former Secretary of Defense Robert McNamara to help him understand just how the United States became involved in Vietnam. *The Pentagon Papers* revealed the secrecy, the double dealings, and actions of questionable legality by officials in the Eisenhower, Kennedy, and Johnson administrations.

Although the papers did not treat the Nixon era, the president felt that they tended to raise questions about his own Vietnam policies. In addition, he worried that his reputation as a defender of law and order had been thrown into a bad light by the disclosure of the papers during his administration. Such disclosure might hurt his chances for reelection. Therefore, Nixon strongly believed that the papers' publication should be halted immediately and that Daniel Ellsberg should be made an example of. The president decided to attack on both fronts.

Nixon's first move was to have the courts enjoin, or legally stop, the *Times* and *Post* from printing segments of the papers. His grounds for this action were that the papers revealed secret material, the release of which would imperil national security. On this front he enjoyed mixed success. The New York court upheld Nixon's view and forbade the *Times* to print more segments of the papers. But the Washington, D.C., court refused to enjoin the *Post* from printing the papers. The issue was laid before the U.S. Supreme Court on June 26. On June 30, the Supreme Court upheld the *Times'* right to print the documents in accordance with the First Amendment guarantee of freedom of the press.

The Nixon administration then moved to an illegal offensive against Daniel Ellsberg, who had been indicted in Los Angeles on charges of theft and espionage. The administration wished to use the trial to discredit Ellsberg, as well as the whole quick-withdrawal movement. Therefore, Nixon officials hired a group of specialists who were known as "plumbers" because their job was to stop "leaks" of information that the administration wanted to keep secret.

The plumbers, composed of a half-dozen men, were headed by former CIA agent E. Howard Hunt and former FBI agent G. Gordon Liddy. On Labor Day, 1971, the plumbers broke into the office of Ellsberg's psychiatrist in Los Angeles. Their mission was to search his files for confidential reports that would show Ellsberg to be neurotic or otherwise disturbed. Such files could be used to discredit not only Ellsberg but the entire radical left by association. Thus Nixon could take credit as the defender of national security against the lunatic fringe.

But on this front, too, the Nixon forces were stymied. The plumbers were unable to find the desired reports. Yet, the efficiency with which the plumbers operated prompted Nixon officials to consider other areas of activity for their talents.

Shortly after midnight on June 17, 1972, the plumbers struck again. On this occasion they were assigned to break into the Watergate building in Washington, D.C., and to plant bugging devices in the Democratic party headquarters. An alert guard discovered the break-in and called the police. The plumbers were caught. Administration officials tried to cover up their involvement, but it was impossible. Although the famous Watergate scandal would not hit the headlines until after Nixon had won the 1972 election, it ultimately would have far-reaching effects. It would result in more convictions of highly placed officials than in any prior presidential administration. Eventually Richard Nixon himself would be forced to resign, the only chief executive ever to do so.

Ironically, the Watergate hearings brought to light the plumbers' role in the burglary of Daniel Ellsberg's psychiatrist. This fact prompted the judge presiding over the Ellsberg trial to dismiss all charges against Ellsberg on the grounds of "improper government conduct."[2]

The close relationship between Vietnam and the Watergate scandal is pointed out by Barry Sussman. Sussman wrote, "It seems certain that if not for Nixon's appetite for political gain out of Ellsberg [and his theft of *The Pentagon Papers*], there would never have been a Watergate affair . . . ."[3]

Thus, just as Vietnam had caused the downfall of President Johnson, so would it help to destroy the career of President Nixon.

NIXON'S HISTORIC JOURNEY TO CHINA

But Watergate had not yet happened when Nixon made a triumphant visit to China in February, 1972. Perhaps to help insure that China would not interfere with his fighting withdrawal from Vietnam, Nixon met with Communist Chairman Mao Tse-tung and Premier Chou En-lai. An American president had never journeyed to China. In fact, if an American had suggested such a visit during the prior generation, he probably would have been regarded as a traitor or Communist or both. Indeed, Richard Nixon himself had won his first campaign victory in 1946 by taking a strong anti-Communist position. But the world had changed between 1946 and 1972, and Nixon had changed with it. Although the political right wing still maintained a suspicious hostility toward Red China, Nixon had the courage to break with his past and to seek a basic realignment of American foreign policy.

Perhaps the most curious aspect of the president's seven-day stay in China was that his talks with Mao and the other Red leaders did not center on the Vietnam War. The Chinese apparently cared little about American actions in the south, at

---

2. "Watergate: Now the Stage Is Set for the Full Story," *U.S. News & World Report*, 21 May 1973, p. 17.

3. Sussman, *The Great Cover-Up*, p. 213.

Premier Chou En-lai and President Nixon at a banquet held in honor of the President's visit to the People's Republic of China during February, 1972.

least far less than they had about the American army in Korea immediately across the China Sea from Peking. Instead, their interest centered on Japan and the ability of the United States to keep that once warlike nation on a peaceful course. Of even greater worry to the Chinese was Russia, which had half a million crack troops on China's northern border.

Another major area of Chinese concern was Chiang Kai-shek and his army of half a million men on Taiwan. Taiwan was virtually a U.S. satellite; and as long as Chiang's troops and American warships remained poised just off the China coast, they were potential destroyers of Communist rule. Nixon, however, could not abandon Chiang, the man to whom presidents dating back to Roosevelt had pledged undying support. Taiwan remained, in the words of presidential adviser Henry Kissinger, a "murderously tough problem."

Toward the end of his stay, President and Mrs. Nixon were taken on a tour of a portion of China's Great Wall. Across America millions watched on live television as Nixon walked along the massive ramparts that stretched over the hills and down the valleys as far as the camera could see. At times the

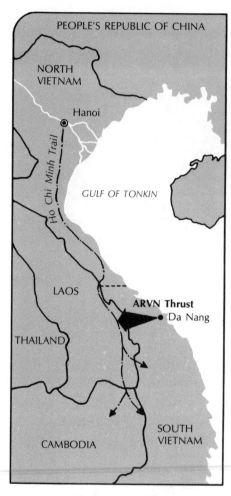

The Laos offensive,
February–March, 1971.

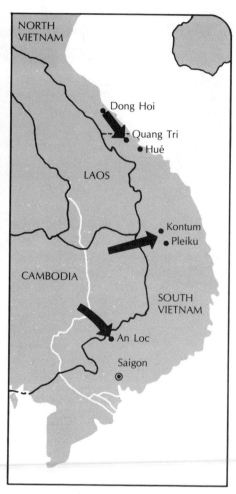

The Vietcong Easter offensive,
April 1972.

cameras panned northward, just as the vision of Chinese defenders had done for more than a thousand years. It then occurred to many Americans that China always had regarded its northern border as the most important. It was from the north that the Mongols, Manchus, and other warlike tribes from the early mists of history had charged into China's heartland. The Great Wall, about twelve hundred miles long, was the most spectacular memorial to China's age-long fear of attack from the north. Vietnam? Vietnam was merely a slumbering region in the distant south from whence no invaders had ever come. There was no Great Wall on the southern frontier.

When the president returned to America, the antiwar groups again tried to stir up the nation against U.S. involvement in Vietnam. The agitators claimed that since China apparently had no designs on Vietnam or on the rest of Southeast Asia, Nixon should withdraw all U.S. forces from Vietnam immediately. Vietnam simply was not worth another American death.

The president, however, still did not view Vietnam in this light. Although he had a firsthand indication of the deep split between the two Communist giants, he would not consider abandoning his South Vietnamese allies. Nor would he abandon the commitments made by four presidents before him. But at the same time he did allow Henry Kissinger to pursue secret peace talks in Paris with a special Hanoi negotiator, Le Duc Tho. When the talks stalled over Kissinger's refusal to accept Vietcong representatives in the Saigon government, it was Hanoi, not Washington, who decided to make another attempt to win the war by force.

THE GREAT EASTER OFFENSIVE

The Easter Offensive, as it became known, opened with devastating effectiveness during the first week in April, 1972. Russian-built tanks and hundreds of artillery pieces hammered their way southward toward the provincial capitals of Quang Tri and the prize city of Hue, ancient capital of all Vietnam. Following close behind were forty thousand North Vietnamese troops in battle formation. The operation obviously was no minor guerrilla attack. "What we've witnessed," said a State Department spokesman, "is an invasion of South Vietnam." The United States, with only seven thousand combat troops out of ninety-five thousand military personnel still in Vietnam, could not give the ARVN any ground support. "It all depends on the will of the ARVN," was the opinion of U.S. officials in Saigon.

During the first weeks of the Easter Offensive the ARVN was unable to stop the enemy. The North Vietnamese force pushed southward until it was just five miles from Quang Tri. As ARVN reinforcements were rushed northward, the Communists launched major attacks in the central highlands aimed at the provincial capital of Kontum and the strategic U.S. air base at Pleiku. No sooner had ARVN units been dispatched in this direction than more Red troops blasted their way out of Cambodia toward yet a third capital, An Loc, just sixty miles from Saigon itself.

Everywhere the North Vietnamese and Vietcong were mauling the ARVN. *Newsweek* magazine warned that "North Vietnam's

Defense Minister Vo Nguyen Giap appeared to be on the verge of accomplishing a military masterstroke." Since it had been Giap who had smashed France's colonial dreams at Dien Bein Phu, any Giap-planned operation could not be taken lightly. His strategy apparently was not only to capture the three provincial capitals but also to discredit the Thieu government. Once these objectives were attained, President Thieu would be replaced by someone more agreeable to the formation of a coalition government in which the Vietcong would share power.

There seemed to be little hope for President Thieu. In the north the ARVN forces retreated in confusion from Quang Tri. As they fell back toward Hue, 100,000 refugees created more chaos. It seemed as if Hue would be an easy conquest. Farther south, government troops had such a tenuous hold on An Loc that Thieu sent his own palace guards into the fight.

As the Communist successes mounted, President Thieu's popular support began to erode. But Thieu, a cool and determined man, did not lose heart. Convinced that he must not lose An Loc, he threw in more and more troops. Although he was warned that Giap was using An Loc as bait to draw off Saigon's reserves, Thieu persisted in his tactics.

Meanwhile, Nixon ordered massive U.S. air support. Six aircraft carriers cruising off the coast launched a thousand fighter-bombers that cascaded thousands of tons of bombs on the enemy. Among these bombs were the new, deadly "smart bombs," guided directly to their targets by laser beams. Nixon also carried the war into North Vietnam by directing U.S. planes to hit Hanoi and U.S. warships to mine Hanoi's harbor, Haiphong. It was a chilling gamble because Russian ships were frequent users of the harbor.

Congress stormed, and Senator Edward Kennedy along with eighteen other congressmen joined one thousand demonstrators on the Capitol steps. But the Russians, perhaps fearing that a hostile reaction might push the United States and China closer together, did not voice much objection. China, too, remained silent—perhaps, some surmised, because Nixon had hinted that he would withdraw U.S. troops from Taiwan after the problem of Vietnam was solved. Thus Nixon's artful diplomacy had enabled him to adopt aggressive tactics that Johnson would never have been able to undertake.

During June the North Vietnamese offensive began to lose its steam. American air power had been extremely effective—more so than Giap had anticipated. And the ARVN, having survived the initial onslaught, put up such a surprising defense that Giap

Two Broncos of Light Attack Squadron Four flying low in search of enemy activity. If such flights spotted major enemy troop concentrations or supply depots, they radioed in a squadron of heavily armed fighter-bombers.

could not take Hue, Kontum, or An Loc. Reports of huge Red losses began to come in—some estimates ran as high as forty thousand men.

Gradually it became obvious that the Easter Offensive was a failure. The North Vietnamese simply lacked that extra ounce of muscle needed to push to their objectives. The prolonged years of war had strained their resources. For the Tet Offensive of 1968 the Communists had 267,000 men available, but for the Easter Offensive they could muster only 200,000. They were also short of supplies, possibly as a result of the U.S.–ARVN strikes into Cambodia and Laos. But the failure of the Easter Offensive also must be laid at the feet of Defense Minister Giap.

Giap had conducted the siege of Dien Bien Phu brilliantly in 1954. But he was no Guderian or Patton. If he had used his tanks to achieve a breakthrough after taking Quang Tri, the prize of Hue would have been his. Many observers thought that if the ARVN lost this center of Vietnamese loyalty, the Thieu government might well have fallen. Instead, Giap plodded cautiously forward, using his tanks as portable forts, ignoring the basic tactic of mobility. Accordingly, the ARVN troops were given time to rest and regroup. Time also was given to the American carriers to reach the area. Before Giap could close his fist on Hue, American air power had demolished nearly every one of his precious tanks.

By July the offensive was over, and the Paris peace talks were resumed. In October, 1972, Henry Kissinger announced that peace was at hand—just in time for the presidential elections, muttered the supporters of Democratic candidate George McGovern. But, regardless of whether the approaching peace settlement was politically motivated, President Nixon was keeping his 1968 campaign promise to get the United States out of Vietnam. Nixon's role in Vietnam and his impressive peace missions to China and Russia earned him an electoral victory in November that nearly topped Johnson's record-breaker of 1964.

Later in November, Kissinger returned to Paris, supposedly to sign the treaty. Thus apparently ended the longest and one of the most controversial wars in American history. Although more than fifty-five thousand Americans had lost their lives (fifteen thousand of them during Nixon's administration), the United States achieved what the president called "peace with honor."

★ CHAPTER SIXTEEN ★

The Peace That Wasn't: 1973

Early in December, 1972, loudspeakers in Hanoi began blaring warnings. The peace negotiations at Paris were breaking down, they said, and the Americans were threatening to destroy Hanoi, a city of nearly one million inhabitants. The people of Hanoi, who knew and feared American air power as the result of nearly eight years of intermittent bombing, started packing their meager possessions. For two weeks, while Henry Kissinger and Le Duc Tho wrangled over certain issues newly raised by South Vietnam's President Thieu, the citizens of Hanoi trudged out into the countryside. There they awaited the roar of approaching B-52 bombers. Meanwhile within the nearly deserted capital, soldiers readied their anti-aircraft defenses. Massive shipments of Russian weapons had made Hanoi the most heavily fortified city in the world.

Kissinger wired home that he could not gain acceptance of Thieu's demand that the treaty contain a provision for the withdrawal of Hanoi's 145,000 troops from South Vietnam. Neither would Hanoi back down from its own new demand that the 473 American prisoners of war would not be freed until Saigon released its 150,000 military and civilian POWs.

President Nixon held tense consultations with officials of the State Department, Defense Department, and the Central Intelligence Agency. He had just been reelected on the promise of immediate peace. What would happen if he renewed the bombing? Would there be riots on the campuses? And could the bombing force Hanoi to withdraw its troops and thus also force it to abandon its dream of uniting Vietnam?

But the president had never been one to flinch from using power. He sent Hanoi a seventy-two-hour ultimatum. He waited until December 18. When his ultimatum was not accepted, he

Secretary of State Henry Kissinger and Le Duc
Tho shake hands in Paris following the announcement that the two men had reached an
agreement to end the Vietnam cease-fire violations. The Paris peace talks would not produce a
treaty until January, 1973, and then only after
U.S. bombers had reduced Hanoi to ruins during
December, 1972.

unleashed the most devastating bombing offensive since
Nagasaki.

THE CHRISTMAS RECESS AIR OFFENSIVE

Giant B-52 Stratofortresses from bases in Guam and Thailand
soon held Hanoi in their sights and bombs rained down on the
North Vietnamese capital. Entire blocks of factories, warehouses,

and homes were blasted into rubble. Smoke and flames billowed skyward. Explosions rumbled far out into the countryside, where most of Hanoi's population listened in awe. Day after day, with a brief halt for Christmas, the mighty Stratofortresses made high-altitude bombing runs over the smoldering city. When a certain target eluded them, fast lower-flying fighter-bombers were called in to hit it with precise, laser-guided bombs.

The North Vietnamese fought back. Russian ground-to-air missiles were hurled at the Stratofortresses. Special U.S. planes, equipped with electronic-jamming gear, tried to interfere with the missiles' guidance systems and usually were successful in sending them astray. But there were too many missiles to deal with. They began homing in on the bombers. When the missiles struck, the great planes disintegrated in brilliant flashes that scattered wreckage for many miles. Several of the multimillion-dollar planes and their crews were destroyed each day.

Nevertheless, the air offensive continued for two weeks. By December 30, when Nixon called it off, there were no military or industrial targets worth hitting in the leveled city.

The bombing began and ended while Congress was recessed for the Christmas holiday. When the legislators returned, they were incensed that the president once more had taken offensive action without securing congressional approval. "I have never seen a Congress open in such an ugly mood," remarked New Hampshire's veteran Republican Senator Norris Cotton.

Immediately Senators Clifford Case of New Jersey and Frank Church of Idaho began work on a bill that would carry the Defense Appropriations Act one step further. That act had prohibited the military use of federal funds without congressional approval. Now, the Case-Church Act set a time limit at the end of which Congress would cut off all money for war-making in Vietnam. If such an act had been passed earlier, the war could have been terminated years sooner.

Meanwhile, Kissinger and Tho were meeting again in Paris. Laboriously they hammered out an agreement. On January 27, 1973, representatives of North and South Vietnam, the National Liberation Front, and the United States at last put their names to the document designed to end the war. On this day all fighting was to stop.

THE PEACE TREATY

At first glance the treaty seemed an American victory. Almost none of Hanoi's basic terms were met. Thieu was not removed as

American B-52s—like the ones above showering 750-pound bombs on a suspected VC stronghold—pounded Hanoi daily for two weeks during Nixon's 1972 Christmas air offensive. When Nixon ordered a halt to the air offensive, Hanoi (facing page) lay in ruins.

South Vietnam's president; the Vietcong were not included in a coalition government; and American aid to South Vietnam was not eliminated. Saigon remained in control of seventy-five percent of the South Vietnamese population, and Hanoi acknowledged the existence of an independent South. These concessions represented a tremendous retreat from Hanoi's initial demand for one united nation. The Seventeenth Parallel was settled upon as a fixed border between North and South until reunification by peaceful means could be achieved. However, a further concession by Hanoi made it unlikely that peaceful reunification would come soon: Hanoi granted South Vietnam's right to decide its own future through an election to be conducted under the existing government, which meant that the vote was certain to support Thieu and the ARVN. In addition, the treaty promised the immediate release of American POWs, a major goal of the Christmas bombing.

President Nixon, addressing the nation, spoke of the treaty in glowing terms. "Now that we have achieved an honorable agreement," he said, "let us be proud that America did not settle

for a peace that would have betrayed our allies; that would have abandoned our prisoners of war; or that would have ended the war for us but would have continued the war for the 50 million people of Indochina."

The president also gave an accolade to Lyndon Johnson, who had died just a few days before the signing of the treaty. "No one would have welcomed this peace more than he," Nixon said. "And I know he would join me in asking for those who died and for those who lived: let us consecrate this moment by resolving together to make the peace we have achieved a peace that will last."

But the treaty was not as rosy a piece of literature as Nixon described. Hanoi was allowed to keep its 145,000 troops in the South. The Christmas bombing did not shake Hanoi from this resolve. These troops, plus about 50,000 VC and nearly 100,000 part-time VC civilian fighters, constituted a great danger to Saigon. The United States, on the other hand, was obligated to withdraw all its troops and advisers from South Vietnam within sixty days, as well as to dismantle all its military bases in the country. The United States promised to stop bombing North Vietnam and to remove the mines it had planted in North Vietnamese waters. Furthermore, the United States would henceforth "not continue its military involvement or intervene in the internal affiars of South Vietnam." The only aid the United States

Armaments and supplies being unloaded at Da Nang in accordance with the peace treaty. The U.S. continued supplying armaments to the ARVN until the fall of Saigon in 1975.

could give South Vietnam was to supply replacement armaments and munitions. Thus South Vietnam was to be strictly on its own. Many American officials gave Saigon barely a fifty-fifty chance of surviving under the conditions of the treaty.

There seemed to be little likelihood that the treaty would end the conflict. However, an attempt to implement the treaty was made in the creation of the Council of National Reconciliation and Concord. This council was to organize "geniunely free and democratic general elections." But right from the beginning, the council, composed of representatives from Saigon and the National Liberation Front, were unable to agree on what sort of elections were to be held. The VC desired district elections to select representatives to the legislature. This would have given them oversized representation from the numerous rural areas they controlled. Thieu, however, demanded a national election for president, which would have given him a renewal of power to the complete exclusion of the VC. Since the treaty stipulated that the council operate only on a basis of unanimity, it was obvious that no elections would be held. This deadlock put the matter back to where it had been in 1956 and left the Vietcong no recourse except force.

With the elections bypassed, other portions of the treaty quickly fell into the rubbish heap. The treaty called for the demobilization of the VC and ARVN armies "as soon as possible." It called for "North and South Vietnam [to] promptly start negotiations with a view to reestablishing normal relations." It called for the United States to "contribute to healing the wounds of war and to postwar reconstruction of the Democratic Republic of [North] Vietnam." None of these clauses was ever carried out. However, in fairness to President Nixon, he did try (but failed) to get Congress to agree to a $2.5 billion program to aid Hanoi.

TO WAR AGAIN

The year that followed the treaty found Vietnam again convulsed with hard fighting. Many of the highest U.S. military authorities had predicted that Saigon would fall easy prey to the Reds. The huge infusion of U.S.-donated planes, tanks, guns, and other military hardware just prior to the signing of the treaty, however, seemed to bolster the ARVN war machine and spirit. Also, the presence of four thousand Americans gathering intelligence and supervising the repair of the U.S.-made equipment was of immeasurable aid to the ARVN in its surprising resistance to the VC.

Those people who felt the full fury of the continuing war were the peasants. Thousands were killed as the armies fought across their farms and through their hamlets. Neither the VC nor the ARVN troops seemed to care any longer about the civilians. As the fighting continued during the next few years, the VC began kidnapping peasants living in ARVN country. The VC had a great deal of territory but few people. The kidnapped peasants were put to work growing food for the VC. The ARVN, for their part, swept through the countryside herding the farmers back into the relocation areas. The peasants, caught between the two forces, had no choice but to accept war as a way of life. They grew accustomed to the VC bothering them by night and the ARVN by day. Meanwhile, the peasants continued to tend their rice paddies, to marry, and to have families. Despite the hardship of perpetual war, babies were born and survived, and the population of South Vietnam increased to 17 million.

Despite the horrors of war, life went on.

An ARVN soldier fires a submachine gun to familiarize himself with the weapon. As U.S. troops were withdrawn from Vietnam, the ARVN began taking on more of the responsibility for defending South Vietnam.

★ CHAPTER SEVENTEEN ★

Lingering Drumbeats

A month after the peace treaty had been signed, Secretary of State Henry Kissinger sat before NBC's television cameras. A dapper and precise man, Kissinger spoke with a slight German accent, a wry wit, and unobtrusive mannerisms. Kissinger was America's man of the hour because he had negotiated the long-sought peace treaty with North Vietnam. And he was America's most admired man—so said a Gallup poll. Always at ease in any company, Kissinger was relaxed with his interviewer, Barbara Walters.

During the course of the program, interviewer Walters asked Kissinger many questions. One question was, "Now that the United States is disengaged in Vietnam, would you object if North Vietnam took over South Vietnam?"

Kissinger did not hesitate with his answer: "We are not opposed to the unification of Vietnam in principle, if Vietnam is unified by peaceful means. If the performance of one part or the other part is so clearly superior to that of the other that it tends to achieve moral superiority over the other, that is not an American concern."

Such a statement would have been shocking, even treasonable, in 1965, the year of Pleiku and of President Johnson's stepped-up involvement. Johnson would have disagreed sharply with Kissinger. Didn't Kissinger know, Johnson would have demanded, that the whole war began because Diem and Eisenhower had refused to allow a Communist takeover by peaceful means when the elections of 1956 were canceled? Didn't Kissinger know about the Domino Theory and Communist dreams of world conquest? But Johnson was dead, and it was Kissinger who now directed U.S. foreign policy.

Near the end of the TV interview, Kissinger offered his summary of American involvement in the war. He said that the

Barbara Walters interviewing Secretary of State Kissinger on NBC's Today Show.

"general lesson we have learned" is that "domestic security and guerrilla warfare ought to be the task of the government concerned. . . . The guerrilla lives with his own population. The foreigner can never compete with him on that level."

Kissinger voiced not only the administration's opinion of the ultimate futility of Vietnam but also the thoughts of most of his viewers. Never had a war's ending resulted in such an empty feeling. The termination of World War I, for those who still remembered, had brought a buoyancy at America's success on European battlefields. World War II had brought wild elation at the victory over the ruthless dictatorships. Korea had brought the satisfaction of stopping communism cold.

But Vietnam? It brought none of these elevating sensations. Only one word could describe the feelings about the years, the expense, and the lives lost. The word was *disillusionment*.

DOMESTIC EFFECTS OF THE WAR

Although the peace treaty of 1973 did not end the fighting for the Vietnamese, it did for the Americans. The conflict had brought the most profound changes to the American way of life of any event since the Civil War. The United States had been accustomed to viewing its mission in the world as the defense of righteousness. Wilson, for example, had called upon the nation to fight the "war to end all wars" and "to make the world safe for democracy." Franklin Roosevelt championed the crusade to crush the Axis powers, Germany, Japan, and Italy. And even Truman in Korea had the noble goal of preventing the spread of communism.

Vietnam, on the other hand, had no such sense of mission. Despite the deaths of more than 55,000 Americans, the wounding of about 304,000 more, the loss of 8,600 aircraft, and the expense of $140 billion, the war had not checked the Communist menace to South Vietnam. Service in Vietnam was looked on by many as a degrading experience. One-half million disgruntled servicemen received bad discharges. The number of men who chose to evade the draft was likewise high—an estimated 200,000 compared to only 16,000 in World War II. Even most of those men who had served well regarded themselves simply as mercenaries doing the job for which they were being paid. Many of them cared little for the Vietnamese, whom they called "gooks" and "dinks." As for the American public, it was shocked and dismayed by reports of merciless bombings of civilians, of the defoliation of a fifth of Vietnam's forestlands, and of massacres like My Lai. Other nations were critical of the American role in Vietnam. Some formerly pro-U.S. countries went so far as to compare the United States with Nazi Germany.

Americans themselves seriously began to question not only their nation's international role, but also what seemed to be the deteriorating quality of life at home. Not only had the United States become mired in Vietnam, but at home John and Robert Kennedy, Martin Luther King, Jr., and the students at Kent State University had been brutally, senselessly gunned down.

The disillusionment arising from the war showed up in many other ways, too. Students, unable to bring an immediate end to the war, turned to violence and to drugs. A new subculture evolved—one based on marijuana, disrespect for authority, criticism of the country, and a profound disdain of the armed forces. Desertion from the army ran high. And up to sixty percent of those who did not desert preferred to smoke marijuana or to take stronger drugs, which the Vietnamese supplied at cheap prices, to fighting the VC. Discipline in the army was lax: the men wore disheveled uniforms, and they often scoffed at their officers. Some reporters and military authorities thought the only

Students demonstrating to end the wars against Vietnam and women.

thing that held the army together were the huge, expensive service facilities, which kept ninety percent of the men lounging in the rear.

Yet whether the men fought or not, merely serving in such an unpopular war seems to have been a permanently unnerving experience for many. A 1974 poll of 2.1 million Vietnam veterans showed that half of them felt their lives were not going well. Only a quarter of the nonveterans in the same age group held this view of their lives.

It was not only the students and the young army men who experienced disillusionment arising from the war. People everywhere began to lose faith in the persons and institutions that hitherto had been regarded as providing moral leadership for the nation. Polls showed a staggering devaluation of the office of the president, which fell from forty-one percent approval in 1966 to barely nineteen percent in 1973. Confidence in the Supreme Court dropped during this period from fifty-one to thirty-three percent and in business executives from fifty-five to twenty-nine percent.

The disillusionment with the war helped to bring about changes in other areas of American life. Churches normally could expect to increase their membership as the national population rose. But this was not the case during the 1960s, when the population grew by thirteen percent. Large numbers of Americans turned away from religion, which they apparently felt lacked relevance in this era of confused morality. The membership of the United Presbyterians, the United Church of Christ, the American Lutherans, and the Protestant Episcopalians declined up to eight percent between 1964 and 1973. Roman Catholic membership leveled off, and the proportion of church-going Catholics in the total population dropped to twenty-three percent.

Disillusionment with the war also was one factor that helped to bring about a profound change in family life. During the nine years of U.S. involvement in Vietnam, the divorce rate nearly doubled, reaching an all-time high. One out of four marriages ended in divorce. And because of the high divorce rate, improved methods of birth control, and inflation, the birth rate decreased. This event seemed destined eventually to end the confident, upward surge of population that had characterized the United States from the very earliest colonial days. America, its ideologies, and institutions were being questioned, tested, and changed.

The rise of the Women's Liberation Movement can also be traced, in part at least, to the Vietnam War. Women active in the antiwar groups of the 1960s often found themselves relegated to menial tasks. They were expected to run the mimeograph machines, paint the posters, and supply the refreshments while the men debated theory and decided on tactics. For many such women, fighting for their own rights became as important as fighting to end the war, and into this new fight they carried much valuable political know-how.

Encouraged by the Women's Liberation Movement, many women began seeking alternatives to homemaking. One result was an increased enlistment of women in the armed forces. Beginning in 1971, the services began offering women a far greater number of opportunities than ever before. Consequently, the number of women in uniform rose from two and a half percent to nearly eight percent in only three years. Officials expected that the total number of women in uniform soon would climb to more than 100,000.

In some ways the war had a beneficial influence on the American economy. The stimulus of a $135 billion military industry spurred a strong upsurge in production. The gross national product doubled in the 1960s, and the average American family had $9,000 more yearly to enjoy than before the war. This prosperity, however, was not all that it seemed. Taxes were increased to support the war, and a spiral of inflation, based largely on government borrowing, ate gaping holes in many incomes.

Another effect of the war was the growing influence of the Pentagon in the economic life of the nation. Some observers feared that American prosperity was becoming increasingly more dependent on the preparation for war. To these observers, one of the most alarming facts was that at the end of the war military expenses were not reduced. The Pentagon, instead, spent larger amounts of money on the development of more expensive weaponry.

While the turbulence of the 1960s undermined some people's faith in Amercan ideologies, it did not entirely dampen student idealism. The experience of the McCarthy presidential campaign was rewarding to those who took part. It also was a revealing application of student power to the American political arena. Student participation in politics provided a precedent for other student activities. For example, students and other young people worked hard for the Democratic, antiwar candidate, George McGovern, during the 1972 presidential elections. Also, student resistance to the draft persuaded Congress to end the draft and to set up an all-volunteer army in 1973. The new volunteer army—being better equipped, trained, and paid—offered excellent career opportunities, especially to men and women from low-income families.

The Vietnam War had a significant influence on the Negro population. Most obvious was the role of black men in the army. In World War I blacks had rarely seen action, and in World War II they had fought in segregated units. In Vietnam, however, blacks not only were completely integrated into the armed forces but often fought in numbers that far exceeded their eleven percent of the nation's general population. This larger participation was especially true in the army, where blacks comprised seventeen percent of all U.S. infantrymen during the closing years of the war.

Black servicemen often volunteered for the most dangerous duty. They had a newborn pride in themselves, exemplified by the "black is beautiful" motto. Nonetheless, black servicemen complained that they were being passed over for promotion. They made up less than four percent of the officers in the army, less than two percent in the air force, and a bare nine-tenths of one percent in the navy. This situation, however, began to change in the post-Vietnam all-volunteer services.

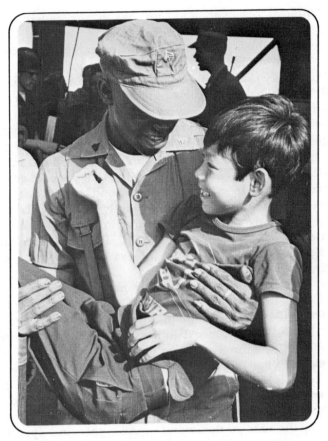

A marine lending a helping hand to a Vietnamese refugee.

The Vietnam years also altered the situation of the Negro at home. The war contributed to an atmosphere of aggressiveness, in which militant and nonmilitant black groups began to make demands. Consequently, blacks began winning better job opportunities, educational facilities, and a greater share in the political process. The number of Negro white collar and professional workers soared from twenty-two to almost forty percent of the black population between 1960 and 1973. The proportion of black college graduates rose from five to more than twelve percent in the same period. And the blacks, who were virtually unrepresented in politics in 1960, claimed by 1973 a senator, 16 congressmen, 108 mayors, and 1,142 other local officials. Although the United States was far from being integrated by 1976, most indications pointed to the Negroes' eventually finding their place in the American mainstream.

The Latinos, however, did not benefit as much from the changes brought about by the war. The 7.5 million Mexican-Americans and the 1.5 million Puerto Ricans had long achieved equality in the armed forces, though few had become officers. But at home they found themselves segregated into urban barrios or rural "serape belts" because of their low incomes, about thirty percent below the national average. The Latinos' main problem stemmed from their poor education. This difficulty, caused to a large degree by the unwillingness of Anglo schools to conduct classes in Spanish, resulted in a high school drop-out rate of up to three-fourths. The average Latino had eight years of schooling, compared with nearly ten for blacks and twelve for Anglos. Having less education and consequently fewer skills, Latinos had little choice except to seek out menial work—work that had high rates of seasonal unemployment. This situation, in turn, resulted in the number of Latino jobless being twice as high as the national average.

Latino militancy developed slowly in the ferment of the war years. César Chavez led the way. Chavez won a significant victory for the Mexican-American farm workers in California. The militant leader Reies López Tijerina organized the Alianza Federal de Pueblos Libres in New Mexico. And Rudolfo "Corky" Gonzales, a former prizefighter, started the Crusade for Justice and La Raza Unida in Denver, Colorado. One of the chief goals of these leaders was to bring out Latino voters so that a Latino power base could be laid in the political arena.

Even so, the road to achieving equal rights and opportunities promised to be difficult for the Latinos, one of whose leaders complained that they were fifteen years behind the blacks.

INTERNATIONAL EFFECTS OF THE WAR

The war reshaped international politics. Vietnam demonstrated the weakness of Communist unity. Apparently, neither Russia nor China felt much loyalty to North Vietnam since their contributions to Ho Chi Minh's war effort were minimal. While the U.S. had spent about $40 billion to aid its South Vietnamese ally, Russian and Chinese aid to North Vietnam amounted to only around $2 billion and $1 billion, respectively.

The Vietnam War brought into focus the very real differences between Russia and China. It became clear that the two Communist giants were not working together for world domination. On the contrary, they were more fearful of each other than

Egyptian President Anwar Sadat greeting U.S. Secretary of State Henry Kissinger who has journeyed to the Middle East to seek an end to the 1973 Egyptian-Israeli war.

they were of the capitalist nations. With this realization, the era of the Cold War, dating back to the Truman administration, finally came to an end.

But Vietnam did more than highlight the split between Russia and China. It also tended to fray the alliance of Western Europe with the United States. Although the United States maintained 300,000 troops in Europe as part of the NATO defense force, the nations of Western Europe no longer felt obligated to follow the American lead in Asia. Neither the British nor the French sent combat troops to Vietnam as they had to Korea nearly fifteen years earlier. Some members of the European Common Market began taking a course more independent from, and sometimes in competition with, the United States. Such developments could become quite serious if they destroyed NATO, the cornerstone of American foreign policy.

By the early 1970s it became clear that Vietnam had helped to cause a basic reshuffling in the international lineup. The new lineup was nearly as earth-shaking as that resulting from World War II, which saw Germany and Great Britain replaced by the United States and Russia as the world's dominant powers. For nearly thirty years the United States and Russia had politically divided the world between them. Now Western Europe and China were on the rise. Their combined population far outstripped that of the United States and Russia, and, in addition, they had the potential to outproduce them in goods. Instead of two world leaders, the stage was being set for four major power blocs.

To further complicate the international picture was the formation of lesser but nonetheless powerful political and/or economic Third World power blocs. These blocs were formed by the emerging nations of Africa and Asia. When acting in concert, these countries had political clout in the United Nations General Assembly. Other Third World nations, such as the Arab oil-producing states, had economic clout. By refusing to sell their petroleum products during the early 1970s, they persuaded Western Europe and the United States to reassess their stance on the Middle East Arab-Israeli conflict.

Thus in international relations, as with domestic affairs, the VietnamWar and the rise of Third World nations marked a major historical turning point.

Nothing would ever be the same again.

CHAPTER EIGHTEEN

The Final Collapse: 1975

The villagers watched in dismay as ARVN troops staggered down the road toward them. There was no roar of enemy artillery, no twang of rifle fire. No battle had been fought, and no defeat administered. Yet on they came—by the hundreds, by the thousands, by the tens of thousands.

Some ARVN troopers sat in disheveled groups atop American-made tanks. Others crammed themselves into military trucks. A few rode bicycles that they had stolen from Vietnamese peasants. Many simply trudged down the road in no formation and with no officers to discipline them.

As the soldiers flooded through the villages, they could offer no reason for their retreat. All they knew was that they had been ordered to abandon their mountain strongholds and to march to the coastal areas. They had left their heavy guns and most deadly weaponry at their fire bases. At one base, 90 tanks and 250 pieces of artillery, all in perfect condition, were left to the enemy. At an airfield 45 fighter-bombers stood in smart rows awaiting enemy pilots.

As the troops from the highlands passed through the countryside, the inhabitants began to mutter among themselves. Had Saigon abandoned them? Panic flickered, then flamed within them. Hurriedly, they gathered up their possessions, put them on their backs, and joined the throng fleeing toward the coast. At Pleiku, once the site of a large U.S. air base, more than a hundred thousand frightened civilians jammed the road in a column of four thousand bikes, carts, cars, trucks, and buses. Men, women, children, babies, old folk, cripples, the blind, and the sick—everyone scrambled off. There was confusion and utter dispair among them. "Why is this happening?" an old man asked

ARVN and civilian refugees retreating from the Central Highlands to coastal cities as the Vietcong launch their final offensive to take Saigon.

a correspondent. "Every soldier I have known is brave. Yet they have not fought. Why have they ordered this withdrawal?" It was a question no one on the dusty road could answer. And so the panic grew.

THE UNWISE WITHDRAWAL

The withdrawal originated on direct orders from President Nguyen Van Thieu in mid-March, 1975. Thieu had intended only to remove his forces from eight of South Vietnam's most isolated provinces. He had planned then to concentrate these troops in the remaining thirty-six provinces, where most of the population, as well as nearly all of South Vietnam's agricultural resources, were located. The defense of the mountain provinces had become a serious drain on Thieu's resources, largely because of the buildup of North Vietnese troops and the distressing decrease in American military aid.

Thieu's orders for withdrawal had been given without the advice of his American advisers, who undoubtedly would have warned against making such a move without long and detailed preparation. Yet the theory behind the withdrawal was sound. A similar "enclave" strategy had found favor with General James Gavin, the U.S. Army's top research expert, and Colonel Anthony Herbert, author of *Soldier*.

But Thieu made little or no preparation for the withdrawal. His men knew only that they had been ordered to retreat from strong positions which had not been attacked. As they saw it, the order could only mean that the ARVN had suffered a grave defeat somewhere. In merely a matter of days, nearly the entire ARVN force in the north firmly believed that it had been defeated.

To add to the growing disaster, Thieu made other more grievous moves. Fearing that the retreat might undermine his far from popular rule in Saigon, Thieu recalled two of his best divisions from the north to Saigon. Here they would be used to repress any possible challenge in Saigon. This order further added to the feeling in the north that Thieu was abandoning the area.

The garrison at Hue was particularly dismayed by the removal of the elite divisions. This was the garrison that had made a gallant defense of the city during the vicious Tet Offensive in 1968. The garrison had fought violently for weeks to drive the enemy back into the jungle. But in March, 1975, Thieu's tactics had so demoralized the soldiers of Hue that they abandoned the ancient capital of all Vietnam without a fight. Quickly the fleeing garrison disolved into the mass of panic-stricken refugees trudging toward Da Nang. Thereupon the garrison was lost as a fighting unit.

The abandonment of Hue delivered a grave psychological blow. Hue was not only South Vietnam's third largest city, but it was also the sentimental capital of all Vietnam. With its magnificent palaces and miles of massive, French-built walls, Hue was the symbol of the strength, permanency, and legitimacy of the South Vietnam government. "To think of South Vietnam without Hue," sobbed a Saigonese physician, "is to think of a body without a heart."

The loss of Hue, especially without a fight, was a blow from which Thieu's subjects never recovered.

THE WITHDRAWAL BECOMES A ROUT

The disorganized mass of dispirited soldiers and civilians from Pleiku, Hue, and other cities, towns, and hamlets descended on Da Nang. Thieu undoubtedly had counted on Da Nang, Vietnam's second largest city and once one of America's most important bases, to serve as a keystone in his coastal defenses. But the avalanche of refugees completely disrupted all city organization,

ARVN and South Vietnamese refugees crowded aboard (front to back) the tugboat *Pawnee*, a barge, and the *Pioneer Contender*, an American freighter.

and, worse still, infected the defending troops with the malady of defeatism.

The Communists were surprised by the unexpected and sudden collapse of Thieu's mountain troops. Consequently, the enemy had not had time to organize a strong thrust at Da Nang, a city now convulsed by utter demoralization. Soldiers filled the streets, plundering and shooting at will. "The looting started at an American club and a French brewery," reported one eyewitness. "[The soldiers] roamed the streets robbing people and shooting wildly. . . . By Saturday morning the streets were littered with burning vehicles—and with the bodies of people killed by the soldiers."[1]

The defense organization of Da Nang broke down completely. Even the generals gave up any thought of repelling the enemy. Instead, these men and their junior officers joined the populace at the chaotic waterfront, hoping ships would be available to carry them south to safety.

The Da Nang waterfront became a horror. Hundreds of thousands fought and clawed at each other in their attempt to board anything from ocean-going freighters to garbage scows towed by tugs. Many ships had no food or water for the crowds that occupied every inch of deck space. By the time the Vietcong's gold-starred flag was fluttering atop Da Nang's city hall three days later, ninety thousand refugees, floating southward, soon would spread the panic to other towns.

The ARVN who escaped from Da Nang were only a fraction of those who had retreated there. Because of the northern debacle, Thieu lost more than 500,000 troops, the cream of his 1.1 million-man army. In addition, Thieu left the enemy more than $1 billion in weaponry. Thus, in one blinding stroke, the Vietcong and North Vietnamese had been transformed from poorly equipped underdogs into the dominant force.

THE FAILURES OF PRESIDENT THIEU

Despite the disaster, Saigon and twenty-seven of South Vietnam's forty-four provinces still held out. All would not have been lost if a concerted effort to inspire the will to resist had been made at this time. But Thieu's officials refused to stop their game of corruption long enough to meet the emergency. Thus, though the army desperately needed new recruits, young men could still easily avoid service by paying a bribe to the proper officials. Although supplies were precariously low, American shipments found their way into the hands of black-market politicians. Although fuel was scarce, profiteers with government connections had plenty to sell to motorcyclists who biked freely about Saigon.

Thieu himself provided no leadership that might have rallied the people to him. He did nothing to crack down on the corruption of those close to him. Neither did he present a bold, confident

---

1. Quoted in *Newsweek*, 14 April 1975, pp. 21–22.

front to his countrymen. On the contrary, he retired from public view into moody isolation within his Saigon palace. There, he apparently gave more thought to how he might cling to his presidency than to how he could inspire his people or guide his generals. While the army cried for reinforcements in the north, Thieu kept some of his best troops riding about Saigon to put down demonstrations. On the other hand, the suspicious president, fearful that certain generals might move against him, kept many of his best officers in distant, exposed positions. He neither informed them of his overall strategy nor, on some occasions, even returned their telephone calls.

AMERICA AND THE FALL OF SOUTH VIETNAM

By early April the Communists were massing before Xuan Loc, a town of 100,000 just forty miles from Saigon. If Xuan Loc fell, the best tank road would lie open to the capital. On April 10, while Thieu mustered his last line of defense at Xuan Loc, President Ford appeared on American TV. He staunchly maintained that South Vietnam still could be saved if Congress would pass an immediate appropriation of $722 million in emergency military aid. In addition, Ford was considering the reintroduction of American troops—up to six full divisions, it was rumored. The avowed purpose was to help evacuate the six thousand Americans in Saigon, but Ford's critics knew that this large force might be used for combat once it arrived. All that prevented such action was the important War Powers Act, passed over Nixon's veto in November, 1973. The War Powers Act prohibited the military engagement of U.S. forces overseas for more than two days without congressional approval. President Ford, continuing his televised speech, said "I ask the Congress to clarify immediately its restrictions on the use of U.S. military forces in Southeast Asia."[2]

Meanwhile in Saigon, President Thieu was crying out for more supplies to replace those ($1 billion worth) lost during the disastrous retreat. Such a replacement had been promised in the 1973 treaty. Thieu insisted that U.S. congressmen must honor the treaty commitment if they wanted to "keep from earning the label of traitors."[3] In Hanoi, the Communist leaders watched U.S. aid dwindle. According to the chief of staff of the North Vietnamese

---

2. Quoted in *U.S. News & World Report*, 21 April 1975, p. 81.

3. "Thieu to U.S.: Don't Be Traitors," *Chicago Daily News*, 4 April 1975, p. 1.

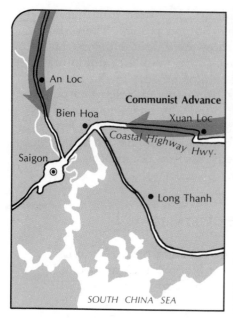

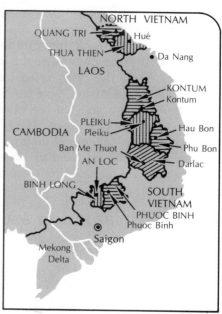

The last days of Saigon, April 1975.

The eight provinces ordered abandoned by South Vietnam's President Thieu. While Thieu's strategy was sound, his execution of it was so inept that he lost both his army and government.

army, this drop in aid was an important factor in Hanoi's decision to go on the offensive.[4]

Despite Ford's and Thieu's urgings, neither Congress nor the American people would go along with them. The depth of public feeling was revealed by a Harris poll. The poll reported that three-fourths of the American people were against further Vietnamese military aid and the reintroduction of U.S. troops. Congress, reflecting this viewpoint, refused to provide either a tempering of the War Powers Act or the $722 million Ford desired. With that refusal, America washed its hands of Vietnam.

On April 17, Cambodia fell to Communist forces. If Saigon needed a seal of doom, that event was it. After that date there was not the slightest doubt that South Vietnam would quickly follow its northern neighbor into the Communist camp.

The death agonies of South Vietnam were painful to watch—particularly for most of the 2.1 million U.S. veterans who had

---

4. Quoted in *Newsweek*, 10 May 1976, p. 57.

given so much to save it. "All it seems to come to is a waste of lives," was one comment. "All we've done is create a lot of homeless people and orphans. I feel terribly sorry for the people over there."[5] War guilt welled up throughout America as newspapers and TV showed an ever increasing tide of helpless and bloody Vietnamese stumbling into Saigon. A hastily organized airlift began bringing fifteen thousand war-orphaned children to the United States, where they were eagerly adopted by American families.

THE BATTLE OF XUAN LOC AND THE RESIGNATION OF THIEU

Zero hour approached at Xuan Loc. To reinforce the line, Thieu even sent his precious Saigon security forces into action. A seesaw battle raged for several days, and the ARVN actually repulsed the enemy. But it was a hollow victory. Vietcong and North Vietnamese infantry, never bound by roads, tramped through nearby rubber and banana plantations to post themselves near the rear of Xuan Loc. Although enemy tanks could not yet break through, the threat of encirclement was enough to prompt the ARVN to flee the city. As the ARVN fled, they left behind more than half of their comrades, either dead or wounded.

On April 21 it became clear that Xuan Loc was lost. Saigon was doomed. Only then did Thieu reluctantly decide to step down from the presidency.

Thieu's resignation speech was a bitter attack against the United States. He maintained that the treaty worked out in 1972 and 1973 "was an agreement by which the U.S. sold South Vietnam to the Communists." Thieu had signed the document only because President Nixon had assured him that if "Communist North Vietnam renewed its aggression and violated the agreement, the Americans would react violently and immediately to check the aggression." Nixon furthermore promised, said Thieu, that the United States would "provide abundant military and economic aid to the South Vietnamese people." The Americans had not lived up to either guarantee, Thieu stormed. "This amounts to a breach of promise, injustice, lack of responsibility and inhumanity toward an ally who had suffered continuously—[it represents] the shirking of responsibility on the part of a great power." With the end of his presidency at hand,

---

5. Quoted in the *Chicago Daily News*, 5 May 1975, p. 1.

Nguyen Van Thieu publically resigning as president of South Vietnam and bitterly denouncing the United States as untrustworthy.

Thieu now was ready to stick the "traitors" label to American policy makers.[6]

Thieu flew to sumptuous safety in Taiwan, and new politicians took over the South Vietnamese government. But it was obvious their tenure of office would be short. On April 23, President Ford himself stated bluntly that the Vietnam War was finished as far as the United States was concerned. With Congress refusing further military aid and with Ford "unfortunately" (to use his word) hamstrung by the War Powers Act, all the president could do now was to evacuate the Americans from Saigon. Ford also

---

6. Quoted in *U.S. News & World Report*, 5 May 1975, p. 2.

would evacuate as many loyal South Vietnamese as possible. On April 29, as 150,000 jubilant Vietcong and North Vietnamese troops massed around Saigon, the Americans started a frantic airlift.[7]

There was great anxiety throughout America. Could the U.S. citizens be evacuated before the enemy knifed into Saigon? And would the South Vietnamese troops permit the evacuation or would they turn their guns on the American "traitors"?

As the climax approached, America went through an almost convulsive reappraisal of who was to blame for the catastrophe in Vietnam.

---

7. *U.S. News & World Report*, 5 May 1975, p. 19.

CHAPTER NINETEEN

The Fall of South Vietnam: Accountability

Almost everyone agreed that much of the blame for South Vietnam's fall must be shouldered by President Thieu. It was, after all, Thieu's bungled withdrawal from the highlands that was undeniably the immediate cause of the collapse. It was largely his fault that the ARVN was ill prepared for such a change of strategy. And it was Thieu's personally recalling the two elite divisions from the north to Saigon that led to the abandonment of Hue, psychological capital of Vietnam. Furthermore, the disastrous results of the withdrawal pointed to the fact that Thieu and his clique had done little, if anything, to put the ARVN into proper fighting trim.

Western observers had said many times that the ARVN had too many colonels and generals whose only qualifications were that they came from wealthy families aligned with Thieu. The army brass was rife with corruption. There was, for example, General Dang Van Quang, Thieu's special assistant, whose wife made a fortune from protection fees paid to her by the brothels in the Mekong Delta. And there was General Ngo Dzu, who pocketed vast sums from peddling heroin. Hundreds of thousands more dollars found their way into officers' pockets from American supplies stolen from government warehouses. Corruption in the ARVN was so bad that Colonel Anthony Herbert admitted that he feared giving his invaluable starlight-scope gun sights to South Vietnamese officers. He felt certain that some of these officers would quickly sell the scopes to the Vietcong!

While many ARVN officers made illegal fortunes, the common infantrymen, who made up the backbone of South Vietnam's 1.1 million-man army, were scandalously underpaid. A special 1974 report by the U.S. defense attaché in Saigon stated, "It is quite

A South Vietnamese editor burning newspapers because government officials were preparing to confiscate the papers. Such confiscations were not rare, nor was the imprisonment of "political enemies" under the repressive Thieu regime.

clear that [ARVN] personnel are forced to live at less than reasonable subsistence levels." This condition, the report continued, "has caused a deterioration of performance, which cannot be permitted to continue if it [the ARVN] is to be considered a viable military force." The report estimated that a full ninety-two percent of the soldiers believed their pay would have to be *doubled* before they could meet just the basic needs of food, clothing, and shelter for themselves and their families!¹

Thieu and his ruling clique did nothing to remedy the corruption. In fact, they encouraged it, because the officers involved were thereby cemented to the regime. Thus, even as the Communist offensive opened in the early spring of 1975, ARVN

---

1. Quoted in the *Christian Science Monitor*, 1 April 1975, p. 1.

officers were permitted to force their soldiers to pay juicy bribes to secure special favors or safer duty. With the army in such discontent, it is no wonder that the soldiers lacked the will to stand up to the VC and the North Vietnamese regulars.

Thieu had long known that the enemy was planning to attack. Complete superiority in the air provided his fliers with clear views of the North Vietnamese construction work that was slowly turning the Ho Chi Minh Trail into a highway for trucks. Fliers also reported the laying of a long pipeline to pump oil to storage tanks located well within South Vietnam's borders. To hold the loyalty of the frontier provinces against the VC and North Vietnamese buildup, Thieu should have set up efficient programs to improve the peasants' living conditions. However, no effective attempt was made by Saigon. Far from it. Often Saigon seemed to go out of its way to make enemies of the villagers. More than once ARVN forces blew apart villages merely because they were suspected of harboring VC. So great was the resentment aroused by ARVN tactics that Thieu's men sometimes had to take rice for Saigon from the delta farmers at gunpoint!

Thieu's regime also made many enemies within Saigon and the other major cities, where the government's main power base lay. The regime ruthlessly censored newspapers, and it was not unusual for long blank columns to appear on front pages. Thieu's security police kept a tight lid on antigovernment activity—200,000 political prisoners eventually were confined in filthy jails. When the people tried to protest, they were met by fierce government repression.

Not only Thieu's tactics but also his personality made him unfit to rule South Vietnam during this time of crisis. One reporter who knew the president well remarked on his "arrogance, inability to compromise, penchant for secrecy, suspiciousness and high tolerance for corruption." Thieu was a man, continued the reporter, "who lost touch with his people and his troops, relying on a small group of trusted advisers who served him well but his country badly."[2]

THE FAILURE OF THE UNITED STATES

Thieu's shortcomings notwithstanding, the United States also must shoulder its share of blame for the fall of South Vietnam.

---

2. Larry Green, "Onetime Asian Strongman Comes to an Inglorious End," *Chicago Daily News*, 21 April 1975, p. 8.

Thieu probably could have been removed at any time if the United States had given a nod to the many highly placed South Vietnamese who hated him. The United States, however, preferred to keep Thieu because he was a strong ruler. American officials did not want to risk having a series of weak rulers like those who had followed Diem in 1963. Thus, if Thieu continued to give his nation poor leadership, American backing was at least partly responsible.

The United States also contributed to the collapse of ARVN military forces. American advisers, schooled in the massive bombardments of World War II and the vaunted "Meatgrinder" of Korea, failed to realize fully that Vietnam was an entirely different kind of war. American advisers taught the ARVN officers to rely on bombs, chopper gunships, and long-range artillery to deal with the enemy. When a bombardment was over, U.S. and ARVN troops would move forward in mechanized troop carriers supported by long lines of tanks. This tactic had two unfavorable results. First, the ARVN became chained to its artillery and air bases. And, second, the ARVN was dependent on the few good roads for movement. Gut fighting and personal hand-to-hand combat were not part of ARVN tactics. The army grew soft and shied away from the tough, close-contact fighting practiced by the VC and North Vietnamese.

The Communists gained tremendous advantages from their mode of fighting. Having no air support and very little artillery, they carried most of what they needed on their own backs. Thus they could use the many narrow trails to circle around behind the road-bound ARVN. Bombs and shells presented no insurmountable problem, because the guerrillas could disperse quickly through wide areas of the jungle or slip into a maze of tunnels that had been easily dug into the soft earth.

The most serious criticism of U.S. advisers is that they did not revise their tactical training of ARVN troops upon seeing that the Meatgrinder was ineffective in Vietnam. They should have known that if the tactic had not worked for half a million U.S. troops supported by the most sophisticated arsenal in the world, there would be little likelihood of its working for ARVN. And there would be no likelihood of the tactic working after U.S. troops had left and the supply of military hardware was no longer limitless.

The problem of tactics caught up with Thieu early in 1975. Indeed, the reason for his initial withdrawal from the highlands was the fact that his road-bound, equipment-heavy frontier troops could no longer be supplied. The Communists had grown strong enough to ambush ARVN convoys almost at will. And to

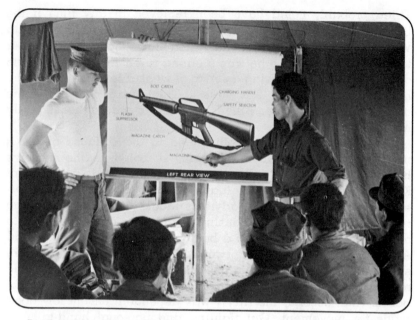

As President Nixon withdrew U.S. troops, American advisers supervised the training of a greater number of ARVN recruits. The recruits above are being taught how to use and care for the M–16 rifle.

make the situation worse, the Communists now had new Russian-made portable rockets to shoot down Thieu's supply choppers. As a result, most military experts agree that Thieu had little choice except to abandon his exposed forward bases.

The U.S. Congress also did its share to undermine South Vietnam's ability to resist. In 1972, Congress spent $7 billion on Vietnam; but in 1973, following the departure of American troops, it gave Thieu only $1.1 billion in military aid. A year later Congress reduced this figure to barely $700 million. To maintain the complex equipment the Americans had given him, Thieu was forced to take parts from working equipment. Tanks and trucks were junked for lack of parts. Ammunition was sometimes so low that ARVN gunners had to ration it. For an army that once had been motorized and had had unlimited firepower, the decline in American aid was not only distressing but crippling.

While the South Vietnamese were feeling the pinch, North Vietnam was receiving more and more aid from Russia and China. This aid increased to unparalleled proportions by 1974, when an estimated $1.6 billion reached Hanoi. General Giap and his men put this material to good use, especially the Russian heat-seeking, antichopper rockets. Although the United States had recently developed a chopper against which the Russian rockets were ineffective, the chopper had not been rushed into mass production. In addition, Giap and the Communist leaders were much more efficient than the corrupt Thieu regime. The North Vietnamese troops were inspired by Communist dogma and their desire to reunite their homeland. To the Communists their noble goals were well worth their sacrifices. The common ARVN foot soldier, as pointed out earlier, could see no goal for his government except the enrichment of the many corrupt officials.

WATERGATE AND VIETNAM

Even with all its problems, South Vietnam might have survived if it had not been for a completely unforeseen event that threw all predictions askew. This event was the Watergate affair.

When the Watergate break-in first came to light during the 1972 presidential campaign, it had no effect on Nixon's political strength. Indeed, in November Nixon won an overwhelming victory over George McGovern, the Democratic candidate. This victory emboldened Nixon to conduct the massive Christmas bombing of Hanoi. As a result of Nixon's fierce determination to stand by Saigon, the North Vietnamese returned to the conference table with slightly subdued demands. The result was the 1973 treaty that was supposed to end the war.

President Thieu had been extremely reluctant to sign the treaty. Thieu probably was persuaded to sign the treaty only by Nixon's firm assurances in writing that he would "respond with full force" if North Vietnam violated the peace by sending more troops into South Vietnam. Not once but several times Nixon wrote Thieu of his "absolute assurance" to take "swift and retaliatory action" against truce violations by Hanoi.[3] In view of Nixon's devastating Christmas bombing, it was clear that the president would not hesitate to bring the full fury of the U.S. Air Force to Thieu's aid.

There was, of course, the problem of the War Powers Act, which forbade such military action without congressional approval within two days. But administration spokesmen were quick to question the legality of a law that encroached on the

---

3. Robert Gruenberg, "Nixon's Viet Vow Dismissed As Semantics by White House," *Chicago Daily News*, 1 May 1975, pp. 1, 8.

president's constitutional power as commander-in-chief. If Nixon had remained at the zenith of power, it is highly probable that he would have sent aid in defiance of the act.

But as the Watergate affair grew into a national scandal during the summer and fall of 1973, Nixon became cautious. Now he could not take any action that might further reduce his support in Congress, where rumors of impeachment were arising. Thus, even through mid-1973 intelligence reports revealed that about 55,000 more North Vietnamese troops had infiltrated south, Nixon dared not honor his promise to Thieu.

Nixon's declining political strength and Congress's determination to give South Vietnam only the barest military and economic aid emboldened Hanoi to try again for total victory. The peace treaty was completely disregarded as North Vietnam's troop strength in the South rose from the permitted 145,000 to 220,000 in the spring of 1974 and to 300,000 by February, 1975. The movement of Communist soldiers down the Ho Chi Minh highway was so great that North Vietnam had almost no troops left at home to defend itself. One observer remarked that Hanoi was sending everyone south except the girl scouts.

It was a bold gamble on Hanoi's part. A sudden U.S. air offensive on the great caravans of troops and vehicles lumbering southward could have been disastrous. An American-ARVN amphibious landing at Haiphong could have quickly captured Hanoi. Yet Gerald Ford, who replaced Nixon in August, 1974, was not an elected president and lacked even Nixon's capabilities for action. He dared not disregard U.S. public opinion. A recent poll had indicated that four out of five Americans were against any increase in military aid to Saigon—to say nothing of renewed American troop involvement.

THE AMERICAN EVACUATION

And so President Ford stood by helplessly while South Vietnam disintegrated. In mid-April, Xuan Loc fell. Then the Vietcong and North Vietnamese began forming a vise around Saigon. By now the question had become not how to save Saigon, but how to evacuate the six thousand remaining Americans. Word was secretly passed to the Americans that special buses would pick them up at predetermined street corners and carry them to the U.S. Embassy for a flight out by chopper. Officials hoped that the Americans could sneak away before Saigon learned of the operation. But it was impossible to keep the news from sweeping over the city. Thousands of South Vietnamese who loyally had

An American helicopter crewman helping evacuees off ladder to the roof of a Saigon building, April 29, 1975. This evacuation site was one of many in the downtown area from which Americans and foreign nationals were ferried to U.S. navy ships lying off the coast.

served the United States hurried to the embassy grounds. Before long a huge mass of frantic men, women, and children was shrieking to be taken aboard one of the eighty-one choppers that began landing around midday on April 29.

Among those Americans observing the last disturbing hours of America's presence in Vietnam was Bob Tamarkin, reporter for the *Chicago Daily News*. Below is the setting as Tamarkin viewed it:

> The scene at the [embassy] wall was brutal. Marines and other embassy personnel threw Vietnamese people off the wall. One official drew his revolver, stuck it point blank in the face of a young Vietnamese boy and screamed: "Get down, you bastard, or I'll blow your head off."

The marines brought the butts of their rifles down on the fingers of those trying to climb the walls. Elderly women and children who were being pushed up by the sheer force of bodies beneath them became enmeshed in the barbed wire [looped along the top of the wall], their skin punctured with bloody wounds.

One official who had thrown a young girl from the wall three times finally gave in. "I couldn't take it any more. I felt sorry for her . . . . I couldn't play God any more."[4]

Tamarkin kept a journal of the frantic, chaotic termination of the U.S. presence in Vietnam:

> 9:40 P.M. As helicopters circled overhead, their red lights blinking off and on, orange flames and thick smoke poured out of the embassy's smoke stack. The remaining documents and papers, some collected since 1954, when the United States established its embassy in Saigon, were being burned.[5]

After a chopper was jammed with up to ninety persons—nearly twice the normal load—it took off for the forty-five-minute trip to one of the carriers standing offshore. After quickly unloading its human cargo, it headed back to Saigon, landing on the embassy roof or in the parking lot.

By midnight the Communists were moving forward, and the muffled sound of artillery and small arms could be heard in the distance. Yet there were still thousands of South Vietnamese outside the embassy walls screaming to be taken aboard on the choppers. "One young Vietnamese boy and a man tried to squeeze through the gate," Tamarkin reported. "They were beaten, brutally."

> 4:15 A.M. Ambassador Martin appeared in the lobby. . . . He spoke to no one, but stood waiting for the elevator to the sixth floor for the last time. . . . An air of deep depression surrounded [Martin and his aides] as they walked into the elevator. About 15 minutes later, a marine helicopter carried off the ambassador . . . officially ending America's presence in South Vietnam. . . . Lightning from monsoon rains in the distance lit up the sky. . . .[6]

---

4. Bob Tamarkin, "Diary of South Vietnam's Last Hours," *Chicago Daily News*, 6 May 1975, p. 6.

5. Tamarkin, "Diary."

6. Tamarkin, "Diary."

At 5:15 A.M. a radio message informed the remaining Americans that the airlift was to end with the next chopper. The pilots had been flying fourteen hours without rest. But no word was to be given the South Vietnamese for fear they might riot. Instead, the marines at the wall walked casually into the embassy, bolting the doors behind them. Not even the loyal Vietnamese fire crew on the roof knew they were being left behind. Tamarkin walked beneath the whirling chopper propellers and took his place inside.

> My chopper lifted off, its red lights blinking, and headed toward the South China Sea. The passengers, including me, sat stoically in the dark, tired and numb. Some were dazed, finding it difficult to believe that the Americans were pulling out in this manner, skulking away in the darkness.
> Below in the courtyard, where the big choppers had been loading, the headlights from the cars and trucks surrounding the parking lot were still on to light the way for the choppers.
> Hundreds of Vietnamese looked up, waiting for the next one.
> It never came.[7]

Less than three hours after the Americans had disappeared into the night, the first Communist soldiers marched triumphantly into Saigon. Russian-made tanks battered down the gates of the presidential palace. Soon the gold-starred flag of the Vietcong floated from the masthead. Saigon was renamed Ho Chi Minh City. And, after a short period of rule by the NLF, South Vietnam was formally absorbed by North Vietnam on July 2, 1976.

AFTERMATH

And so it was over at last. For the first time in America's history the nation had not fought a war to a satisfactory conclusion. Not only had Vietnam been lost, but there remained the disquieting problem of what to do with the more than 130,000 South Vietnamese who had managed to escape the Communists. Many had been ferried out of the country on U.S. helicopters. But more had braved choppy waters in tiny boats to reach American ships plying the South China Sea.

Even as the refugees were being housed in temporary camps in California, Florida, and Arkansas, Americans viewed these newcomers with mixed feelings. True, we had some sort of obligation

7. Tamarkin, "Diary."

South Vietnamese refugees waiting in line for lunch at Camp Pendleton, California, May, 1975. During the months that followed, thousands of Vietnamese families were relocated in cities throughout the United States.

to them, but on the other hand they were arriving in the midst of a severe postwar recession. Many Americans, especially those who were jobless or were barely eking out a living, feared that the Vietnamese would compete with them in the diminished job market. Others were wary of the dread diseases with which the Vietnamese were believed to be infected. A few disliked them just because they were "Orientals," and in Florida there was some talk of organizing a "Gook Klux Klan." Whatever the reason, a poll in May, 1975, revealed the disturbing fact that fifty-four percent of the Americans resented the presence of the South Vietnamese in the United States. Only after repeated reprimands from President Ford and other concerned Americans did the public conscience finally accept the refugees.

Perhaps the South Vietnamese were merely victims of the overall disillusionment with the war's frustrating conclusion.

There was a general bitterness about the entire affair, particularly among former servicemen who had to live with the scars of war on them. One of these men was Matt Senizaiz, who as an infantryman had been machine-gunned in the leg. After seven and a half years of pain and worry, he had recently learned that his leg might have to be amputated. As South Vietnam crumbled, Senizaiz poured out his feelings to a *Newsweek* reporter:

> It was all those Ivy League dudes with great educations that thought all this [war] up; and then, when it didn't work, they just went off to fancy jobs and left us with our dangling legs. It was an intellectuals' war, except 55,000 of *us* had to die. And for what?[8]

That question might well haunt America for decades to come.

---

8. *Newsweek*, 14 April 1975, p. 34.

Bibliography

KOREA

Acheson, Dean. *The Pattern of Responsibility: From the Record of Secretary of State Dean Acheson.*. Edited by McGeorge Bundy. New York: W. W. Norton, 1969.

Angle, Paul M. *The Uneasy World.* New York: Fawcett World Library, 1964.

Crofts, Alfred, and Buchanan, Percy. *A History of the Far East.* New York: Longmans, Green, 1958.

Eisenhower, Dwight D. *The White House Years.* Vol. 1, *Mandate for Change, 1953–1956.* New York: New American Library, Signet Books, 1963.

Fehrenbach, T. R. *This Kind of War: Korea, a Study in Unpreparedness.* New York: Simon & Schuster, Pocket Books, 1964.

Greene, Felix. *China.* New York: Ballantine Books, 1962.

Halle, Louis J. *The Cold War As History.* New York: Harper & Row, 1967.

Herbert, Anthony B., with Wooten, James T. *Soldier.* New York: Dell, 1973.

Higgins, Marguerite. *War in Korea: The Report of a Woman Combat Correspondent.* New York: Doubleday, 1951.

Jones, Charles, and Jones, Eugene. *The Face of War.* Englewood Cliffs, N.J.: Prentice-Hall, 1951.

Kennan, George F. *Memoirs, 1925–1950.* Boston: Little, Brown, 1967.

Lincoln, Eric C. *The Negro Pilgrimage in America: The Coming of Age of Black America.* New York: Praeger, 1969.

Link, Arthur S. *American Epoch.* New York: Alfred A. Knopf, 1955.

MacArthur, Douglas. *Reminiscences.* New York: McGraw-Hill, 1964.

Miller, Merle. *Plain Speaking: An Oral Biography of Harry S. Truman.* New York: Berkley, 1974.

Phillips, Cabell. *The Truman Presidency.* Baltimore: Penguin Books, 1972.

Rees, David. *Korea: The Limited War.* Baltimore: Penguin Books, 1970.

Roper, Elmo. *You and Your Leaders: 1936–1956.* New York: William Morrow, 1957.

Russ, Martin. *The Last Parallel: A Marine's War Journal.* New York; Holt, Rinehart & Winston, 1957.

Truman, Harry S. *Memoirs.* Vol. 2, *Years of Trial and Hope.* New York: Doubleday, 1958.

Truman, Margaret. *Harry S. Truman.* New York: Simon & Schuster, Pocket Books, 1974.

Williams, William A. *The Tragedy of American Diplomacy.* New York: Dell, 1962.

VIETNAM

Austin, Anthony. *The President's War.* Philadelphia: J. B. Lippincott, 1971.

Calley, William L., Jr., and Sack, John. *Lieutenant Calley: His Own Story.* New York: Grosset & Dunlap, 1970.

Donovan, James A. *Militarism, U.S.A.* New York: Charles Scribner's Sons, 1970.

Duncan, Donald. *The New Legions.* New York: Random House, 1967.

Effros, William G., ed. *Quotations Vietnam: 1945–1970.* New York: Random House, 1970.

Eisenhower, Dwight D. *The White House Years.* Vol. 1, *Mandate for Change, 1953–1956.* New York: New American Library, Signet Books, 1963.

Evans, Rowland, and Novak, Robert. *Nixon in the White House: The Frustration of Power.* New York: Random House, Vintage Books, 1972.

Fall, Bernard B. *Last Reflections on a War.* New York: Doubleday, 1967.

Fall, Bernard B. *Viet-Nam Witness, 1953–1966.* New York: Praeger, 1966.

FitzGerald, Frances. *Fire in the Lake.* Boston: Little, Brown, 1972.

Fulbright, J. William. "Reflections: In Thrall to Fear." *The New Yorker,* 8 January 1972, pp. 41–62.

Gettleman, Marvin, ed. *Vietnam: History, Documents, and Opinions.* New York: Fawcett World Library, 1965.

Gettleman, Marvin, et al. *Conflict in Indochina: A Reader on the Widening War in Laos and Cambodia.* New York: Random House, 1971.

Goldman, Eric. *The Tragedy of Lyndon Johnson: A Historian's Personal Interpretation.* New York: Alfred A. Knopf, 1969.

Greenhaw, Wayne. *The Making of a Hero: The Story of Lieutenant William Calley.* Louisville, Ky.: Touchstone, 1971.

Halberstam, David. *The Best and the Brightest.* New York: Random House, 1972.

Heller, Deane and David. *John Foster Dulles.* New York: Holt, Rinehart & Winston, 1960.

Herbert, Anthony B., with Wooten, James T. *Soldier.* New York: Dell, 1973.

Hersh, Seymour. *Cover-up: The Army's Secret Investigation of the Massacre at My Lai Four.* New York: Random House, 1972.

Higgins, Marguerite. *Our Vietnam Nightmare.* New York: Harper & Row, 1965.

Ho Chi Minh. *Ho Chi Minh on Revolution: Selected Writings, 1920–1966.* Edited by Bernard B. Fall. New York: Praeger, 1967.

Johnson, Haynes, and Gwertzman, Bernard M. *Fulbright: The Dissenter.* New York: Doubleday, 1968.

Johnson, Lyndon. *The Vantage Point: Perspectives of the Presidency, 1963–1969.* New York: Holt, Rinehart & Winston, 1971.

Khrushchev, Nikita. *Khrushchev Remembers.* Boston: Little, Brown, 1970.

Lacouture, Jean. *Ho Chi Minh: A Political Biography.* New York: Random House, 1968.

Lacouture, Jean. *Vietnam: Between Two Truces*. New York: Random House, Vintage Books, 1966.

Lederer, William J., and Burdick, Eugene. *The Ugly American*. New York: W. W. Norton, 1958.

Ly Qui Chung, ed. *Between Two Fires: The Unheard Voices of Vietnam*. New York: Praeger, 1970.

Mailer, Norman. *Miami and the Siege of Chicago*. New York: New American Library, Signet Books, 1968.

Newman, Bernard. *Background to Viet-Nam*. New York: New American Library, Signet Books, 1965.

The Pacific Rivals. New York: Weatherhill/Asahi, 1972.

Raskin, Marcus G., and Fall, Bernard B., eds. *The Viet-Nam Reader*. New York: Random House, 1965.

Sale, Kirkpatrick. *SDS: Ten Years Toward a Revolution*. New York: Random House, 1973.

Schell, Jonathan. *The Military Half: An Account of Destruction in Quang Ngai and Quang Tin*. New York: Alfred A. Knopf, 1968.

Schlesinger, Arthur M., Jr. *The Bitter Heritage*. Boston: Houghton Mifflin, 1967.

Schlesinger, Arthur M., Jr. *A Thousand Days: John F. Kennedy in the White House*. New York: Fawcett World Library, 1967.

Schoenbrun, David. "Journey to North Vietnam." *Saturday Evening Post*, 12 December 1967.

Sheehan, Neil; Smith, Hedrick; Kenworthy, E. W.; and Butterfield, Fox, eds. *The Pentagon Papers*. New York: Bantam Books, 1971.

Sorensen, Theodore. *Kennedy*. New York: Bantam Books, 1966.

Sussman, Barry. *The Great Cover-up: Nixon and the Scandal of Watergate*. New York: New American Library, Signet Books, 1974.

Taylor, Telford. *Nuremberg and Vietnam: An American Tragedy*. New York: Bantam Books, 1971.

Thich Nhat Hanh. *Vietnam: Lotus in a Sea of Fire*. New York: Hill & Wang, 1967.

Tran Van Dinh. *No Passenger on the River*. New York: Vantage Press, 1965.

Vo Nguyen Giap. *People's War, People's Army: The Viet Cong Insurrection Manual for Underdeveloped Countries*. New York: Praeger, 1962.

Walker, Daniel, et al. *Rights in Conflict*. New York: New American Library, Signet Books, 1969.

White, Theodore H. *The Making of the President: 1964*. New York: Atheneum, 1965.

White, Theodore H. *The Making of the President: 1968*. New York: Atheneum, 1969.

White, Theodore H. *The Making of the President: 1972*. New York: Atheneum, 1973.

Zeiger, Henry. *Lyndon B. Johnson: Man and President*. New York: Popular Library, 1963.

Index

dies, 229; how his view of Vietnam
differed from Kissinger's, 233
Joint Chiefs of Staff, U.S., 29, 31; on
Cuban invasion, 132; on
Cambodian invasion, 197
Joy, Turner, U.S. admiral, at Korean
peace talks, 77
Joy, Turner, U.S. destroyer. See
Turner Joy

Kaesong, site of first Korean peace
talks, 77
Kahn, Nguyen, ARVN general, and
overthrow of Diem, 140; his shaky
government, 165; is overthrown,
167
Kennan, George, criticizes U.S. policy
in Korea, 32
Kennedy, Edward, U.S. senator, on
Cambodian invasion, 198;
demonstrates against bombing
Hanoi, 222
Kennedy, Jacqueline, at Vienna, 135
Kennedy, John F., U.S. president, 89;
meets Diem, 121; becomes
president, 128–29; and world
problem areas, 130–32; does not
heed de Gaulle's warning about
Vietnam, 132–34; meets with
Khrushchev, 134–35; steps up U.S.
presence in Vietnam, 136–37; and
Cuban Missile Crisis, 138; knows
of plot to overthrow Diem, 140–42;
supports Strategic Hamlet
Program, 151–53; sends Green
Berets to South Vietnam, 154;
assassination of, 143; in *Pentagon
Papers*, 216
Kent State University, killings at,
199–201
Kentucky, antiwar riots in, 199
Khrushchev, Nikita, Soviet premier,
and Geneva Conference (1954),
115; meets with Kennedy in
Vienna, 134–35; and Cuban
Missile Crisis, 138
King, Martin Luther, Jr., as civil
rights leader, 190; opposed to U.S.
involvement in Vietnam, 235
Kissinger, Henry, U.S. secretary of
state, on invasion of Cambodia,
197; secret peace talks on Vietnam
War, 221; at Paris peace talks, 224,
225, 227; interviewed by Barbara
Walter, 233–34
Korea. See North Korea and South
Korea
Korean War, 21–94; as related to

Vietnam War, 126, 169
Kosygin, Aleksei N., Soviet premier,
at Hanoi, 167
Krause, Allison, killed at Kent State
University, 201

Laos, occupied by France (1887), 99;
enters French Union, 103–4; at
Geneva Conference (1954), 115,
117; Communist offensive in, 131;
Johnson urged to invade, 191;
ARVN invades, 213
Latin America, 86
Latinos, and urban segregation, 240;
high school drop out rate, 240;
Alianza Federal de Publos Libres,
240; La Raza Unida, 240; César
Chavez, 240; Reies López Tijerina,
240; Rudolfo Gonzales, 240
League of Oppressed Peoples of
Asia, founded by Ho Chi Minh, 102
Lebanon, 89
Lederer, William, coauthor of *The
Ugly American*, quoted, 112–13
Lenin, Nikolai, influence of his
writings on Ho Chi Minh, 101
Liddy, G. Gordon, and Watergate,
217
Lie, Trygve, U.N. secretary general,
22
Lodge, Henry Cabot II, ambassador
to South Vietnam, role in the
overthrow of Diem, 140–42
Loi Le, early Vietnamese ruler, 97
Luc, Do, VC infiltrator, diary quoted,
144–45
Lutheran Church, declining
membership during 1960s, 237

MacArthur, Douglas, 21–27; compares
North Korean attack on South
Korea with Japanese attack on
Pearl Harbor, 21; discusses South
Korean retreat, 25; shares blame
for poor condition of U.S. troops,
27; his early Korean strategy,
25–27, 37; his Inchon strategy,
41–43; the Inchon landing, 44–45;
crossing the 38th parallel, 47;
drive toward Yalu River, 48; meets
with Truman at Wake Island,
51–56; thrown back by Chinese
intervention, 56–63; relieved of
command, 69; welcomed home in
the United States, 69; regarded as
possible presidential candidate,
69; advice to Kennedy about
Vietnam, 129